The Importance of Insight

Essays in Honour of Michael Vertin

EDITED BY
JOHN J. LIPTAY JR AND DAVID S. LIPTAY

Written in honour of Michael Vertin, the distinguished philosopher and Lonergan scholar, *The Importance of Insight* brings together a number of thoughtful essays by leading figures in Lonergan scholarship. These essays investigate Lonergan's articulation of insight and hot it can be applied to the fields of cognitional theory, theology, ethics, and politics. The contributors address issues emerging from the post-Enlightenment crisis of meaning and value, as well as more specific contemporary concerns such as the nature of Christian revelation, the articulation of Church doctrine, and the ethical training health care professionals should receive.

By indicating what there is to be gained by understanding and applying insight in a number of different contexts, this collection highlights the relevance of Lonergan's thought to the contemporary intellectual and cultural milieu and, at the same time, makes a significant contribution to the development of Lonergan's thought itself. *The Importance of Insight* thus offers a window into cutting-edge Lonergan scholarship and some of its central concerns and preoccupations.

JOHN J. LIPTAY JR is an assistant professor in the Philosophy Program at St. Thomas More College, University of Saskatchewan.

DAVID S. LIPTAY is a PhD candidate in Religious Studies at Syracuse University.

Michael Vertin. Photograph by D'Arcy Glionna.

Edited by JOHN J. LIPTAY JR and
DAVID S. LIPTAY

The Importance of Insight

Essays in Honour of Michael Vertin

UNIVERSITY OF TORONTO PRESS
Toronto Buffalo London

Toronto Buffalo London
Reprinted 2017

ISBN 978-0-8020-9217-5 (cloth)
ISBN 978-1-4875-8725-3 (paper)

Printed on acid-free paper

Lonergan Studies

Library and Archives Canada Cataloguing in Publication

The importance of insight : essays in honour of Michael Vertin / edited by John J. Liptay Jr and David S. Liptay.

(Lonergan studies)
Includes bibliographical references.
ISBN 978-0-8020-9217-5 (bound). – ISBN 978-1-4875-8725-3 (pbk.)

1. Lonergan, Bernard J. F. (Bernard Joseph Francis), 1904–1984. 2. Insight. 3. Theology. 4. Ethics. 5. Political ethics. I. Vertin, Michael, 1939– II. Liptay, John J. Jr III. Liptay, David S. IV. Series.

B995.L654146 2007 121 C2006-906836-4

This volume has been published with the help of a grant from St Thomas More College, University of Saskatchewan.

University of Toronto Press acknowledges the financial assistance to its publishing program of the Canada Council for the Arts and the Ontario Arts Council.

University of Toronto Press acknowledges the financial support for its publishing activities of the Government of Canada through the Book Publishing Industry Development Program (BPIDP).

Cover photograph courtesy Lonergan Research Institute, Regis College, University of Toronto.

Contents

Introduction

This volume of essays has two different but related purposes. First, it is intended as an expression of gratitude to and esteem for Michael Vertin, professor emeritus of the departments of Philosophy and the Study of Religion at the University of Toronto. For over thirty years Vertin has been, in the words of one of his colleagues, 'the ideal teacher-scholar,' and remains widely respected and admired for the commitment and integrity he brings to both these roles. These papers themselves testify to Vertin's dual influence insofar as they are written not just by long-term colleagues drawing on his published work, but also by some of his former students. For those who know Vertin, it should come as no surprise that our contributors address him not only as a teacher and fellow scholar, but as a friend.

This volume is also intended as a significant contribution to the study of Bernard Lonergan's thought, and, in particular, looks to attest to the importance of Lonergan's articulation of insight itself, and to how it can be applied in the fields of cognitional theory, theology, ethics, and politics. In these respects, the volume addresses teaching and scholarly concerns that have been central to Vertin's work, and provides a wide spectrum of scholarly perspectives on the book that, as Philip McShane rightly suggests, 'has haunted his life' – Lonergan's *Insight*. Collectively, these essays not only demonstrate the importance of insight, but also speak to Vertin's scholarly commitment to and highlight his considerable efforts in expounding and communicating that importance.

Joseph Michael Vertin was born on 25 September 1939 in Breckenridge, Minnesota, the oldest of seven children of Joseph Matthias and Kathleen Vertin. Vertin received his primary and secondary education in the local schools at Breckenridge, and during this period was active in the Eagle

Scouts – an affiliation that he claims is as significant to him in personal terms as his doctorate in philosophy. Upon graduation from high school, he entered St. John's University in Collegeville, Minnesota, where he declared himself as a math and physics major. In the second term of his third year, Vertin went to learn Latin with the Jesuits at Loyola in Chicago. When he returned to St. John's, it was as a diocesan seminarian, and he then switched his major to philosophy, keeping math and physics as minors. Because he did so well in his undergraduate studies, he was sent in 1962 to the Catholic University of America in Washington, DC to study theology. It was there, during these studies, that Vertin first encountered the book that was to change his life: Bernard Lonergan's *Insight: A Study of Human Understanding*. Given his interests and background in the sciences, Vertin was intrigued when he heard that Lonergan's book illustrated the values of these disciplines for the study of theology. At the time, this seemed to a young seminarian not simply new but groundbreaking. Vertin's initial encounter with *Insight* helped confirm his suspicion that his philosophical studies had been cut short or, at any rate, that he needed to deepen and broaden his philosophical training. So, after an interim year teaching physics at a Washington high school, Vertin enrolled in a master's program in philosophy at the University of Toronto, and proceeded to pursue doctoral studies there. And while he did not yet know it, his days as a seminarian were over – although he was to return to Catholic University for one year to complete the licentiate in theology he had begun there, and to continue thinking about returning to the priesthood.

During his graduate studies in Toronto, Vertin had the opportunity to meet the person whose book had inspired him to pursue further philosophical studies: Bernard Lonergan. And while Lonergan's book had inspired him to continue with philosophy, Lonergan himself endorsed the topic Vertin chose to pursue in his doctoral thesis. Vertin was already intrigued by the Belgian Jesuit Joseph Maréchal; Lonergan suggested that he investigate whether Maréchal took the stance that human knowing was by way of intellectual intuition – something that Lonergan himself professed to be unclear on. To this day Vertin recalls his exchange with Lonergan, and it is worth hearing this as he remembers it:

> 'How's your Kant?'
> 'Not bad.'
> 'How's your French?'
> 'I can read French pretty well.'
> 'Then go for it!'[1]

Vertin did indeed 'go for it,' and in 1973 defended his dissertation 'The Transcendental Vindication of the First Step in Realist Metaphysics, according to Joseph Maréchal,' with Lawrence Lynch and Joseph Owens as his supervisors; he reached the conclusion, subsequently relayed to Lonergan, that Maréchal does not in fact maintain that human knowing takes place by intellectual intuition. Vertin was eventually hired on as assistant professor at the University of Toronto, in which his duties were given the unusual but appropriate division of two-thirds in the Department of Philosophy and one-third in the Department for the Study of Religion. It was in his capacity as assistant professor, in a Lenten lecture series at St Michael's College in 1974, that he first worked with the person who was to become his life-long collaborator: Margaret O'Gara. The two were married two years later on 24 April 1976. Not only did his marriage mark a change in his state of life, but he now had someone with whom to share a newly articulated vocation to an *academic* ministry, a spousal colleague with a shared vocation. Vertin came to realize that what he understood to be a call to the *priestly* ministry was in fact a preliminary manifestation of a vocation to a *pastoral* ministry that was *academic* in orientation.

Vertin has had, over the course of some thirty years of teaching, a profound influence on undergraduate and graduate students at the University of Toronto. His students invariably, and almost to a person, remark on his teaching acumen and commitment – as we ourselves discovered while we were his students. His teaching excellence was, in fact, acknowledged at a university-wide level when in 1997 he won the University of Toronto's prestigious Faculty of Arts and Science Outstanding Teaching Award, and when in 2004–5 he was awarded the Students' Administrative Council/Association of Part-Time Undergraduate Students Teaching Award (an award he was nominated for in 1984–5). He was also recognized in 2003–4 as Teacher of the Year at his own college, St Michael's. Vertin has brought this teaching excellence to bear upon a wide range of course material at both undergraduate and graduate levels, and in addition has given careful and insightful supervision to a number of doctoral students, two of whom – Cynthia Crysdale and William Sullivan – are contributors to this volume. While these courses and dissertations address diverse themes, central to each of them has been the thought of Bernard Lonergan.

Vertin is also an important and influential Lonergan scholar from the standpoint of his own published writings, and has made available seminal Lonergan-related material through the editorial work he has assumed. As editor, he has ensured, by means of three separate books, that many important studies by Lonergan's greatest disciple, Fr Frederick E. Crowe, SJ, receive an appropriately wider readership. While grateful for Vertin's labours on his behalf, Crowe was concerned that Vertin was diverting energy from his own original work.[2] Yet Vertin found time to publish a significant number of articles on metaphysical, epistemological, ethical, and methodological themes in Lonergan in leading scholarly journals, many of which are regarded as very significant contributions to the explication and development of Lonergan's thought.[3] Indeed, several of the contributions to this volume make use of, develop, or proceed in light of Vertin's work. Accordingly, the very title of this volume, *The Importance of Insight*, intends to capture the focus of Vertin's teaching and scholarly career, the central theme and preoccupation that he has called attention to in all his published work; for Vertin is convinced that at the heart of empirical disputes over a broad range of disciplines and issues is the philosophical problem of articulating an adequate theory of knowledge, and Lonergan's pivotal contribution in this regard must be his emphasis on insight. Just as Vertin's own publications address both foundational concerns regarding insight and the relevance of those concerns as applied to more concrete philosophical and empirical disputes, so, too, do the essays in this volume. The contributors, from their chosen areas of concentration, join with Vertin in showing the importance of what is to be gained by understanding and applying insight.

The volume's first section, entitled 'Understanding Insight,' investigates insight in both historical and contemporary contexts. Fr Matthew Lamb sets Lonergan's work within its historical context and emphasizes how Lonergan is concerned with *transposing* the achievements of the past (especially those of Augustine and Aquinas), not with rejecting them. To make a genuine transposition, it was necessary for Lonergan to return to the texts of the past themselves to discover the realities to which they refer. In this way, Lonergan did not allow modern assumptions to distort his understanding of the ancients and medievals, and, in grasping and making explicit their achievements, avoids the pitfalls of modern and postmodern epistemologies. Lamb suggests that Lonergan's method provides a solution to the Enlightenment project's intellectual atrophy by transposing into contemporary terms Aquinas's understanding of skills and virtues. Mark Morelli directs his attention to articulating the crisis of meaning that pervades our contemporary world. This crisis is the result of a rejection of a classical understanding of philosophical foundations by Enlightenment and post Enlightenment figures, and a subsequent confusion as to how to move forward in philosophy and our culture at large. Like Lamb, Morelli insists that the way out of this crisis lies not in a rejection of nor an uncritical return to the classical ideal, but in a *transposition* of it. Specifically, Morelli suggests that Lonergan's solution is not spelt out as a propositional foundation but as an operational one, requiring from each of us self-appropriation. Morelli, however, realizes that each of us is caught up in this crisis of meaning and faces obstacles to implement our own dynamic operational structures, and thus proposes ways to overcome them. Now insofar as insight is an element of our cognitional process, it is necessary for us to advert and attend carefully to it. For that reason, Fr Robert Doran SJ's and S.J. McGrath's essays complement these two context-setting pieces by examining more closely Lonergan's conception of insight or, more particularly, the data on which it sets to work. Doran's essay looks to re-evaluate the prevalent understanding of the empirical level of consciousness, insofar as its contents are thought to be merely sensible in act and not intelligible in act. Doran argues that there is some kind of minor formal and actual intelligibility that is given to us in experience and, thus, at the level of empirical consciousness. The very data of our experience, according to Doran, are already invested with meaningfulness, and this meaningfulness mediates our reception of those data. In this way, Doran incorporates into Lonergan's own account Heidegger's account of *Verstehen*, points out the value of doing so, and shows that it can in fact be found in Lonergan. McGrath, like Doran, is interested in expanding our conception of the empirical level of consciousness. His concern is that the role of the image in Lonergan is importantly downplayed, and seen merely in its relation to insight – not as something that possesses excessive meaning. The failure to attend to this excess of meaning could lead, McGrath argues, to a conceptualism that Lonergan himself strenuously opposed. McGrath, with the help of Heidegger, utilizes Aquinas's notion of *illuminatio* to explain how and that the image has a pre-conceptual intelligibility, and argues that there is – and *must be* – a place for this understanding of the image in Lonergan.

The volume's second section highlights the role that insight can play in theology. Fr Frederick Crowe, SJ, in an essay that models the medieval *quaestio*, takes up the question of whether or not God is free to create. On the one hand, God is good and the Dionysian axiom has it that 'the good is self-diffusive,' suggesting that God is obligated to create. On the other hand, Crowe accepts the Vatican I teaching that God freely created the spiritual and material worlds. Crowe shows how this problem can be resolved by harmonizing the positions through an analysis of human activity as an analogue to the divine activity. Insofar as Crowe seeks to determine what we can understand of God's activity in this present life, he is explicit in his appeal to the importance of insight. So too is Charles Hefling in his study of how revelation is possible. As a systematic theologian, Hefling aims at understanding, and questions, with Aquinas, how *this* understanding is different from the understanding of other disciplines. By way of an answer, he looks to the notion of revelation itself, and asks how we are to understand it today; drawing on the later Lonergan, Hefling suggests that we understand it through Christology, specifically through an analysis of Christ's self-knowledge. For Hefling, revelation is possible because Christ's beatific knowledge gives him a unique insight into the inexpressible, and he is able to express this insight in human language and acts. The act of insight can also be used, as Margaret O'Gara explains, to elaborate a correct understanding of the nature of reception – that is, the manner in which the people of God come to accept a given statement or teaching as an authoritative expression of the apostolic faith. O'Gara highlights how, at present, there is a conflict regarding what the act of reception entails. What is at issue in this conflict is the precise role of the faithful in reception. Whereas the Anglican–Roman Catholic International Commission assigns an important role to the faithful in reception, the Vatican has difficulties with this formulation. O'Gara argues that the conflict arises due to a fundamental epistemological misunderstanding and commitment on the part of the Vatican, and suggests that these can be corrected through an appropriation of Lonergan's theory of knowing.

'Insight in Ethics and Politics,' the volume's third section, addresses the role that insight plays in grasping, not creating, objective value, which in turn informs our actions in the ethical and political realm. Fred Lawrence shows how Lonergan's ethics shares, with rival and competing ethical approaches, an appreciation for the role of values and authenticity; he also notes that Lonergan shares with these other approaches the understanding that values and authenticity cannot be *based* upon premodern commitments or world views. Lawrence argues that, unlike Lonergan's, these other approaches do not provide adequate alternative criteria by which these values can be affirmed and authenticity itself attained. What is at issue for Lawrence is a correct understanding of the subject, one that allows us, as Lonergan's does, to appropriate ourselves as intelligent, rational, and responsible. In this way a criterion is identified that allows for the possibility of self-transcendence and the achievement of personal and communal authenticity, despite the fact that personal and global influences often promote unauthenticity. Cynthia Crysdale is similarly concerned with the issue of self-transcendence, and with articulating it as an ethics grounded in risk, gratitude, and, ultimately, love. Crysdale wants to undermine basic assumptions that she finds embedded in our culture, and which distort our understanding of moral deliberation. To correct this misunderstanding, she first emphasizes that there is an element of risk involved in the attempt to instantiate values in our action, so that we do not have complete control over the consequences of our actions. But the element of risk, for Crysdale, is not ultimately problematic, because the same insight that grasps possible values enables us to grasp actual values; we do not bear sole responsibility for creating values, then, because the values that we seek to instantiate are actual values that we have first grasped. Crysdale goes on to maintain that authentic moral deliberation requires a religious dimension, moving us beyond considerations of the merely human good. William Sullivan and John Heng suggest that at least an understanding and appreciation of Crysdale's conclusion is a necessary requirement in the moral education of health care professionals. They maintain that, generally speaking, health care professionals lack authentic subjectivity, and this gives rise to a mentality that overemphasizes a realm of facts deemed to be arrived at independently of the person, and that considers moral values as simply the subjective preferences of the patient. Sullivan and Heng point out, through an overview of Lonergan's transcendental method and an elucidation of 'deliberative insight,' that there is inescapable subjective component in both knowing facts and grasping values, and that health care professionals should be educated to understand this. Moreover, Sullivan and Heng share Crysdale's concern that an overemphasis on problems and possible values to be instantiated leads to a neglect of actual, present values – including spirituality – that provide the necessary context for moral decision-making in health care. Kenneth Melchin's essay also offers an elaboration of Lonergan's notion of value, but here the focus is on how value can and ought to inform and underwrite democratic pluralism. As Melchin points out, democracy poses a challenge for ethics: on the one hand, it is committed to certain high ethical ideals, but on the other hand, by embracing pluralism it has also unfortunately embraced ethical relativism. This challenge has proven difficult, even impossible, for many ethical theories to resolve, insofar as they maintain that values are privately held and inherently relative. By showing how Lonergan's scale of values can be related to the operations of our consciousness, Melchin explains how we can understand the relationship among these values, and how they are hierarchically ordered. Since values are apprehended in a manner that each person can verify for herself, Melchin maintains that they are capable of informing democratic discourse.

The volume concludes with Philip McShane explaining why *Insight* is in need of rescue. In a complex essay, the distillation of a lifetime of grappling with *Insight*, McShane claims that '*Insight* is to be rescued by the gradual development of functional specialization as a dominant and differentiated pattern of global culture.' In addition to spelling this out in greater detail, McShane provides a further context for understanding the volume's previous essays.

We would like to close by thanking a number of people. First, we extend our deepest gratitude to Margaret O'Gara, who warmly embraced the idea of this *Festschrift*, helped us to shape it, gave it its title, agreed to contribute an essay, and managed – without lying! – to keep it a secret from Michael for as long as we needed. Her assistance to us was indispensable, and enabled us to assemble a much better tribute than we could have managed on our own. Next, we would like to thank all of the contributors, who graciously and eagerly agreed to participate in this project for Michael. It was a pleasure and an honour for us to work with some of the most thoughtful and respected members of the Lonergan scholarly community; the fact that they all agreed to contribute, and to contribute such outstanding pieces, exceeded our wildest expectations. We thank them for their cooperation and professionalism as well as for discreetly managing to keep word of this project from Michael. This volume would not have been possible, however, were it not for the early enthusiastic response given it by the University of Toronto Press's Ron Schoeffel, who was unwavering in his support of the project from its inception to its completion, and generously offered his time and expertise to us whenever we asked. We are grateful also to two anonymous readers for the University of Toronto Press for providing us with extremely perceptive responses to our manuscript and making many helpful suggestions, as well as to Terry Teskey for her invaluable editorial assistance.

Finally, we remain grateful to Michael Vertin for altogether different reasons. This *Festschrift* has its origin in a discussion we had several years ago about one of the most influential and gifted teachers under whom we have been privileged to study. Michael is both a consummate teacher and a deeply respected interpreter and developer of Lonergan. His service and contribution to the University of Toronto's academic community and the global Lonergan community, and, in addition, his profound influence on the lives of hundreds of former students, make him a most worthy subject for a *Festschrift*. As editors, we hope this collection is a fitting tribute to Michael Vertin's career, and to what he holds to be Lonergan's most significant contribution to the scholarly world: the importance of insight.

John J. Liptay Jr
David S. Liptay

Notes

1 For this quotation, and Vertin's own account of his relations with Lonergan, see Michael Vertin, 'Remembering Bernard Lonergan,' *Lonergan Research Institute Bulletin* 13 (1998), 3 4.

2 As Crowe himself notes in his *Three Thomist Studies*, ed. Michael Vertin (Boston: Lonergan Center of Boston College, 2000), 'The catalogue of his writings is already long – the card index in our Lonergan Research Institute shows some forty items under his name, and it lists only those works of his pertaining to Lonergan. One might expect and hope that he would pursue creative studies of his own instead of sacrificing time and energy ... to further the work of another' (p. xix).

3 For a list of Vertin's publications, including his editorial work, see the bibliography at the end of this volume.

PART ONE

Understanding Insight

Matthew Lamb

Lonergan's Transpositions of Augustine and Aquinas: Exploratory Suggestions

To set up the *Sitz im Leben* of this essay, I recall how, during the very first visit I had with Fr Bernard Lonergan at the Gregorian in Rome during the early fall of 1964, he asked if I had studied the early dialogues of St Augustine, especially the *Soliloquies*. Twenty years later, as some of us were sharing memories after Lonergan's funeral, several remarked how he stated that as he got older he became more Augustinian. While there is little in the written archives about his study and reading of Augustine, there are massive materials charting his reaching up to the mind of Aquinas. Both Lonergan's reference to Augustine and his well-documented indebtedness to Aquinas indicate a pedagogical starting point for any students wishing to understand Lonergan's achievements.

As I look back on my years of teaching and writing on Lonergan's work, I have found that many students who read Lonergan's *Insight* and/or *Method in Theology* fail to appreciate the explanatory character of his cognitional theory because they did not engage in any in-depth study of his earlier works on Aquinas. Instead they misread him by not fully appreciating how his call to intellectual conversion challenges all modern and postmodern variations on Cartesian and Kantian themes. In contrast, students who have studied both Aquinas and Augustine have tended to attain a more profound grasp of Lonergan's achievement.

The work of Michael Vertin has been an aid in overcoming such misreadings of Lonergan, in his contributions to our understanding of the significance of Lonergan's work for our times. In his honour, but without the clarity of his prose, I should like to explore Lonergan's contributions as efforts at transposition. I have worried over the decades that graduate students and colleagues have not had the long years of study of the great achievements of the past that were accorded those of us who had religious communities to support years of learning.

One cannot transpose what one does not know. Lonergan himself was explicit about the importance of transposition for the renewal of Catholic intellectual life.[1] The new is 'analogous to the old,' Lonergan wrote, and therefore the new 'can preserve all that is valid in the old' and therefore 'can achieve the higher synthesis mentioned by Leo XIII in his bull *Aeterni Patris: vetera novis augere et perficere,* augmenting and perfecting the old by what is new. To that end we must labor and for it we must pray.'[2]

The work of transposition indicates the Catholic character of Lonergan's work. By that I mean the importance of realizing that the higher fulfils and corrects but does not negate the lower; the newer does not negate but enriches the older. Transposition is not done once and for all; it is as ongoing as the method based on authentic interiority in any historically aware culture.[3] The reason for a constant return is the stark contradictions between the ancients (embracing the Greek and Roman philosophers, the Greek and Latin Fathers, and the Medievals) and the moderns who have been so influential in shaping modern and postmodern cultures (Machiavelli, Hobbes, Spinoza, Locke, Descartes, Rousseau, Nietzsche). Central issues are the rejections by the moderns of ancient understandings of nature, along with the ancients' love of wisdom as spiritual exercises, ways of living that attune the mind and heart to the whole of reality. For moderns only particulars exist, and any grouping or explanatory unification is an act of the will rather than a discernment of the mind. Power as force and domination replaces wisdom as the path to follow, and this 'philosophy' has rooted itself in nearly all facets of modern life and grounds the modern and postmodern form of this longer cycle of decline. Lonergan realized that this longer cycle of decline would require ongoing efforts at retrieval and transposition rooted in long-term commitments and self-sacrifice.[4]

For recovery and transposition to effectively address the longer cycle of decline, theology would need to recover an intellectual prestige that attracts such students into its difficult yet rewarding studies on a larger scale that could then publicly address the interface of civilizational and religious trends. However, that scale has not existed for some time. Theology long ago lost the intellectual prestige it enjoyed when it was heralded in the universities of Europe as the *Regina scientiarum* – the queen of the sciences. Nietzsche provides a key to understanding the dethroning of theology when he lumps theology with metaphysics and cognitional theory as not truly scholarly or scientific because these disciplines do not rely on the five senses to know what is real. Hence, he concludes, theology thrives on falsehoods.[5] An argument in this study will elucidate how, since the

Enlightenment, higher aspects of intelligent and rational activity have tended to atrophy, thereby contracting intellectual life to a see-saw between empiricism and idealism. This contraction of intelligence has also led to important misunderstandings of ancient and medieval theologians – and it was a life-long effort of Lonergan to correct those misunderstandings, and the all-too-modern and postmodern contraction of consciousness that has resulted in such great difficulties for religious and ecclesial life today.[6]

Lonergan on Transposition

Lonergan always – both before and after *Method in Theology* – emphasized that his work was a transposition rather than a rejection of the achievements of the great Catholic theologians, especially Augustine and Aquinas. At the end of *Verbum* he states clearly that, having established what the *vetera* really were in the intellectualist position of Aquinas, there was another task he would undertake, namely, that 'one can aim at a transposition of his position to meet the issues of our own day.'[7] He then confidently asserts: 'A completely genuine development of the thought of St Thomas will command in all the universities of the modern world the same admiration and respect that St Thomas himself commanded in the medieval University of Paris.'[8] Given the stark faculty debates in Paris, one wonders if Lonergan did not write that more as a warning than an encomium.

Transposing the great achievements of the past is not something invented by Lonergan. In the 1967 introduction to the book publication of his Verbum articles he acknowledged the debt Aquinas owed to Augustine and how deftly Aquinas inserted the Augustinian 'subject' into an Aristotelian self-knowledge of the soul.[9] However, Lonergan does give attention to the very nature of this transposition and the need to understand it. In a 1979 lecture entitled 'Horizons and Transpositions' he situated transpositions within the context of the horizon analysis.

> Now a change of horizon takes us out of the field of deductive logic. As long as one is simply logical, one remains within the same horizon. As soon as one changes one's horizon, one begins to operate in virtue of a minor or major change in one's basic assumptions. Such a change may be just a jump but also it may be a genuine transposition, a restatement of an earlier position in a new and broader context.

If a genuine transposition is the restatement of an earlier position in a new context, how are we to differentiate between genuine and inauthentic transpositions? He goes on:

> Finally, be it observed that a change of horizon cannot be demonstrated from a previous horizon. So the genuineness of transpositions cannot be a simple logical conclusion. What is basic is authenticity. It is a summit towards which one may strive and, only through such striving, may one come to some imperfect participation of what Augustine and Aquinas named Uncreated Light.[10]

This indicates that Lonergan was not merely using a figure of speech when he spoke of reaching up to the mind of Aquinas. Indeed, it is one of many texts of Lonergan that shows how he took the 'intellectual light itself which we have within us,' which later he transposed into 'the pure and unrestricted desire to know,' as indeed 'nothing else than a certain participated likeness of the Uncreated Light.'[11] The reflective insight of judgment knows a reality not by 'taking a good look' (what Lonergan calls knowledge by confrontation) but by grasping that the evidence is sufficient, the conditions are *de facto* fulfilled (knowledge by identity). One of the basic and central points that Lonergan makes is that genuine transpositions rest on knowing the realities referred to in the texts one is studying.

Thus, transposition is not a translation or transliteration from one set of texts to another. Rather, it involves judgment and thus knowledge of the realities referred to in the texts one is studying. Reaching up to the mind of an Augustine or an Aquinas means reaching up to the realities they knew.

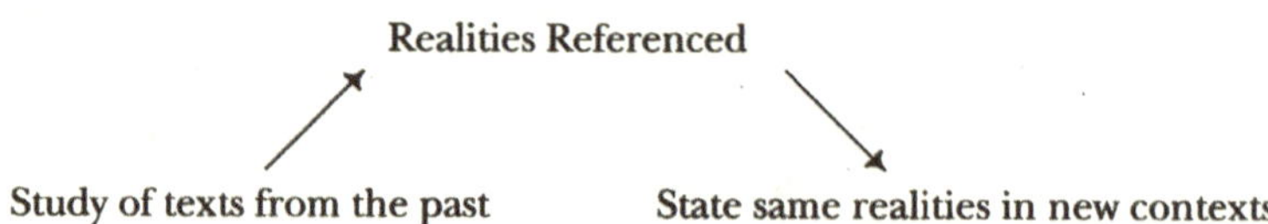

To some degree, the failure of Thomist and Augustine scholars to recognize and accomplish this transposition is what marks aspects of the 'earlier' and 'later' Lonergan. There has been much written about the 'earlier' and 'later' Lonergan, the shift that occurred between *Verbum* and *Insight* on the one hand and *Method in Theology* on the other. The writings of Lonergan in the 1940s and 1950s seem more intent on casting the transposition as one that would build upon working out what in a 1955 article he calls the 'isomorphism' between Thomism and modern developments.[12] His writings in the early period were marked by a willingness to engage Thomist philosophers and theologians as allies in the task of the Leonine transposition: *vetera novis augere et perficere.*

By 1973, however, Lonergan could write of 'the passing of Thomism' in the wake of Vatican II, and analyse its causes in a lecture entitled 'The Scope of Renewal.'[13] Just as Lonergan carefully distinguished between classicism and the great classics, the study of which he always recommended, so he distinguished Thomism from Aquinas and Augustinianism from Augustine.[14] While it is usual for Lonergan to be grouped with so-called transcendental Thomists influenced by Maréchal, he was in fact much more strongly influenced by his study of Plato, Augustine, and Aquinas than the work of Maréchal.[15] Lonergan recalled that when he came to hear of Maréchal's approach, he did not really study it so much as recognized Maréchal's treatment of judgment as confirming what he was more familiar with, namely, Augustine's key notion of *veritas* and Aquinas's notion of *esse.*[16] It was Lonergan who set Michael Vertin on his doctoral dissertation project by asking him to see if Maréchal espoused intellectual intuitions – a question he would hardly ask if he had studied the Belgian philosopher extensively himself.[17] Vertin's research uncovered some similarities but also important differences between Maréchal and Lonergan.[18]

These differences between Lonergan and the transcendental Thomists have long roots. In Lonergan's 1975 'Aquinas Today: Tradition and Innovation,' as well as in the above-mentioned 1979 article 'Horizons and Transpositions,' he writes of the 'emergence of method' in the thirteenth-century Schoolmen: the technique of the *quaestio* 'resulted in a method, for it attracted a group of specialists following a common procedure in a determinate field of investigation.'[19] But the subtleness of the method of the *quaestio* in the work of Aquinas gave way to a conceptualist deductivism and nominalism that prepared the way for a radical Enlightenment. The later scholastics paid little attention to the interplay of the *ratio inferior* and *ratio superior* and how Aquinas's cognitional theory mediated these in the objective abstraction of grasping the *species qua* in the phantasm illumined by active or agent intellect.[20] A conceptualist logicism infected metaphysics with a deductivism that was not attentive to Aristotle's own scientific practices, as Patrick Byrne has shown.[21] To recover Aquinas, Lonergan discovered, would require a profound change in oneself that many Thomistic scholars never achieved.

Lonergan's reaching up to the mind of Aquinas changed him profoundly. He realized that to recover the wisdom of Aquinas in more students of Aquinas, and bring the fruit of that recovery to the issues of our time, required making the intellectual, moral, and religious dimensions of Aquinas's intellectual achievements explicit. This meant going back to a premodern, ancient and medieval, cognitional theory wherein *theoria* was a speculative-contemplative wisdom fostering the self-knowledge of the soul. In this task Augustine's narratives of his own intellectual, moral, and religious conversion proved a foundational guide. Augustine's intellectual conversion to the Truth, moral conversion to Goodness, and religious conversion to God revealed in Christ Jesus, together with the doctrinal theology of Athanasius, grounded the shift towards theory in Thomas Aquinas.[22] This threefold conversion process of Augustine becomes in Aquinas the fundamental importance of the intellectual, moral, and theological virtues.[23]

Lonergan's call for intellectual, moral, and religious authenticity transposes the ancient and medieval call to live by what is highest. For the philosophers this was reason as highest *quoad nos* – and indeed it is what Lonergan in *Insight* analyses as the appropriation of rational self-consciousness. But for theologians what is highest *quoad se* is the Triune God revealed in Jesus Christ as the way, the truth, and the life. Lonergan analyses this in how the supernatural solution to the problem of evil sublates the humanist quest for the good life into an absolutely supernatural fulfilment in eternal life.[24] The 'law of the cross' in *De Verbo Incarnato* is a masterful transposition of the theologies of Augustine and Aquinas on how only the God who creates can redeem us by bringing life out of death and good out of evil – it shows how the only intellectually satisfying solution to the massive histories of evil and suffering is a Christ-centred theology of history rather than any philosophy of history.[25]

However, what is highest theologically cannot be reached without a continuity with the genuine achievements of the past. This is certainly true for systematic theology, as Lonergan argues in *Method in Theology*. In this context he evaluated his own early work:

> I have done two studies of the writings of St. Thomas Aquinas. One on *Grace and Freedom*, the other on *Verbum*. Were I to write on these topics today, the method I am proposing would lead to several significant differences from the presentation by Aquinas. But there also would exist profound affinities. For Aquinas' thought on grace and freedom and his thought on cognitional theory and on the Trinity were genuine achievements of the human spirit. Such achievement has a permanence of its own. It can be improved upon. It can be inserted in larger and richer contexts. But unless its substance is incorporated in subsequent work, the subsequent work will be a substantially poorer affair.[26]

Unfortunately, the serious scholarship on past achievements of the human spirit in systematic theology has declined over the past decades, as these achievements were left to historians who had no more than a common-sense scholarly grasp of the historical contexts.[27]

Method as a Transposition of Virtues, Skills, and Habits

In many respects Lonergan's *Method in Theology* is an outline of the enormous tasks of transposition. The first phase outlines what has to be done to retrieve the past, and the second phase what has to be done to transpose the genuine intellectual, moral, and religious truth, goodness, and holiness transmitted from the past into the present. This task of transposition itself resulted from Lonergan's recovery of the theoretical achievements of Aquinas by attending to the acts and objects of human intentional consciousness. The following recalls key elements in the self-knowledge of the human soul:

Soul → Powers – faculties < { Intellect / Will } > Habits < { Good (Virtues) / (Vices) Bad } > Act ←→ Objects

Lonergan's recovery of these acts and objects and transposition into intentionality or, to use the Augustinian term Lonergan preferred, 'interiority,' is anything but Kantian or Cartesian. Such transposition is rooted in attentiveness to the aspects of the self-knowledge of the soul that fall within human conscious experience, in other words, the acts and objects of consciousness.[28] This was the key in Lonergan's transposition. As he states in *Method in Theology*: 'And if modern theologians were to transpose medieval theory into the categories derived from contemporary interiority and its real correlatives, they would be doing for our age what the greater Scholastics did for theirs.'[29] This move is not the modern move to epistemology, but the cultivation of a heightened awareness of what we do when we know as Lonergan sketched it out in the first two chapters of *Verbum*. This is clear by his phrase 'and its real correlatives' – the object specifies the act. This is a transposition rooted in Aquinas and Augustine, not in Kant and Descartes.

Lonergan saw the objective abstraction in Aquinas's attention to the light of active intelligence illumining the human imagination, so that the intelligibility of the object is grasped (*species qua*); from this 'insight' the mind understands the universal in the particular (*species quae*), whereby the mind intelligently formulates the universal common to many in the concept or inner word (*species in qua*). The inner word can then, through the reflective understanding of weighing the evidence, be related to the universal in the particular and the evidence provided by the senses and the objective abstraction of the *species qua*.[30]

It is the light of active intelligence that grasps through reflective insight the sufficiency of the evidence, and so knows the intelligible and the universal in the particular. Hence, in contrast to nearly all modern epistemologies, there is no antinomy between the universal and the particular, no contradiction between the singular and the species and genus to which it belongs. The reflective insight of judgment knows the real. This knowledge is by identity; there is no Cartesian gulf between knower and known. Lonergan follows Aquinas when he states how by that light of active intelligence we can know truly and unchangeably very changeable and contingent things and events.[31] This modern gulf and all of its variations has severely hampered theology in its ability to reach up to and transpose the past.

Lonergan's development of method thus is a direct challenge to this deformation. His preliminary definition of method is really seeking to find a wise integration of the theological specialties by asking theologians to attend to their acts or operations. 'A method is a normative pattern of recurrent and related operations yielding cumulative and progressive results.'[32] And method is really a transposition of Aquinas's teaching on skills and good habits into terms that contemporaries could grasp by attending to their operations and objects.

No human being can avoid forming habits, good or bad, for our faculties are naturally oriented to act, and actions or operations are either ordered (good) or disordered (bad). How do we know we have habits? We act in a certain way with ease. How do we know if the habit is bad? The easy acts are simply repetitive, tending to degenerate our minds and souls. How do we know they are good habits? The related and recurrent acts tend to uplift our minds and souls. So Lonergan's definition of method is a differentiated way of showing how method in theology means acquiring sets of sets of intellectual and moral virtues as well as skills. Nor can we exercise those virtues in theology without receiving the gifted theological virtues. Without a living faith, along with sets of acquired intellectual and moral virtues, Catholic theology ceases. We in fact have nothing but reflections on dead texts in a very dead and deadening God-free, faith-free, privatized study of religion.

The eight functional specialties, then, are sets of sets of skills and virtues needed to recover and transpose the great achievements of the past. Lonergan attends to the related and recurrent acts or operations in each. For instance, foundations is an explanatory theoretical analysis of intellectual, moral, and religious conversion, and needs metaphysics since there is no one-to-one correlation between conscious acts and natural realities and revealed realities. Indeed, there could not be such a correspondence short of the *lumen gloriae.* For Lonergan, as for Aquinas, the science of theology will always be a science subaltern to Divine Knowledge and the knowledge of the Blessed in heaven.[33] Without acquiring metaphysical wisdom theologians would be unable to understand fundamental aspects of their tasks as Lonergan outlines them in *Method in Theology*. This is especially the case with foundations, where Lonergan sees metaphysics as playing a role in articulating the explanatory nest of terms and relations in the 'general theological categories.'[34] This metaphysically articulated foundation affects all the other specialties such as doctrines, where the ongoing discovery of mind requires attention to the 'fully metaphysical context' and the dependence of an explanatory interiority on metaphysics as what we know when we know.[35] And it affects the twofold positive function in systematics, where metaphysics provides both a heuristic structure and a criterion for proper distinctions between literal and metaphorical meaning, and between what is notional and what is real.[36]

I realize this is only a most rudimentary sketch. There would be much work to indicate how skills and good intellectual, moral, and theological habits interact in each of the eight functional specialties. It could be helpful to see how Lonergan is doing this in order to fill out key operations needed in each of the eight.[37] There is much assistance in this if we study carefully Aquinas's analysis of the intellectual, moral, and theological virtues.

The Two Phases of Functional Specialties as a Transposition

The two phases of functional specialty are transpositions of long and complex traditions in Catholic theology. St Augustine's *De Doctrina Christiana* develops the *via inventionis* (the first three books) and the *via doctrina* (Book IV). Aquinas takes these two ways – variously termed *via inventionis* and *via judicii* or *ordo disciplinae* – and shows how they are operative in speculative and practical sciences, and links them to the *ratio inferior* and *ratio superior*, to the intellectual virtues of *intellectus* and *sapientia*.[38] Lonergan transposes these in *De Deo Trino II* as a twofold movement to attain the end of theology: the way of discovery or analysis as we seek to attain knowledge, and the way of ordering what we have learned as a way of synthesis or *doctrinae seu disciplinae*.[39]

Further transpositions of the interplay of these two ways or phases could greatly benefit our understanding of theology. In other words, attending to how the related and recurrent operations are operations of intellectual, moral, and theological virtues would indicate how the first phase is influenced by the 'unity of the virtues.' This would result in a theological capacity to use researches, interpretations, histories, and dialectics of scholars more wisely, especially those writings authored by those who do not believe. For example, St Augustine had no problem using the Donatist Tyconius's *Rules* in the way of discovery; and, of course, the Fathers and Schoolmen drew upon all types of sources as they sought to fulfill their theological responsibilities.[40] In doing this they followed Augustine's wise admonition to his students: while these should be read by students to understand the revealed mysteries more fully, the students 'should not expect from them what they do not have to offer.'[41] Transposing his advice can give us much-needed wisdom in our own day.

The transposition of good theological habits and skills for Lonergan resulted in the distinction of the functional specialties only to relate them so that theological collaboration would be able to show the unifying order of theological and metaphysical wisdom. This transposition of the nature of theology really responds to a severe deformation that arose in the last of three developments of theology that Lonergan briefly outlined in his remarks on the ongoing discovery of mind.[42]

Developments

Scriptural	→ Doctrinal	→ Theoretical	→ Historical
WORD OF GOD	AS TRUE	AS INTELLIGIBLE	AS TRANSFORMATIVE

The first development led to the differentiation or development of doctrine and creed from Sacred Scripture. If the Bible as the Word of God is true, then questions arose that could not be answered simply by quoting the Bible. The great Trinitarian and Christological councils, beginning with Nicea (AD 325), realized that to assure that the Word of God in Scripture is true, one had to invoke other than biblical terms.

As this doctrinal and creedal development continued, there were questions that arose about the inner intelligibility of the many doctrines and creeds. These questions led to the second development, which differentiated theoretical *Summae* from collections of doctrines and creeds. An essential question was the extent to which this differentiation of theoretical theology would succeed in being faithful both to the scriptural and doctrinal, on the one hand, and to the exigencies of intelligence and system, on the other hand. Theology is both wisdom requiring holiness and goodness and a science, a scholarly discipline, requiring intelligence and theory. The great figure representing this integration was Thomas Aquinas.

However, the synthesis of wisdom and science in Thomas Aquinas required intellectual, moral, and theological virtues that were not adequately practised and deepened in subsequent theologians. Despite efforts to counteract it, nominalism spread, replacing wisdom with increasingly fragmented attention to particulars in isolation from their natures and ends within the universe of being. Metaphysics was increasingly dominated by a conceptualism that eclipsed the acts of judging and the knowledge of being.

With the Renaissance, Reformation, Counter-Reformation, and modern periods a new development was increasingly needed. What arose was the third development, but it was seriously lacking because the nominalistic heuristics that had all but destroyed metaphysical wisdom could not genuinely recover the tradition. Hence, the concern with history was initiated by disputes and questions that tended to fragment and cut off Scripture, Doctrines, Creeds, and *Summae* from their sapiential context. The previous two developments – doctrinal and theoretical – were called into doubt and ignored by many scholars in the name of a greater attention to empirical data. Any living continuity with the great theological traditions of the past was broken by nominalism, and so the doctrinal and theoretical traditions were devalued into purely 'textual' and 'verbal' matters. To gauge the depth of the break between the ancients and the moderns is most important, for it indicates that the third development, designated as 'historical,' calls for a profound recovery of the religious, moral, and intellectual practices of the ancients.[43]

Since we are all living in this modern and postmodern period, the analysis of the ancient texts requires attention to the realities those texts affirm if we are to break from the contracted version of history that we have inherited. Lonergan emphasizes the transformative aspect of the historical development: intellectual, moral, and religious conversion and practices must be made explicit and foundational. Once again, the key to the historical development is that the later developments do not negate the former, but build upon them in new contexts. Pope Leo XIII caught this in his famous *vetera novis augere et perficere.*

A view of this third development as historical transposition contrasts with what the noted historian of the modern Enlightenment, Peter Gay, called 'the new paganism'[44] – a judgment recently deepened and extended in Jonathan Israel's massive *The Radical Enlightenment.*[45] Enlightenment thinkers, faced with the so-called wars of religion, made fateful mistakes. They blamed religion, defining religion by its abuse rather than by the wisdom and holiness of its saints and scholars. They kept the bath water and threw out the baby. That is, they critiqued and privatized religion and provided totally secularized versions of culture, while inscribing warfare into all of nature and history. They were quite explicit in their rejections of the ancient wisdom in favour of mathematical and empirical-encyclopedic studies concentrated on disparate individual data. Sciences and intellectual formation were cut off from any concern for wisdom as a metaphysical attunement to the whole of reality. The whole of nature was dissected into data so scattered that ongoing discoveries could only be summarily brought together by the alphabet in the new encyclopedia. Natural things became fragmented data in the service of pervasive and dominative technologies. The nominalism that started shortly after Thomas Aquinas grew into an entire social and cultural horizon that affected all facets of our Enlightened world.

Early on in its existence this 'new paganism' turned its habits and skills towards the Bible, breaking it up into so many scattered texts. Spinoza warned that, like nature, the Bible was not a whole, and the truth question had to be avoided at all costs. The meaning of a text would only be by reference to other texts. As with science, so truth was identified with power, not wisdom, and so Scripture was divested of its truth as the Word of God revealing the mysterious realities of creation and redemption.[46] Rather, the Bible, like nature, was reduced to what is accessible only by sense data. This reductionism dates from the Enlightenment and Benedict de Spinoza's *Theologico-Political Treatise.*

Spinoza's view is consonant with that of the Enlightenment's faulty understanding of time and history. The Enlightenment tended to contract human time consciousness to a sensate present. This was a natural outgrowth of nominalism. It failed to mediate history as a sapiential whole in ways genuinely open to the new without negating the old. The fixation of the Enlightenment upon the present moment, set up in opposition to the past, not only mirrored the hyperindividualism of autobiography in the Enlightenment (e.g., Rousseau's *Confessions*), but also accounts for the emergence in Spinoza's *Theologico-Political Treatise* of the historical-critical methods. Neither nature nor history is open for Spinoza. They both are fixed and necessary chains of events. Confronted with the religious pluralism of his day, Spinoza sought to privatize faith and show how the Scriptures were to be empirically studied, as nature is. As he writes: 'I may sum up the matter by saying that the method of interpreting Scripture does not widely differ from the method of interpreting nature – in fact, it is almost the same.'[47] Such an interpretative study of the Scripture restricts itself to the texts alone. No appeal can be made to faith, for that is private and personal, sharply separated from reason. Faith plays no role in the interpretation of Scripture.

There are two major premises of historical and textual criticism for Spinoza. (1) Do not treat the Bible as a whole; do not treat books of the Bible as wholes; break up the text into discrete parts. One text is to find its meaning only by relation to other texts. For the universal rule is only to accept as meanings of the texts what anyone can perceive from studying the history of that text. (2) The truth question is rejected in any and all interpretation of the Bible. The texts are not to be taken as true when they are referring to any realities not perceptible by the human senses. Spinoza makes clear that biblical interpretation does not concern itself with the truth of the texts, but only with perceptible meanings. Therefore, the birth of the historical-critical methods is to treat the Bible as any other text. As Newton's mechanics sought only three-dimensional perceptible motions, so Spinoza's canons of interpretation recognize only those perceptible textual meanings found in the Scriptures as a perceptible book:

> We are at work not on the truth of passages, but solely on their meaning. We must take especial care, when we are in search of the meaning of a text, not to be led away by our reason in so far as it is founded on principles of natural knowledge (to say nothing of prejudices): in order not to confound the meaning of a passage with its truth, we must examine it solely by means of the signification of the words, or by a reason acknowledging no foundation but Scripture.[48]

Spinoza anticipates here a postmodern severe restriction to intertextuality, 'all we have is texts.' Little wonder, then, that he would restrict faith to an obedience and piety, the assent of faith to obedience, an act of will, not an intellectual act. Theology is founded on obedience to revelation and has no power ever to oppose reason. While philosophy and reason are concerned only with knowledge and truth, theology is totally separate, concerned only with obedience and piety. The teachings of the Scriptures, as Spinoza cynically remarks, need not be true, they need only promote pious and obedient acts. This is to make faith not an assent of our intelligence to Divine Intelligence, but an act of our will submitting to a blind power. This was part of the dramatic shift from wisdom to power that occurred as a consequence of nominalism. Nominalism claims that there can be no such things as universals except as mere 'names' or 'nouns' – only individual things exist. Universals are only constructs of the mind, and, as the empiricists (e.g., Hume) claimed, of less 'reality' than what we contact with our senses. Lonergan's work on the twofold phases of functional specialization offers important elements in the task of overcoming the fragmentation of modernity and postmodernity by transposing the wisdom of the ancients and medievals. Little wonder that of the eight, only history needed two chapters.

Concluding Remarks on Nature and Analogy

In addition to Lonergan's important transposition of skills and good habits into method, along with the *via inventionis* and *via judicii* to the two ways of a functionally specialized theological method, two further transpositions that he initiated and that are important for theology should be noted and further studied. The first is his recovery of a genuine notion of nature. In many ways the tasks set by what Pope John Paul II called 'the new evangelization' are more daunting than those facing the Greek and Latin Fathers and Schoolmen. For they could appeal to major philosophers who had a wise understanding of nature and had influenced their intellectual cultures. Our contemporary cultural world has no interest in wisdom or in nature as a whole created by God. As Pierre Manent has pointedly written:

> In the beginning, the world was without form and void, without laws, arts, or sciences, and the spirit of man moved over the darkness. Such, in brief, are the first words man speaks to himself when, rejecting alike both Christian law and pagan nature, he decides to receive his humanity only from himself and undertakes to be the author of his own genesis. Hobbes, Locke, and Rousseau give us three synoptic versions of this genesis that all proclaim the same good news.[49]

The new evangelization will require a recovery and transposition of Aquinas's sapiential understanding of both nature and grace. Towards this, Lonergan's transposition of the Aristotelian-Thomist understanding of nature in terms of emergent probability is an enormous resource in need of further study and application. By way of example, I would call your attention to the publications of Giovanni Sala on natural law where he indicates how Lonergan's work illumines the importance of living according to Catholic moral teachings and natural law.[50] Sala clearly shows the importance of the chapters on metaphysics in *Insight* for explanatory understanding of human interiority.[51]

A final area in need of further work in transposition has to do with the difference between metaphor and analogy, and how this relates to the affirmative and negative sides of theological and philosophical statements about God. Lonergan follows Aquinas in affirming that God is incomprehensible but not that God is unknowable.[52] Analogy differs from metaphor as knowledge of being and reality as intelligible differs from sense and imagination. The *via negativa* in regard to metaphors (e.g., God is a rock, a shepherd) denies exactly what was literally affirmed, that is, it relates to metaphorical judgments, in order to see that it was only a figure of speech (e.g., rock means fidelity, shepherd means caring).

When, however, we affirm that God is being, truth, love, goodness, simple, and so on, what is denied is *not* what is literally affirmed. The *via negativa* does not relate to the judgment, which is true, but rather relates to the act of our understanding, which is finite and limited. What is denied is the limitations of our understanding, not the truth of our knowing in true judgments. The judgment that affirms God as being, truth, love, goodness, simple, and the like, is completely certain and not metaphorically provisional. The apophatic dimension does not touch the judgment itself but rather the first act of the mind, our understanding of what we have truly affirmed; what is denied is only our limited understanding of what being, truth, goodness is. Incomprehensibility of God is not the same as unknowability. This, as Lonergan saw, following Augustine and Aquinas, is central to the fact that the light of faith heals and elevates, but never negates, the light of reason.

The teaching and writings of Michael Vertin attest to both the importance of the tasks set us by Lonergan's transpositions and the imperatives of intellectual, moral, and religious conversions if they are to be genuinely met. Lonergan's work of transposition began the labour of resolving many of the modern and postmodern contractions that have made a genuine theology so difficult and foreign to many students. He was able to grasp in method the key habits and skills underpinning the theological life, and in the two phases of theology, along with the transposition of metaphysical wisdom, he found the keys to recovery and transposition itself that heals the serious deformations of religious and theological truth generated by the modern and postmodern truncations of theological and philosophical wisdom.

Notes

1 See Bernard Lonergan, 'The Scope of Renewal' and 'Horizons and Transpositions,' both in *Philosophical and Theological Papers 1965–1980*, vol. 17 of *Collected Works of Bernard Lonergan*, ed. Robert C. Croken and Robert M. Doran (Toronto: University of Toronto Press, 2004), 282–98, 409–32.

2 Ibid., 298.

3 See my 'Will There Be Catholic Theology in the United States?' *America*, 162 (26 May 1990), 523–34. See also 'The Catholic Theological Society of Amer ica: Theologians Unbound,' in *Crisis: Politics, Culture, and the Church*, 15, no. 11 (December 1997), 36–7; and 'The Catholic Theological Society of America: A Preliminary Profile,' *The Fellowship of Catholic Scholars Quarterly* 21, no. 2 (Spring 1998), 8–10; responses to Fr Hollenbach in *Crisis: Politics, Culture and the Church* 16, no. 2 (February 1998) 3, 14; Sr Farley in *The Fellowship of Catholic Scholars Quarterly* 21, no. 4 (Fall 1998), 2–5. Over the past four decades seventy five per cent of dissertations have been done on twentieth-century themes and figures and ten per cent on nineteenth-century themes and figures. Of the remaining fifteen per cent, most were on the Bible. See Walter Principe's plaintive presidential address to the CTSA in 1991 and my response, 'History and Systematics: A Response,' *The Proceedings of the Catholic Theological Society of America* 46 (1991), 98–107.

4 See his *Insight: A Study of Human Understanding*, vol. 3 of *Collected Works of Bernard Lonergan*, ed. Frederick E. Crowe and Robert M. Doran (Toronto: University of Toronto Press, 1992), 250–67.

5 See Friederich Nietzsche, '"Reason" in Philosophy,' sec. 3 of *Twilight of the Idols*, and *The Antichrist*, sec. 9.

6 For an exposition of the need for an ongoing retrieval and transposition of Aquinas, see Wayne Hankey's 'Denys and Aquinas: Antimodern Cold and Postmodern Hot,' in *Christian Origins: Theology, Rhetoric and Community*, ed. Lewis Ayres and Gareth Jones (London: Routledge, 1998), 139–84.

7 The same is stated in the epilogue of *Insight*, 769–70: 'After spending years reaching up to the mind of Aquinas, I came to a two-fold conclusion. On the one hand, that reaching had changed me profoundly. On the other hand, that change was the essential benefit ... One can hope to reach the mind of Aquinas, and once that mind is reached, then it is difficult not to import his compelling genius to the problems of this later day.'

8 Bernard Lonergan, *Verbum: Word and Idea in Aquinas*, vol. 2 of *Collected Works of Bernard Lonergan*, ed. Frederick E. Crowe and Robert M. Doran (Toronto: University of Toronto Press, 1997), 227.

9 Ibid., 3–11.

10 Lonergan, *Philosophical and Theological Papers 1965–1980*, 410.

11 Lonergan, *Verbum*, 85–6, 91–101; see p. 66: 'For the spirit of inquiry within us never calls a halt, never can be satisfied, until our intellects, united to God as body to soul [*Summa contra Gentiles* 3, c. 51], know *ipsum intelligere* and through that vision, though then knowing aught else is a trifle [*Summa Theologiae* 1, q. 12, a. 8, ad 4m], contemplate the universe as well.' See also p. 105, where Lonergan points out how Aquinas's metaphysics has embedded within it the facts of cognitional theory based upon psychological facts. On the transposition of this into the pure and unrestricted desire to know, cf. *Insight*, 372–5, 659–67, 767–8.

12 Bernard Lonergan, *Collection*, vol. 4 of *Collected Works of Bernard Lonergan*, ed. Frederick E. Crowe and Robert M. Doran (Toronto: University of Toronto Press, 1988), 133–44.

13 Lonergan, *Philosophical and Theological Papers 1965–1980*, 282–98.

14 See my 'The Notion of the Transcultural in B. Lonergan's Theology,' *Method: Journal of Lonergan Studies* 8, no. 1 (1990). Note also how he distinguishes Aquinas from his commentators in, e.g., *Method in Theology* (Toronto: University of Toronto Press, 2003), 280.

15 Lonergan has been too casually lumped together with the 'movement or school' of transcendental Thomism. R.J. Henle's study of the movement indicates that Lonergan has sources other than it. See his *The American Thomistic Revival* (St. Louis: St. Louis University Press, 1999), 348ff.

16 Bernard Lonergan, 'Insight Revisted,' *A Second Collection*, ed. William F.J. Ryan and Bernard J. Tyrell (London: Darton, Longman & Todd, 1974), 265: 'I was sent to Rome for theology, and there I was subject to two important influences. One was from an Athenian, Stefanos Stefanu, who had entered the Jesuit Sicilian province and had been sent to Louvain to study philosophy

at a time when Maréchal taught psychology to the Jesuit students and the other professors at the scholasticate taught Maréchal. Stefanu and I used to prepare our exams together. Our aim was clarity and rigor – an aim all the more easily obtained, the less the theses really meant. It was through Stefanu by some process of osmosis, rather than through struggling with the five great *Cahiers*, that I learnt to speak of human knowledge as not intuitive but discursive with the decisive component in judgment. This view was confirmed by my familiarity with Augustine's key notion, *veritas*, and the whole was rounded out by Bernard Leeming's course on the Incarnate Word, which convinced me that there could not be a hypostatic union without a real distinction between essence and existence. This, of course, was all the more acceptable, since Aquinas' *esse* corresponded to Augustine's *veritas* and both harmonized with Maréchal's view of judgment.'

17 See 'An Interview with Michael Vertin,' Lonergan website, http://www.lonergan.on.ca/interviews/vertin.htm.

18 Michael Vertin, 'Maréchal, Lonergan and the Phenomenology of Knowing,' in *Creativity and Method: Essays in Honor of Bernard Lonergan*, ed. Matthew Lamb (Milwaukee: Marquette University Press, 1981), 411–22.

19 Lonergan, *Philosophical and Theological Papers 1965–1980*, p. 421. See also Bernard Lonergan, *A Third Collection*, ed. Frederick E. Crowe (New York: Paulist Press, 1985), 35–54.

20 See Lonergan, *Verbum*, and note how *ratio inferior et superior* play into the *via inventionis et via judicii vel doctrinae* in Thomas Aquinas's *Summa Theologiae* 1, q. 79, aa. 8 and 9.

21 Patrick Byrne, *Analysis and Science in Aristotle* (New York: State University of New York Press, 1991).

22 These three conversions are especially clear in St Augustine's *Confessions*, Books V through IX; see also Ernest Fortin's several essays on Augustine in *The Birth of Philosophic Christianity*, ed. J. Brian Benestad (New York: Rowman & Littlefield, 1996), 1–120. On the movement towards theory, cf. Lonergan's 'The Origins of Christian Realism,' in *A Second Collection*, 239–61. The foundational reality of intellectual, moral, and religious conversion is in Lonergan's *Method in Theology*, 267–94.

23 Cf. Thomas Aquinas, *Summa Theologiae* 1-2, qq. 55–67; 2-2, 1–170.

24 Lonergan, *Insight*, 747ff.

25 See Bernard Lonergan, *De Verbo Incarnato* (Rome: Gregorian University, 1964), 445–85; see also my 'Eternity and Time,' in *Gladly to Learn, Gladly to Teach: Essays in Honor of Ernest Fortin*, ed. Michael P. Foley and Douglas Kries (Lanham, MD: Lexington Books, 2002).

26 Lonergan, *Method in Theology*, 352.

27 For example, in the preface of his oft-cited biography of Augustine, Peter Brown admits that he has not scaled the heights of Augustine's *De Trinitate*. This becomes evident when he fails to understand the profound struggles Augustine had with intellectual conversion, as narrated in the *Confessions*, interpreting these as a change from a 'literary career' to one in philosophy. Brown puts Augustine's own designation of this as a conversion in quotes,

remarking that in its final form this career change was 'most idiosyncratic' (*Augustine of Hippo* [Berkeley: University of California Press, 1975, second printing], 101 ff.). Little wonder, then, that Elaine Pagels, who relied so heavily on Brown's presentation of Augustine, would further distort Augustine's achievements in her *Adam, Eve, and the Serpent* (New York: Random House, 1988), 98–154. We now have graduate students and theologians writing on Pagels, so we are at the stage of popularization of a common-sense popularization (Pagels) of a common-sense popularization (Brown). This is but one small example of how theology is impoverished today.

28 See the massive works of Giovanni Sala contrasting Lonergan and Kant. Kant excluded the *ratio superior* to which Lonergan calls our attention.

29 Lonergan, *Method in Theology*, 327–8.

30 Lonergan, *Verbum*, 71–8.

31 Cf. *Summa Theologiae* 1, q. 84, a. 6 ad 1: 'For the light of agent intellect is needed by which we can know unchangeable truth in changeable things, and distinguish the things themselves from the [sensible] likenesses of things.' For many other texts on how this light is operative in judging correctly, cf. Lonergan, *Verbum*, 90–103.

32 Lonergan, *Method in Theology*, 4.

33 See Bernard Lonergan, *De Deo Trino*, vol. 2 (Rome: Gregorian University, 1964), 249ff.; Lonergan, *De Verbo Incarnato*, 332ff.; Guy Mansini, 'Understanding St. Thomas on Christ's Immediate Knowledge of God,' *The Thomist* 59 (1995), 91–124.

34 Lonergan, *Method in Theology*, 287.

35 Ibid., 308–9, 316.

36 Ibid., 343.

37 A transposition of the sets of virtues might also assist in Michael Vertin's exploration of the two phases in human living; see his 'Acceptance and Actualization: The Two Phases of My Human Living,' *Method: Journal of Lonergan Studies* 21, no. 1 (Spring 2003), 67–86: 'The central thesis of my paper is that there is an important differentiation of transcendental method *before* the one that generates the eight functionally specialized methods. That is to say, the operations that make up my concrete human living, together with their objects, emerge in a normative pattern not only of four levels but also of two phases, an *acceptive* phase and an *actualizational* phase; and just as the pattern of the four levels constitutes transcendental method, so the differentiation of the four levels into two phases generates two special methods that may be labeled *acceptive* and *actualizational*, respectively.'

38 See *In III Sententiarum* d. 34, q. 1, art. 2; see also *Summa Theologiae* 1, Prol. & q. 79, a. 9c.

39 Lonergan, *De Deo Trino*, vol. 2, 33ff.

40 See *De Doctrina Christiana* III, chaps. 30ff.

41 Ibid.

42 Lonergan, *Method in Theology*, 302–19.

43 By 'practices' I do not mean external behaviours as much as the interior dispositions and acts of questing, understanding, knowing, loving, and how

these acts are all wisely ordered towards the worship of the Triune God.

44 Peter Gay, *The Enlightenment: The Rise of Modern Paganism* (New York: Vintage, 1968). Gertrude Himmelfarb's *The Roads to Modernity* (New York: Knopf, 2004) seeks to offer a very different notion of the Enlightenment by concentrating on her enlarged version of the British. She does not advert to Israel's work; see n. 45.

45 Jonathan I. Israel, *Radical Enlightenment: Philosophy and the Making of Modernity 1650–1750* (New York: Oxford University Press, 2002).

46 Ibid., 157–274, 445–76; and Benedict de Spinoza, *Theologico-Political Treatise*, trans. R.H.M. Elwes (New York: Dover, 1951). Note Lonergan's remark, 'if one starts speculating on the basis of a Dutch philosophy, one gets into bad problems. The greatest Dutch philosopher, I always tell Dutchmen, was Spinoza,' in *Philosophical and Theological Papers 1965–1980*, 432.

47 Spinoza, *Theologico-Political Treatise*, 99.

48 Ibid., 101.

49 Pierre Manent, *The City of Man*, trans. Marc A. LePain (Princeton: Princeton University Press, 1998), 183.

50 See his *Gewissensentscheidung: Philosophisch-theologische Analyse von Gewissen und sittlichem Wissen* (Vienna: Tyrolia, 1993); 'Lex Naturae e Storia,' *Rivista di Filosofia Neo-scolastica* 63, no. 3 (1971), 241–94; 'I consultori familiari cattolici nella Repubblica Federale Tedesca,' *Rivista Bimestrale de Teologia e Scienze Umane* 4 (1998), 549–69. On the new demographic data indicating a global depopulation, with special relevance to Europe, Japan, China, and India, see Ben Wattenberg, *Fewer: How the New Demography of Depopulation Will Shape Our Future* (Chicago: Ivan R. Dee, 2004).

51 See his *Lonergan and Kant* (Toronto: University of Toronto Press, 1994). Note that the discussion Lonergan has regarding interiority and metaphysics in *Method in Theology*, 120ff., shows how the levels of conscious operations, wherein the higher sublate the lower, can be transposed into metaphysical terms.

52 See Lonergan, *Verbum*, 78–105, and *Method in Theology*, 306–18. Aquinas would always add *quasi-ignotus*, for we know that God is, and we can analogically know divine attributes even though we cannot comprehend them.

Mark D. Morelli

Obstacles to the Implementation of Lonergan's Solution to the Contemporary Crisis of Meaning

There is, then, a rock on which one can build. The rock ... is the subject in his conscious, unobjectified attentiveness, intelligence, reasonableness, responsibility.[1]

It was Bernard Lonergan's view that the challenge facing contemporary philosophy is epochal. It is analogous to the challenge confronted by Socrates, Plato, and Aristotle to complete and consolidate the transition from the 'mythic mentality' to the 'logical mentality.'[2] As philosophy arose and took root in response to the crisis of self-knowledge provoked by the collapse of the mythic superstructure, so philosophy today is called upon to respond creatively to a second crisis in our knowledge of ourselves. But if the present crisis resembles that faced by the Greeks in its epochal dimensions, it differs from it in a fundamental way. The Greek search for foundational self-knowledge was in response to the breakdown of myth. The contemporary quest is for new foundations to replace those laid by the Greeks. The contemporary challenge is to complete and consolidate an epochal transition, which began in the late Renaissance and continues to unfold, from the 'classicist mentality' to the 'modern mentality.'

In *Insight* Lonergan proposed his solution to this epochal crisis.[3] But, as the classical solution and the mentality it fostered differ significantly from myth and the mythic mentality, so the solution proposed by Lonergan rests upon a conception of foundations that differs significantly from foundations of the sort that support the classicist mentality. As the collapse of myth evoked, not a new myth, but the establishment of logical foundations, so the collapse of those logical foundations calls neither for a return to myth nor for another logical foundation. The Greek historical experience was limited to the breakdown of myth. It was an experience of the collapse of *an unreflective, spontaneous mediation of meaning.* It evoked reflection on the adequacy of the mythic mediation of meaning. Our historical experience of the breakdown of the classical mediation of meaning, in contrast, is an experience of the breakdown of a *reflectively achieved effort to control meaning.* The breakdown of classicism evokes reflection, not merely on the adequacy of the classical mediation of meaning, but on the adequacy of the *deliberate control of meaning* imposed by the Greeks and exercised by the classicist mentality.[4] To Lonergan's mind, therefore, the foundation required to meet the challenge of the contemporary crisis of meaning cannot be another *logical foundation* in the classicist fashion. It must be a *methodical foundation* in the distinctively modern fashion. As the Greeks completed and consolidated the transition from the mythic mentality to the logical mentality, we must complete and consolidate the transition from the logical mentality to the methodical mentality. Accordingly, the solution to the contemporary crisis of meaning proposed by Lonergan in *Insight* is not another putatively foundational set of universal and necessary propositions, but a more radically foundational set of prelogical operations, or a *transcendental method.*

Efforts to implement the classicist response to the breakdown of myth, as is well known, met with intense personal, social, political, and cultural resistance. Its implementation required the development of strategies for overcoming this wide-ranging resistance to the new logical control of meaning. Similarly, efforts to implement Lonergan's response to the breakdown of classicism are likely to be resisted, and implementation of the new methodical control of meaning requires the development of appropriate pedagogical strategies. But, as the new methodical controls to be implemented differ radically from the old logical controls, so the nature of the resistance and the obstacles to be overcome are different, and the strategies for implementing the new controls must differ as well.

My purpose in this essay is to trace the general character of the major obstacles to be overcome by the philosopher who undertakes to implement Lonergan's solution to the contemporary crisis of meaning. To this end, I shall describe, first, salient symptoms of the breakdown of the classical control of meaning. Secondly, I shall outline Lonergan's understanding of the epochal shift from classicism to modernity. Thirdly, I shall say a bit more about Lonergan's innovative conception of the type of foundation that is needed to meet the demands of our times. The foundation Lonergan proposes is not to be sought by turning from the offerings of modernism back to those of classicism, nor by turning from the offerings of postmodernism back to those of modernism, nor by turning from the offerings of both modernism and classicism to those of postmodernism. Finally, I shall introduce a nest of terms I find helpful for the exposition of the obstacles, identify two major obstacles, and propose two ways in which those obstacles may be at least mitigated if not thoroughly overcome.

1 Symptoms of the Breakdown

Symptoms of the breakdown of the classical control of meaning are manifested both at street level, so to speak, and in the higher reaches of our culture. In the culture at large the effects are revealed most clearly by the unchecked spread of a mood of untroubled tolerance for relativistic utterances, both cognitive and moral, and by a seeming obliviousness to their often blatant inconsistency with the meaningful uttering itself. At the more sophisticated, philosophical level of our culture, they appear in a variety of ways. Most telling are the ongoing controversy surrounding foundations and the related, less prominent, but nevertheless persistent and simmering conflict surrounding the data, method, and aim of philosophy itself. Perhaps related to these conflicts is the variety of attitudes taken in contemporary philosophy to the classical mediation of meaning, two of which are especially prominent.

We may distinguish broadly in contemporary philosophic practice between a traditionalist 'right' with an archaist tendency to maintain or to reinstitute classical controls, on the one hand, and a progressivist 'left' that regards these controls as outmoded. The 'left' appears to hold the view that classical controls of meaning have outlived their usefulness and to revel in the liberation of mind and psyche from classical strictures. Inasmuch as it undertakes to question the classical ideal of rationality itself, it evidently discerns the radicality of the breakdown. The 'right,' on the other hand, regards the classical mediation of meaning as possibly in need of updating but as still authoritative and perhaps even eternally valid; and it is suspicious of leftist 'liberation.' If it recognizes the grand scale of the shift going forward, it seems to view it as a declinatory movement and so to resist it. Very broadly speaking, one trend is more or less self-consciously postmodern whereas the other is more or less self-consciously antimodern. But this is a gross distinction. It is intended only to identify major tendencies of the present. Individual philosophers may lean more to the left or more to the right in their actual practice; or they may be engaged in one of a growing number of efforts to unite or reconcile the two tendencies. But these leanings and conciliatory efforts, it appears, are themselves symptomatic of the waning authority of the classical control of meaning. In short, contemporary philosophic practice seems to be an unstable, sometimes volatile, mixture of complementary and radically opposed orientations and methods, and this instability seems to be related directly to the breakdown of the classical mediation of meaning.

These are, however, only symptoms. They are, as it were, only the bulging surface of the groundswell of centuries. If we restrict our attention to these derivative phenomena, the more radical challenge posed by the breakdown of the classical controls of meaning and the rise of modern controls will not be met. For example, we might muster logical arguments against quotidian relativism, but in making such arguments we assume the foundational adequacy of the logical control of meaning, and we presume a similar adherence in our interlocutors. Again, we may attempt eclectic syntheses of the doctrines of the philosophic schools of the present, but such eclectic aggregation presupposes the controls governing the way these schools mediate their doctrines. To Lonergan's mind, if the demands of our times are to be met successfully, we philosophers must eschew as short-sighted and insufficiently radical the symptomatic responses of the progressive philosophical 'left,' the traditionalist philosophical 'right,' and the eclectic philosophical 'centre.' We must undertake to complete, not only intellectually but also practically, the transition to an entirely new set of controls. Such completion requires the identification, assimilation, and accommodation of the epochal shift from classicism to modernity and the articulation of new and more durable foundations.

This philosophic requirement, in Lonergan's view, is to be fulfilled partially by the radical, philosophic taking-possession of oneself that he names critical self-appropriation.[5] Very briefly, critical self-appropriation requires (1) discrimination between two ways of knowing – one perceptual, confrontational, and immediate and the other intelligent, reasonable, and mediating; (2) a grasp of the dynamic structure of intelligent and reasonable knowing, not by cataloguing the abstract properties of knowing as an object for study, but by appropriating one's own intelligent and rational self-consciousness; and (3) a consciousness that is sufficiently cultured and, therefore, capable of discovering, in its own presence to itself in its cognitive performance, the controls of meaning operative in both the classical and the modern mind.[6]

It is this process – the critical self-appropriation of the sufficiently cultured subject – that, Lonergan argues, is the means to the adoption of a new foundational posture proportionate to the demands of our times. But in Lonergan's view this radical shift from classical to modern controls, in its sweeping dimensions, has yet to be assimilated, and the requisite philosophic adaptation by way of critical self-appropriation has yet to be achieved. Obviously, given the present state of things, an effective program of implementation, while not a utopian dream, is still a fairly distant hope. As Hegel might put it, Spirit moves at its own pace and lingers patiently in one-sidedness.

For the most part, then, we have broken with and virtually discarded what Lonergan calls classicist emphases and their accompanying expectations and guiding ideal. I say 'for the most part' because an epochal shift of this sort is not a clean break with the past, as my brief symptomatology of the present illustrates, but a very complex and concrete pattern of lags afflicted throughout by strong tendencies towards symptomatic derailment. Ongoing transformation of actual practices both in the specialized disciplines and in the occupations of the culture at large typically outpaces reflective recognition, assimilation, and articulation of the shifts in ideals, expectations, methods, and techniques upon which they have come to rely. Actual shifts in the way we control our acts of meaning are *lived* before they are *thematized*. Until they are thematized, they elude deliberate assimilation and proportionate accommodation and adaptation.

2 From 'Classicism' to 'Modernity'

What, in more detail, is this radical shift that is manifesting itself variously in the unchecked spread of quotidian relativism, in the 'playful' progressivism of self-styled postmodern philosophy, and in the archaist *gravitas* of contemporary antimodernism? Before I take up this question, it may be helpful to pause to reflect more generally on Lonergan's contrast between 'classicism' and 'modernity.' First, the contrast is not the result of the application by him of an *a priori* typology or periodization in the manner, for example, of Hegel in his *Philosophy of History*. The course of history, for Lonergan, is always and everywhere an admixture of progress-and-decline. Of the contrast Lonergan wrote in 1970:

> I did not think things wrong because they were classicist; on the contrary, I found a number of things that I thought wrong, and, on putting them together, I found what I have named classicism. Again, I do not think things are right because they are modern, but I did find a number of things I thought right and they are modern.[7]

A second point is terminological. Lonergan sometimes uses 'classicist' and 'classical' interchangeably. On one occasion, however, he distinguishes clearly and emphatically the meanings of the two terms. A brief discussion of his usages may help us to avoid a gross misinterpretation of Lonergan's account of the shift from 'classicism' to 'modernity' and of the problem of reorientation with which it confronts us.

2.1 *'The Classical Ideal' and 'Classicism': Terminology*

Lonergan's most detailed accounts of the epochal shift from 'classicism' to 'modernity' occur in his so-called later writings (post 1964–65). But during the period of his transition from the 'earlier' to the 'later' period, he distinguished carefully between the classical ideal, on the one hand, and classicism and its effects, on the other. During that transitional period, moreover, he discussed in some detail his notion of an ideal.

An ideal is a heuristic anticipation of one's goal that determines (a) the method one employs to achieve the goal, (b) one's approach to the goal, and, in the end, (c) the results of one's pursuit of the goal. Lonergan found illustrations of the development of the ideal of knowledge in mathematics, the natural sciences, and philosophy.[8] In brief, the pursuit of knowledge unfolds within a context of anticipations that specify what the unknown will be like if and when it is known. Without such a context, precise questions could not be asked. This context of anticipations constitutes an ideal of knowledge; it gives rise to questions, techniques, and methods, i.e., to cognitive acts of meaning of particular types. In the course of its implementation, the limitations of an operative ideal become apparent in the further questions evoked by its results. Normally the ideal undergoes a change, and so the techniques and methods employed change as well.

As in mathematics and the natural sciences, so in philosophy there are changes in operative ideals that are occasioned by the pursuit of the ideals. But, there is a significant difference that arises from the very nature of philosophy. Inasmuch as philosophy is a comprehensive and reflective discipline, it includes in its reflective sweep the ideals of knowledge and methods at work in the other sciences and disciplines as well as those at work in its own procedures. So it is that Aristotle, for example, relying on Plato's methodological explorations and his own dialectical assessment of incipient scientific inquiry, articulated an ideal of scientific knowledge (*episteme*). So it is that Kant undertook his criticism of the ideal of pure reason modelled on Euclid and at work in the philosophies of Leibniz, Spinoza, and Wolff. So it is that contemporary continental philosophy, now historically conscious, struggles with the post-Kantian realization, first articulated and illustrated by Hegel in his *Phenomenology of Spirit*, that *every* ideal of knowledge, in virtue of its inescapably heuristic character, is bound eventually to be found wanting.[9]

The shift of ideals by which we philosophers are currently challenged is a radical change in the context of anticipations that govern our pursuit of the unknown. Lonergan sometimes refers to the ideal that is being replaced as the 'classical' ideal, and sometimes he refers to it as the 'classicist' ideal. At one stage of his thinking, it seems, he was motivated to distinguish clearly the different meanings for him of the two adjectives. The 'classical' ideal rests upon a distinction between the theoretic life with its apprehension of the abstract and universal, on the one hand, and the practical life with its apprehension of the concrete and particular, on the other. It rests upon a 'theoretic differentiation of consciousness,' a development of the capacity to operate with nests of related terms in which the terms are defined by the relations and the relations are defined by the terms. It presupposes a 'real apprehension,' to borrow Newman's phrase, of theoretical procedures. 'Classicism,' in contrast, he characterizes as 'the fruit of an unsuccessful [classical] education' in which (1) there is no real grasp of theory, of what theory means, or of theoretic procedures; (2) there is no real apprehension of the concrete and particular in its endless variety, detail, and difference; (3) instances are regarded as imperfect examples of universal abstractions; and (4) differences are viewed only as accidental (*per accidens*), while knowledge of the universal is regarded as knowledge of all that is important. In brief, classicism in this more precise sense is something like the *haute vulgarisation* of the hard-won classical ideal of theoretical understanding. The classical ideal emerged with the development and real apprehension of the difference between common-sense procedures for dealing with the concrete and particular, on the one hand, and theoretical procedures for dealing with the abstract and universal, on the other.[10] By the 'classical ideal,' then, Lonergan means a real development of the capacity to perform cognitive acts of meaning; he means the epochal advance known commonly as the Greek discovery of the mind. By 'classicism,' on the other hand, he means the consequences of the appropriation of the language and techniques associated with that advance in the absence of a real apprehension of the nature and requirements of the context of anticipations constitutive of it. 'Classical' is non-pejorative, but 'classicist' is clearly derogatory.

Still another step is required if we are to interpret Lonergan's account of the shift correctly. Classicism is a common caricature of the classical ideal, from which the classical ideal should be distinguished. Obviously, the superficiality of *haute vulgarisation* of any sort should be avoided, and classicism is no exception. But Lonergan also insists that the classical ideal itself, of which classicism is a derailment and an imitation, must be and is being superseded. The discovery of mind is ongoing.[11] 'The Greek differentiation of consciousness,' he wrote,

> was a momentous event in human history, but there is a further element, a further differentiation, in modern consciousness. The Greek differentiation was theory and practice, and that differentiation is not enough to deal with any serious modern problem. The differentiation that we need in order to deal with our problems is threefold: common sense, theory, *and interiority*.[12]

The interior differentiation of consciousness preserves and goes beyond the theoretic differentiation and *a fortiori* beyond its vulgar appropriations.

The emergence of interiority entails a shift of the foundations of our inquiry 'from the realm of theory to the realm of interiority, the realm of *Existenz*, self-appropriation, conversion (intellectual, moral, religious).'[13] So it is that Lonergan proposes critical self-appropriation as the demand of the present age.

With the emergence of the theoretic differentiation of consciousness we were offered self-evident, necessary first principles as the normative foundation for a theoretical critique of common sense (as incipiently implemented in Plato's 'Socratic' dialogues and consolidated in Aristotle's systematic philosophy) and for the products of theory itself. The interior differentiation offers a new normative foundation and reveals 'a necessary function of criticism from the realm of interiority'[14] of both common sense and theory, as well as of the ways in which the two have thus far been distinguished from one another under the governance of either the classical ideal or its *haute vulgarisation*.

Lonergan's analysis of the epochal shift to the standpoint of interiority, then, is not an analysis of a shift from the 'classicist' caricature to the 'modern' mentality. There would be little or nothing to be gained by detailed criticism from the realm of interiority of the superficial stances arising from the *haute vulgarisation* of the classical ideal. Such a critique would succeed only in exhibiting the derailment of the classical ideal and in reinstating in its original purity a classical differentiation of theory and common sense that fails to meet the problems of the present. It is enough to recognize 'classicism' as the *haute vulgarisation* of a real development of the ideal of knowledge and then to move on to implement an interior critique in the proper sense, that is, one whose critical negativity is balanced by a thoughtful recovery and development of the elements of the classical ideal to be preserved in the shift to modernity. So it is that, in his analysis of the epochal shift in the control of cognitive meaning, Lonergan carries out both a suspicious and a teleological hermeneutic of the classical ideal, rather than merely a suspicious hermeneutic of that ideal and of the superficial derailment of it that he names 'classicism.'

It remains that, despite the distinction Lonergan makes between the two adjectives 'classicist' and 'classical' during the transitional stage of his thought, in his subsequent discussions he employs the terms indiscriminately to refer to what has been described here as 'the classical ideal.' In fact, he employs 'classicist' more frequently than he does 'classical' to designate the mentality that is superseded in the transition to modernity. Obviously, a merely negative critique of a caricature of the classical ideal that is being superseded would not bring us to the heart of the matter despite the partial liberation it affords, and Lonergan certainly knew this. It may be that the 'later' Lonergan concluded that the persistence and tenaciousness of the *classical* mentality in the contemporary world, despite the mounting evidence that it has outlived its usefulness, warranted his describing it as an 'ism,' and permitted him to suppress the distinction between 'classical' and 'classicist' in his 'later' writings. Or it may be that he simply took for granted that a successful critique of the classical ideal is *a fortiori* a successful critique of its *haute vulgarisation*. Whatever the reasons, one may safely assume that in the more detailed account of the epochal shift that follows, 'classicism' means the mentality expressed by the classical mediation of meaning that is being superseded.

2.2 From Classicism to Modernity

In his analysis of the transition from the classicist to the modern mentality, Lonergan identifies five related shifts of emphasis at which I have already hinted. The classicist mentality emphasizes (1) the control of meaning and expression by a logic, (2) scientific inquiry of the Aristotelian type, (3) the metaphysical soul, and (4) a fixed and unchanging human nature; and (5) it relies, at least *prima facie* (i.e., it seems to take itself to be relying), upon a foundation consisting of propositions that are to be regarded as self-evident, necessary first principles.[15]

The first four emphases have been or are being replaced by new preoccupations: (1) with the methodical as distinct from, but not exclusive of, the merely logical control of meaning and expression; (2) with scientific inquiry of the modern type; (3) with pre-metaphysical description of the conscious subject, who, unlike the metaphysical soul, enjoys only an intermittent existence but is, when present, nevertheless experientially accessible;[16] and (4) with an emphasis upon human history and upon the constitutive and self-constitutive function of human meaning.

The fifth dimension of this shift pertains most directly to the articulation of new foundations that are to replace propositional first principles. It unfolds as reflection upon the unfolding of the first four shifts of emphasis. The satisfactory completion of the first four transitions depends, in turn, upon the successful completion of the fifth. Moreover, upon the successful completion of the fifth transition depends, not entirely but still in large part, the re-establishment of performative consistency at the level of common-sense living and the reversal of the slide into quotidian relativism, the successful harvesting of the fruits of postmodern suspicion of both classicism and modernity, a successful critical philosophical integration of the classical *vetera* with the modern *nova* that does justice to both, and the successful infusion of philosophic practice with a new relevance to the conduct of life. In short, upon the completion of the fifth transition depends the successful reorientation of contemporary culture both at street level and in its higher reaches. This completing moment would amount to an explicit *intellectual* regrounding and integration of the new ideal, by which a future *actual* integration at the level of concrete *praxis* may be guided and controlled. It would be the successful differentiation of the standpoints, modes of operation, and 'worlds' of common sense, theory, and interiority.

This completing achievement is not to be expected from any philosophical movement that takes for granted that propositional principles are the basis of philosophy, restricts its attention and analytic scrutiny to the conceptual field of propositions, and ignores the nagging problem of the preconceptual, pre-linguistic, and pre-predicative generation of concepts. Nor is it to be expected from any predominantly negative program of philosophical critique. Nor, naturally, may we expect an archaist program to complete the transition, inasmuch as it will regard the classicist and modern mentalities as virtually mutually exclusive contexts of anticipation of the unknown. Precise identification, understanding, and assimilation of the four shifts of emphasis and of the foundational problem they pose require a developed historical consciousness capable of grasping the classicist 'before' and the modern 'after' and of discovering the complementarity of their differing emphases. Adequate formulation and articulation of new foundations presupposes a grasp of the relations of the old propositional foundations to the operative foundations upon which classicism implicitly relied and upon which the new emphases rely with greater or less explicitness. The first four dimensions of the shift, then, occur at the level of lived experience and engagement, whereas the completing fifth occurs only on the philosophic heights of reflective, assimilating thematization of the newly emerging and differently founded flow of lived cognitive experience.

The classical ideal has collapsed or is collapsing, not because it is simply wrong, but because our actual practice has outrun it. Classicism gives relatively adequate expression to the controlling ideal of the actual noetic practice upon which, during the period of its emergence, it reflected, and so it regarded itself with good reason as sufficiently foundational. Given unanticipated modern developments, that ideal and the associated controls of meaning tend to be regarded by the man or woman on the street, for example (who, in any case, has never in any era been a true friend of high cultural ideals), as antiquated and superfluous, or by the postmodernist as both intellectually constricting and socially corrupting. On the archaist, on the other hand, the classicist mentality maintains a tenuous grip despite the new developments. For its historical sense, even if not entirely lacking, seems nevertheless to be of the fairly thin, classicist variety that proclaims 'nothing new under the sun.' Still, one may expect the perduring enthusiasm of the traditionalist for the outmoded ideal and controls to be increasingly dampened as the oversights and omissions of the past continue to be set in bold relief by the ongoing developments of the present. Modern developments will continue to reveal ever more clearly that past claims for foundational understanding and comprehensive integration were excessively abstract, hasty, and even presumptuous.

What is demanded, then, by this critical situation is neither a clean break with the past nor a blinkered denial that modern developments exceed the putatively comprehensive grasp of classicism, but the successful completion of a *transposition* of a traditional melody into a key that can be sung by a modern voice and heard by the differently attuned modern ear.[17]

Clearly, logic is not to be abandoned in the shift to method, but subordinated to methodical procedure. It is to be subsumed and accorded a subsidiary normative role. The truth of the valid conclusion still shares in the truth of its premises, even though the emphasis has shifted from the validity of inferences to the generation of true premises.

Secondly, the Aristotelian scientific ideal of certain knowledge of things through their causes has been abandoned in practice. But Aristotle's predicaments, for example, are still useful in modern scientific description even if they are of limited value for scientific explanation; and neither the Aristotelian analysis of 'what-questions' and 'why-questions,'[18] nor the Aristotelian conception of the formal cause,[19] nor the Aristotelian scientific centrepiece of insight into phantasm are to be discarded.[20]

Thirdly, the metaphysical account of the soul as the first act of an organic body potentially alive[21] does not dissolve into nonsense just because modern attentiveness to the actual flow of lived conscious experience demands the complementary description of conscious subjectivity.

Fourthly, the notion of human nature is not eliminated by a shift of attention to the revelations of the potentialities of that nature in human history – rational, non-rational, and irrational – and by the emergence of an interest to comprehend the human in its concrete, developing or declining actuality.

Finally, assent to the truths of basic propositions is not elicited from concrete subjects by virtue merely of the utterance of sentences. Those truths, like all other truths, must be mediated by a sometimes arbitrary and sometimes reasonable intentional subject who, largely due to classicist preoccupation with the conceptual field, may be submissive and subservient to propositions that place the assent to truth out of the subject's own control. From this realization it does not follow that the propositions expressed in the sentences uttered are not in some still strong sense fundamental, or that the very idea of foundations of any sort is just a classicist pipe dream.

What is required, then, is a successful completion of the fourfold transposition by a fifth that consists of a properly philosophical regrounding.

The timely remedy for the crisis of meaning attendant upon the shift from classicism to modernity is a radical taking-possession of oneself as a sufficiently developed conscious and intentional subject, or critical self-appropriation.

3 New 'Foundations'?

Thus far, my purpose has been to provide the background necessary for the identification and description of major obstacles to the mediation of the sort of radical self-possession Lonergan prescribes and promotes as the fifth moment in the transposition from the classicist to the modern mentality. I do not intend to join the controversy surrounding the issue of foundations. While this large and complicated question must be addressed if we are to respond intelligently and reasonably to classicism's demise, to attempt to address it with thoroughness here would be to essay the very philosophical completion of the epochal shift for which Lonergan calls. Moreover, inasmuch as the contemporary debate is pursued for the most part in terms of a narrow, classicist notion of foundations, to enter into it with a radically different conception of foundations would likely only add to the confusion and further delay the effort of completion. I shall take it for granted that Lonergan's prescription of critical self-appropriation issues from one such attempt at deliberate intellectual completion. Obviously, Lonergan is not advocating either a blinkered, archaist return to an outmoded classicist ideal or the presumptuous casting aside, along with the outmoded classicist notion of self-evident first principles, of every possible notion of foundations. Nor, it should be added, is he advocating an uncritical adoption of the self-understanding of modernity and its consequences for thought about foundations.

The timely, but not final, solution to the problems posed by this massive transposition, in Lonergan's view, is to be found by means of the concrete, modern subject's critical appropriation of the dynamic operational core of its subjectivity. Naturally, the classicist suppositions of immutable truth, of an unchanging human nature, of the incidental nature of all change, of the eternality of principles, and of the permanent validity and applicability of those principles despite the flux of 'accidental' differences, must first be reflectively rejected.[22] Further, the fact that, as Lonergan puts it, 'human living is informed by meanings, that meanings are the product of intelligence, that human intelligence develops cumulatively over time, and that such cumulative development differs in different histories' must be acknowledged.[23] Further still, it must be acknowledged that the premises of cognitive relativism are, as far as they go, true and so should not be summarily dismissed. These premises, as understood by Lonergan, are three:

> (1) the meaning of any statement is relative to its context; (2) every context is subject to change; it stands within a process of development and/or decay; and (3) it is not possible to predict what the future context will be.[24]

Finally, Lonergan argues that the necessary complement to the premises of relativism, contrary to classicist expectations, 'does not consist primarily in further propositions; it is to be found only by unveiling the invariant structure of man's conscious and intentional acts.'[25] Subsequently, the supposedly foundational, self-evident, and necessary propositions of classicism are to be replaced by knowledge of the dynamically structured sequence of pre-logical, pre-predicative, pre-linguistic operations that constitute the normative method of what is loosely, globally, and imprecisely referred to as 'the human mind.'[26]

The crisis of orientation evoked by the transposition from classicism to modernity is to be met by each one of us, or by as many of us as possible, taking possession of ourselves as experiencing, understanding, judging, deciding, and acting subjects. In that process of critical self-appropriation, Lonergan argues, there come to light commitments whose inevitability reveals them to be more than transient historical phenomena like the Aristotelian ideal of science, the Euclidean ideal of geometrical rationality, or the Leibnizian and Wolffian ideal of pure reason. These commitments are invariant, transhistorical imperatives of conscious intentionality.[27] These inevitable, operational commitments constitute the dynamic, normative core of conscious living, and they are named by Lonergan 'transcendental notions.'[28] Once these commitments have been identified in the process of their dynamic unfolding, once they have been understood in their unifying relations, once they have been clearly distinguished from other escapable, transient commitments that stand in no essential relation to the transcendental notions, once they have been reflectively and deliberately claimed by ourselves for ourselves, then the normative thrust of a 'transcendental method' may be expressed in four sequentially related and mutually sublating methodological canons, or 'transcendental precepts': Be attentive; Be intelligent; Be reasonable; Be responsible.[29] Putatively foundational and self-evident declarations that imply a terminal completeness are supplanted by truly foundational, personally appropriated imperatives that imply an original openness.

The process of critical self-appropriation provides the concrete, modern subject with an account of an operational, rather than a propositional, foundation – with a deliberate and methodical posture more fundamental than any logically consistent and coherent 'theoretical stance.' This new position is dynamic without being rootless, flexible without being spineless, open without being relativistic, structurally stable without being rigidly controlled by some eternally fixed belief or set of beliefs. This position is foundational, then, inasmuch as it is a deliberate abiding in inevitable normative commitments; and it is more properly foundational than propositional first principles, because it is the position *out of which* all propositional principles emerge, *by which* they are generated, *by which* they are accepted, and *by which* they are criticized, rejected, or superseded. As Lonergan wrote in *Insight*:

> Nor in the last resort can one reach a deeper foundation than that pragmatic engagement. Even to seek it involves a vicious circle; for if one seeks such a foundation, one employs one's cognitional process; and the foundations to be reached will be no more secure or solid than the inquiry utilized to reach it.[30]

4 Obstacles to Implementation

That, in brief outline, is the Lonerganian solution to the contemporary problem of foundations. No doubt, so brief a sketch gives rise to many important and complex questions. Moreover, nothing has been said about the way in which Lonergan's account of the normative dynamic structure of conscious intentionality performs its foundational function for an epistemology, a metaphysics, and an ethics,[31] let alone about the role it plays as an invariant foundation for Lonergan's proposed collaborative method for contemporary theology and other disciplines that look to the past to move into the future.[32] My limited purpose has been to provide essential background for an understanding of a broad outline of the obstacles the philosopher operating at the level of our times is likely to encounter, should he or she attempt to promote and mediate Lonergan's solution.

Let us suppose, then, that Lonergan's prescription of critical self-appropriation is a relatively adequate response to the contemporary crisis of meaning. In other words, let us suppose that critical self-appropriation is the timely corrective for contemporary disillusionment with proliferating, historically conditioned 'theories,' and that it would meet the contemporary demand for a standpoint that is at once integrated, culturally and historically invariant, and yet open to further, unanticipated developments. Now, implementation of such a revolutionary program, if it is to be a successful intervention in the course of history – i.e., if it is to be more than the projection of one more theory into the already cluttered field of competing theories – will require as a key component the effective promotion and mediation of self-attention, of a 'heightening of consciousness,' as Lonergan calls it; for such self-attention is the means of access to the data of consciousness upon which the standpoint to be promoted is to be built. In that case, obstacles to this heightening of consciousness must be anticipated and strategies for circumventing them must be worked out. In what follows I shall attempt to describe two closely related obstacles to the successful mediation of critical self-appropriation, one posed by the existing field of philosophical objectifications inasmuch as that field is occlusive of normative subjectivity, and another posed by the complex alienation of the contemporary subject who is related problematically to this pre-existing field. Finally, with these obstacles in mind, I shall propose two ways in which these obstructions might be mitigated, even if they cannot, due to the very nature of the solution, be rapidly overcome.

I shall begin by introducing a nest of related terms that seem to me helpful to an adequate exposition of the obstacles. These are: 'infrastructure,' 'superstructure,' 'heightening consciousness.'

4.1 Infrastructure and Superstructure

The notions of infrastructure and superstructure admit application in a wide range of contexts in which the vertical imagery of foundation and that which rests upon the foundation serves to promote understanding. Lonergan's own use of the metaphor is fairly limited; it occurs in only a few articles. While his use of it is not uniform, I think there is a common thread.

Let us mean by 'infrastructure' here the flow of interior operations and events in the field of conscious intentionality as orientated and governed more or less effectively, although not necessarily deliberately, by transcendental notions. By 'infrastructure' is meant, then, the flow of operations, such as perceiving, inquiring, imagining, understanding, formulating, conceiving, hypothesizing, grasping the fulfilment of conditions (or sufficient reasons) for a judgment, judging, deliberating, evaluating, deciding, and choosing. Moreover, it is this flow of operations precisely as orientated by the transcendental notions prior to their objectification in the transcendental concepts of intelligibility, being, and value. By 'superstructure,' on the other hand, let us mean the products, revelations, expressions, articulations, and objectifications of that infrastructural conscious and intentional flow of operations.

We may distinguish, then, two ideal-types of superstructural articulation: one type constituted by symbolism revelatory of the transcendental ground and whose linkage to the infrastructure is reflectively and deliberately maintained; and another type in which once-revelatory symbolism has become untethered, to borrow Plato's apt description, and free-floating, as it were, and thus is regarded as either simply groundless, in any strong sense of 'ground,' or as somehow, yet inexplicably, self-grounding. In the former case, superstructural objectifications continue to reveal more or less successfully their infrastructural origins. In the latter case, in which objectifications are regarded as either groundless or self-grounding, the expressive superstructure has crystallized into a conceptual symbolism that more or less effectively occludes its own infrastructural origins. Naturally, it continues to reveal its origins indirectly; given its actual source, it cannot with complete success do otherwise. In general, every artifact reveals its creator, even in those cases where the creator itself may have taken measures to conceal its originating role. Still, the degree to which superstructural objectifications reveal their infrastructural origins, and the manner in which they do so, are variables and, at the obfuscatory limit, the discovery of infrastructural traces in superstructural objectifications requires a sophisticated dialectical hermeneutic adept at discerning indications of the living infrastructural dynamism in a conceptual field of formulations whose motions, if any remain, are commonly taken to be explicable by some traditional or more recent type of logical mechanics.

The distinction may be stated in another way, and a bit more concretely. It pertains, as already suggested, not to the objectifications *per se* but to the existing subject's intellectual apprehension of them. In the first case, we might say, the subject reflectively and deliberately maintains a living relationship between the field of objectifications and the interior sources objectified, whereas in the second case the objectifications are hypostatized and the living relationship of a dynamic infrastructural ground to a superstructural grounded is, so to speak, forgotten. For example, we may speak either philosophically or in everyday fashion of 'experiencing,' of 'inquiring,' of 'understanding,' of 'judging,' of 'believing,' of 'deciding'; but we may do so either with the concomitant apprehension and the living memory, as it were, of the meanings and references of these words, or we may do so forgetfully, as though the words and their meanings had a life wholly their own, a dictionary life, as it were.

We have, then, a distinction between the ever dynamic, operative infrastructure and the conceptual superstructure, and two ways in which the superstructure may be related to the infrastructure.

4.2 Heightening Consciousness

To speak of the 'heightening of consciousness' is to employ another metaphor found in Lonergan's writings. Obviously, its employment is not unique to Lonergan. The imagery of expanding, enlarging, or raising consciousness has been fairly common currency since the 1960s. Use is made of it outside the properly philosophical domain, and its meanings and associations – psychological, intellectual, moral, religious, mystical, etc. – are many and various.

In Lonergan's usage, the metaphor of heightening consciousness serves several illuminative purposes. It is used sometimes to mean the entire process of critical self-appropriation. That process is a complicated and prolonged application of interior operations to themselves in their intentional relations to a remembered experiential field of strategically chosen instances of conscious and intentional engagement. In other places, it names only the critical initial moment of self-investigative advertence to the infrastructural flow of operations. That initial moment of advertence to myself here-and-now is a necessary first step towards critical self-appropriation. Finally, the metaphor has been interpreted by some as a description of the unfolding of the full range of sequentially ordered operations constitutive of the normative core of conscious intentionality, not in the second-order, so-called introspective mode of self-appropriation, but in the first-order, direct mode of the operative unobjectified infrastructure. In this last case, the relevant heightening is the transition from a normatively prior operation or set of operations to a normatively posterior operation or set of operations. While Lonergan's usage is not uniform, more often than not he uses the metaphor to mean the critical initial advertence to oneself as the subject here-and-now of conscious and intentional operations.[33] This is the usage I shall adopt here.

4.3 Superstructural Obstacles

First, then, we have an infrastructural flow of interior operations and events constituted by the transcendental notions. It is this infrastructural flow *in its normative directedness* that Lonergan means by 'transcendental method.' It also seems to be what Eric Voegelin is getting at when he speaks of the 'luminosity of consciousness.' Fred Lawrence's concise statement of the similarities between Voegelin's 'luminosity' and Lonergan's 'transcendental method' may help to solidify the understanding of what is meant here by the infrastructure.

> What differentiates human being from other conscious beings is that it is a *notion* of its goal. This means that in wonder or in the pure desire to know, consciousness experiences itself precisely as spiritual or intellectual, inasmuch as the unrestrictedness of its intention – completely universal and utterly concrete – entails an anticipatory grasp of the intelligibility, the unconditionality and the absoluteness of being ... This immediately given luminosity of wonder, is not the luminosity of that which it *is already*, but rather of what in its empty

> totality it anticipatorily apprehends and longs for, and what it dynamically seeks. I would say that what is most basically meant by luminosity, therefore, is wonder as involving an experiential knowledge of itself that has not been objectified and so does not involve the objective content of any cognitive act; instead it is an implicit awareness of itself as the principle of such acts, and so it is an inexhaustible background, a tacitly performative awareness.[34]

In the second place, in addition to the luminous transcendental method, there are the superstructural objectifications, revelations, expressions, articulations of that notion-driven or notion-lured infrastructure. Thirdly, the connectedness of these superstructural objectifications to their infrastructural source may be maintained successfully, or the superstructure may become untethered from and, moreover, occlusive of its source. Whereas the transcendental notions constitutive of the normative dynamism of the infrastructure are, Lonergan insists, comprehensive in connotation, unrestricted in denotation, and invariant over cultural change, superstructural objectifications are inevitably determinate, limited in denotation, and historically and culturally variable.[35] The determinateness, denotative limitation, and cultural variability of objectifications pertain to the very nature of conceptual objectifications; they are not due to the subject's forgetfulness of their origins. Conceptual objectification is not per se problematic. However, when combined with the subject's forgetfulness it becomes critically problematic. Once infrastructural origins are forgotten, there remain available only the categorical objectifications in their static determinacy to perform the required foundational, orientating function. But it seems clear that the felt need is for foundations that are not only more comprehensive, less restricted, and more universal than *some particular superstructural objectification*, but for foundations that are more comprehensive, unrestricted, and universal than *any superstructure as such* can ever be. A product can never comprehend, or exceed the boundaries of, or include, its producer. It is important, therefore, that the infrastructural origins be remembered and deliberately recovered. Once they have been hypostatized and have become untethered, free-floating, and supposedly self grounding, the still conscious need for comprehensiveness, unrestrictedness, and historical and cultural invariance stands in danger of occlusive transmogrification. That need may be transmuted into immoderate adherence to the ideal of tolerance that marks quotidian relativism, into the hyperbolic suspicion of postmodernism, into the blinkered nostalgia for the premodern spirit and its objectifications characteristic of archaist antimodernism, or into the resigned conceptualism of formal and linguistic analysis.

To keep alive the memory of infrastructural origins – of the connectedness of superstructural objectifications, not only logically to one another but, more fundamentally, genetically and dialectically to their infrastructural source – is an ongoing communal task. The very nature of objectifications makes it a task that requires the constant vigilance of methodical habit.[36] In our times, though, the challenge is not primarily to preserve a shared living memory, as was the case, say, in the later stages of classicism. The contemporary challenge seems to be to overcome a pandemic amnesia whose source lies not merely in the nature of objectifications *as such*, but in a residual, diehard classicist propensity to lodge foundations in the superstructure rather than to discover them in the infrastructural flow of operations. The ideal and procedures of classicism, insofar as they envisioned propositional, conceptual foundations, were already partially occlusive of the infrastructural foundation. With the collapse of classicism, what was once partially revealed and partially occluded is in danger of being completely obscured. And that is not all. The irony of occlusive objectification is reaching unprecedented heights. As if to ensure that the infrastructure will not be recalled, from the postmodernist side an entirely new spate of conceptual objectifications, with liberating anticlassicist intentions, which devaluate the transcendental notions, 'rationalize' performative inconsistency, and even declaim the death of the infrastructural subject, is being appended to the existing superstructure. Simultaneously, from the hypermodernist side, any residual inclination to take the conscious subject seriously is being redirected by efforts to bring to bear upon what is properly a philosophic crisis of foundations the revelations of neuroscience, as though the crisis of antecedent foundations is likely to be solved by one or another consequent ontology.[37]

With the infrastructure so effectively occluded by the superstructure, there is likely to emerge in the domain of philosophic practice a range of compensatory efforts. First, we may anticipate somewhat reactionary efforts to squeeze from some carefully selected range of existing objectifications a foundational comprehensiveness, unrestrictedness, and cultural invariance that they do not and cannot contain. As such desiccation of the superstructure proceeds, the insurmountable inadequacy of the existing objectifications is likely to become still more evident and troubling. Secondly, and in opposition to this trend, we may expect a somewhat desperate, blanket rejection of the very search for comprehensive, unrestricted, and culturally invariant foundations. On the one hand, then, we may observe a traditionalist return to the classicist past or to some semblance of it, reinforced by an antimodernist reaction against perceived 'nihilistic tendencies' of the present; on the other, we may observe, first, a troubled acquiescence to the prospect of a foundationless future, and then a lightheaded celebration of the purely negative freedom of expression regarded either as absolutely untethered or as firmly bounded by the unbreachable walls of the prison of language. For reasons already outlined, neither of these efforts can rescue us from our contemporary confusion.

The challenge, then, is to bring about a heightening of consciousness, the initial step in Lonergan's critical self-appropriation – a shift of inquiring advertence from the moribund superstructure to the infrastructure-as-infrastructure – that will set the stage for a new pursuit of orientating self-possession. This, in turn, sets the stage for the critical revivification of the existing superstructure by reconnecting it to the infrastructural ground by which it was originally generated and of which it is meant to be the objectification. Again, in Voegelin's language, what is needed is a reattunement to the luminosity of consciousness, to human being in its differentiated openness to being, which recovers self-knowledge from the latency of oblivion. This third alternative is neither a reactionary retrieval and retotalization of classicist objectifications nor a postmodern abandonment of the search for foundations. To the extent that classical thought maintained its connectedness to the infrastructure despite the occlusive pressures exerted by objectification as such, those who opt for the third way will draw sympathetically, to the consternation of postmodernists and the satisfaction of archaists, from classical sources. But, to the consternation of archaists, they will do so without classicist suppositions and emphases. To the extent that modern and contemporary thought correctly apprehends the futility of seeking foundations in the field of categorical objectifications, the completing philosophy will draw from more proximate, modern and postmodern developments.

Philosophically, then, the superstructural obstacle to be overcome is a conceptualism that is marked by three major, interrelated defects. First, conceptualism ignores the dynamic infrastructure, and so it cannot account adequately and convincingly for the generation, development, and radical transformation of concepts and theories. Secondly, inasmuch as it 'overlooks the concrete mode of understanding that grasps intelligibility in the sensible itself,' it suffers from excessive abstractness; it is 'confined to a world of abstract universals, and its only link with the concrete is the relation of universal to particular.' It suffers, finally, from its inadvertent employment of the transcendental notion of being as though it, too, were an abstract concept that differs from others inasmuch as it is 'the most abstract of abstractions, least in connotation and greatest in denotation.'[38]

4.4 Obstacles in the Infrastructure

Finally, we have the disorientated contemporary subject, doubly alienated. It is alienated from the infrastructural ground out of which the superstructural objectifications have emerged, i.e., from itself as an attentive, intelligent, reasonable, responsible, acting subject. Further, it is alienated to some extent from the existing superstructure, which has become untethered and free-floating and in which the transcendental notions are crystallized into a jumble of categorial structures.

It is important not to confuse the disorientated subject of whom I speak with the self-constituting, freedom-affirming, existential subject of whom Lonergan speaks in his later writings. The two subjects differ from one another significantly. Of the latter subject Lonergan writes with sympathetic, if measured, approval as in revolt against an occlusive superstructure. It finds the superstructure uninhabitable, as Kierkegaard, for example, found the 'System' uninhabitable. Its disorientation is cautiously approved because it assumes, although not explicitly, that the authority of objectifications is always derivative authority and that objectifications retain their legitimacy only so long as they remain 'true,' i.e., tethered, to the infrastructural notions. They retain their legitimacy as long as they are, despite their inherent fixity, *held flexibly* and, despite their inherent staticity, *apprehended dynamically*. Accordingly, this type of disorientation is to be regarded as a negative moment in the normative retrieval, albeit incipiently and in rudimentary form, of the infrastructural foundation from the latency of oblivion. It is perhaps similar to the normative disorientation of a Socrates who, in the *Apology*, described himself as 'a complete stranger to the language of this place' (17d). This normative disorientation is a first step towards the preferred outcome of efforts we might make to mediate a heightening of consciousness; and so it differs radically from the disorientation of the subject for whom our mediation serves a need to which that subject is itself almost entirely oblivious.

The radically disorientated subject is doubly alienated. It lives a limbo-like existence neither 'here' nor 'there,' where by 'here' is meant the conscious locus of the infrastructural unfolding of the notions and by 'there' is meant the notion-hardening, occlusive superstructure. This doubly alienated subject is caught between the magma-like flow of transcendental method-as-lived and the hardened, rock-like objectifications of that flow into a superstructure that is too coolly and unnaturally detached. For this subject, the infrastructure surges silently in a dark background, while the superstructure looms oppressively large in an artificially illuminated and falsely illuminating foreground. The doubly alienated subject cannot identify itself comfortably and wholeheartedly either with the unity of the meaning-originating source or with any static, abstract aggregate or theoretical system of accumulated cultural meanings in the existing superstructure.

5 Mediating Critical Self-Appropriation in a Doubly Alienated Subject

The pedagogical aim, it seems to me, must be to promote in the doubly alienated subject a double *periagoge*, a double 'turning around.' First, it is necessary to promote a turn 'inward,' a reillumination by the luminous infrastructure of operative attentiveness, intelligence, reasonableness, and responsibility. Secondly, it is necessary to promote a turn 'back,' by which the reorientated subject reclaims deliberately the superstructural field, de-hypostatizes and so re-naturalizes its contents, de-totalizes the reigning conceptualities, and undertakes attentively, intelligently, reasonably, and responsibly to uncover, restore, and then to maintain the connectedness of the field of superstructural objectifications to its infrastructural origins. The doubly alienated subject must be reintroduced to itself, sensitized to the inherent limitations of the field of objectifications, and equipped with a powerful and effective critique of hegemonous conceptualism. The pedagogical aim, accordingly, is only incidentally a change in the field of objectifications; essentially it is a change in the objectifying subject, a change in the subject's relation to and control of its own acts of meaning.

5.1 The Subject Side: Promoting a Renewal of the Search

Concretely, how are these two turns – the turn 'inward' and the turn 'back' – to be mediated? Self-appropriation requires turning the infrastructural operations as intentional on those same operations as given in conscious experience.[39] This is not a mere exercise in isolated introspection. Self-appropriation is not a suspension of interior performance for the purpose of 'looking inward.' It goes hand in hand with ongoing engagement and self-development. If, as Socrates insisted, the unexamined life is not worth living, it is also true, echoing Nietzsche perhaps, that the unlived life is not worth examining. It is only through engagement with the world and others at the level of one's times that one has access to the conscious experience of the flow of operations to be appropriated. Again, it is only by involvement in the wondering search for intelligibility and truth and the active pursuit of the good that the normative infrastructure constituted by the transcendental notions can come to light, because only then is it actually operative. Accordingly, the mediation of self-appropriation is, in the first instance, the mediation in the contemporary subject of *the renewal of the search*. If the doubly alienated subject is to catch itself in the act of searching, it must first be lured into the search. This, however, presents a knotty practical problem, for the resumption of the search is to be promoted in a subject who is confronted by the imperious presence of a panoply of disconnected and devaluated objectifications and surrounded, more often than not, by other subjects who struggle under their occupation.

Still, while forgetfulness of the infrastructure and outright denial of its existence may modify, disrupt, or truncate the infrastructural process, they do not eradicate it. However severely alienated the subject becomes, it remains that it is *this subject* who is alienated. The alienation itself may be understood dialectically as a manifestation of the persistence of the normative exigencies constitutive of the infrastructure-as-infrastructure. Even the deliberate dismissal of the conscious traces of infrastructural aspirations as vain hopes or futile desires or as expressions of a cleverly disguised will to power, to the extent that the dismissal is meant by the alienated subject to be an attentive, intelligent, critical, and responsible course of action, is revelatory of the normative infrastructure. In short, wherever there are meaning-originating subjects, whatever the state of their self-relation, there are to be discerned traces of the infrastructure. These traces, however, are not to be sought in the *conceptual formulations* of the subject but in its *conscious performance.* Inevitably, it seems, infrastructural traces will remain to which the pedagogue may appeal, and it would appear that this normative residue, inasmuch as it is given in the presence of the subject to itself, is available for pedagogical exploitation.

But because the significance of this residue is more or less habitually denied by the alienated subject, its successful exploitation will require considerable artfulness on the part of the pedagogue; and however artful the pedagogue, it remains that his or her mediative effort is likely to be apprehended by the alienated subject as just one more dominative effort by another theorizing warlord with an ideological interest in the preservation of some abstract principality of the superstructure. Moreover, such artfulness, if it is not to be summarily dismissed as ideological manipulation, will require an interpersonal context of mutual trust. Indeed, the futility of attempting to mediate an 'inward' turn in the alienated subject in the absence of real friendship is illustrated abundantly by the remarkable ineffectiveness of Socrates' exercise of dialectical skill on the doubly alienated Callicles in Plato's *Gorgias,* and by the undertow of violence that makes that dialogue unique in the Platonic corpus. The resistance-softening mutuality of friendship, it appears, is a necessary condition of effective mediation of the 'inward' turn. It is, as Lonergan suggests, in the *personal encounter* that such efforts become effective, rather than in the lecture or in print.[40] It is in the mutual presence of subject to subject in the dramatic encounter that the presence of the subject to itself as subject is heightened most effectively. Moreover, friendships of the specifically modern sort are especially favourable to these efforts. For the modern self who emphasizes its uniqueness, self-disclosure acquires a special significance.[41] The classical approach to friendship values frankness and candour, honesty, and mutual criticism, but it does not regard the revelation of personal intimacies as essential. The modern approach seeks, in addition to the classical values, intimacy, confession, and the communion of subject with subject.

5.2 *The Object Side: Revivifying the Language of Interiority*

Besides this difficulty, there are the further difficulties posed by the climate of the times, which in many ways discourages serious self-attention and truncates autobiographical self-disclosure at the point where revelation of psychological idiosyncrasies might give way to revelations of the normative infrastructure. There are doctrines abroad to the effect that there is no 'substantial subject' to be appropriated; there are long-standing and well-founded reservations about the fruitfulness of the isolated introspection with which, in the long shadow cast by Descartes, critical self-appropriation is too easily confused; there are materialist and other reductionist trends that would substitute, for example, cognitive science for self-appropriation and the language of neuroscience for the 'folk psychological' language that expresses an incipient interiority; there is ubiquitous conceptualism, with its hypostatizing techniques; there is, finally, the crystallized and devaluated condition of the language of interiority itself, which lends weight to the critique of 'folk psychological' self-understanding and invites the transformation of pedagogical inducements to attend to the infrastructural flow into propositions about concepts or about other propositions, i.e., into mere talk about the 'merely subjective' or about a 'ghost in the machine.'

This challenge is to be met by a revivification of the existing language of interiority that makes it more effectively evocative of the interior experiences it was invented originally to objectify. The pedagogical strategy of re-engaging the doubly alienated subject in the search must be complemented by a process through which the superstructural language of interiority in common use is reinfused with the richness of the originating or engendering infrastructural experiences. This revivification of the language of interiority, while it does introduce clarity, coherence, and rigour into the employment of a certain range of ordinary words, does not amount to the construction and prescription of a new theoretical, technical language. Only incidentally will it be a process of defining terms constitutive of the language we employ to objectify our interior lives. Primarily, it will be a process of critically regenerating the extant language of interiority by retethering it to concrete infrastructural operations and events and to their conscious, dynamic relations. It will be a process of reconnecting the existing language of interiority to its infrastructural, transcendental origins.[42] It will be a précising and revaluation of the existing 'folk psychological' vocabulary, a new and complex use of common terms upon which the contemporary subject may draw to talk about itself at once precisely and intimately.[43] The revivification of the language of interiority will constitute an empirically verifiable but still variable nest of terms and relations available to the culture at large. It would serve the pedagogical purpose, not of the classicist mentality whose pedagogical strategy aims to bring about rational conviction through the relatively cumbersome and impersonal mechanics of logical argumentation and relies upon the relatively weak conceptual pressure of valid inference, but of the postpostmodern, post-logical, methodical mentality that aims to mediate critical self-appropriation and pins its faith on the operational pressure of the normative infrastructure. The methodical mentality understands the demise of classicism to be also 'the end of the age of argument.'[44] It promotes critical self-appropriation by objectifying the 'organics' and 'dialectics,' as it were, of personal development and conversion. As it promotes a renewal of the search, a heightening of consciousness, and a 'turn' inward, so also it promotes the revivification of the language of interiority, the reanimation of the ossified superstructure, and the 'turn' back.

Notes

1 Bernard Lonergan, *Method in Theology* (Toronto: University of Toronto Press, 2003), 19–20.

2 See Bruno Snell, *The Discovery of the Mind: The Greek Origins of European Thought*, trans. T.G. Rosenmeyer (New York: Harper & Bros., 1960).

3 Bernard Lonergan, *Insight: A Study of Human Understanding*, vol. 3 of *Collected Works of Bernard Lonergan*, ed. Frederick E. Crowe and Robert M. Doran (Toronto: University of Toronto Press, 1992).

4 On control of meaning, see *The Lonergan Reader*, ed. Mark D. Morelli and Elizabeth A. Morelli (Toronto: University of Toronto Press, 1997), Part 2, sects 4 and 5.

5 See ibid., 11–28, for an overview; see also Part 1, sec. 17 and sec. 7.

6 Ibid., 44. Lonergan's essential pairing of self-appropriation and self-development is one characteristic of his position that distinguishes it radically from Cartesianism.

7 Bernard Lonergan, 'Belief: Today's Issue,' in *A Second Collection*, ed. Bernard J. Tyrrell and William F.J. Ryan (London: Darton, Longman & Todd, 1974), 98.

8 Lonergan draws upon P. Boutroux's *L'ideal scientifique des mathématicians dans l'antiquité et dans les temps modernes* (Paris: Alcan, 1920) to illustrate the notion of a mathematical ideal. See Bernard Lonergan, 'Exegesis and Dogma,' in *Philosophical and Theological Papers 1958–64*, vol. 6 of *Collected Works of Bernard Lonergan*, ed. Robert C. Croken, Frederick E. Crowe, and Robert M. Doran (Toronto: University of Toronto Press, 1996), 147–8. On the ideals in the

natural sciences and philosophy, see *Understanding and Being*, vol. 5 of *Collected Works of Bernard Lonergan*, ed. Mark D. Morelli and Elizabeth A. Morelli (Toronto: University of Toronto Press, 1990), 6–13.

9 Lonergan, in *Understanding and Being*, 11–14, traces this realization back to Hegel.

10 Lonergan, *Philosophical and Theological Papers 1958–1964*, 154–5.

11 Lonergan, *Method in Theology*, 305.

12 Lonergan, *Philosophical and Theological Papers 1958–1964*, 156, italics added.

13 Ibid.

14 Ibid., 159.

15 For an early statement on the transition from logic to method and from Aristotelian to modern science, see Bernard Lonergan, *Topics in Education*, vol. 10 of *Collected Works of Bernard Lonergan*, ed. Frederick E. Crowe and Robert M. Doran (Toronto: University of Toronto Press, 1993), 146–57; and, more recently, *A Second Collection*, 15–16, and *A Third Collection*, ed. Frederick E. Crowe (New York: Paulist Press, 1985), 135–40. On the transition from human nature to human history, and from propositional principles to transcendental method, see *A Second Collection*, 2–7; on historical-mindedness, *A Third Collection*, 169ff.; on the transition from soul to subject, *Verbum: Word and Idea in Aquinas*, vol. 2 of *Collected Works of Bernard Lonergan*, ed. Frederick E. Crowe and Robert M. Doran (Toronto: University of Toronto Press, 1997), Introduction, and *A Second Collection*, 69ff.; on the unfolding of these transitions in theology, *A Second Collection*, 55ff.

16 That is, in the generalized sense of the term 'experience' as employed by Lonergan to include conscious experience of oneself as subject.

17 On the 'transposition' of classical Thomism, for example, see Lonergan, *A Second Collection*, 49–52.

18 Aristotle, *Metaphysics* VII, 17.

19 Aristotle, *Physics* II, 3.

20 Aristotle, *De anima* III, 7.

21 *Ibid.*, II, 1, 412 b 4–5.

22 On classicist suppositions, see *The Lonergan Reader*, 403.

23 On historicity, see ibid., 438.

24 Ibid., 439.

25 Ibid.

26 Lonergan, *Insight*, chap. 11 on self-affirmation. For a summary of general foundational categories, see Lonergan, *Method in Theology*, 285 ff.

27 On the inevitability of these commitments, see Lonergan, *Insight*, chap. 11.

28 If the contents of the transcendental *notions* are objectified, we form the transcendental *concepts* of the intelligible, the real, and value. See Lonergan, *Method in Theology*, 11–12.

29 Lonergan, *Method in Theology*, chap. 1.

30 Lonergan, *Insight*, 356.

31 *Insight* is Lonergan's foundational effort.

32 See Lonergan, *Method in Theology*, esp. chap. 5, for his account of eight functional specialties.

33 Ibid., 15.

34 *The Beginning and the Beyond: Papers from the Gadamer and Voegelin Conferences*, Supplementary Issue of *Lonergan Workshop*, vol. 4, ed. Fred Lawrence (Chico, CA: Scholars Press, 1984), 62.

35 Lonergan, *Method in Theology*, 11–12.

36 This seems to be the point of Plato's strictures on writing in the *Phaedrus* and the *Seventh Letter*, in which there is so much interest at the present time.

37 Bernard Lonergan, *Phenomenology and Logic*, vol. 18 of *Collected Works of Bernard Lonergan*, ed. Philip J. McShane (Toronto: University of Toronto Press, 2001), 311–12: 'The justification of a horizon cannot rest on the *consequent* ontology, on the realities known within the horizon ... If we let each one justify itself by the realities of its consequent ontology, we would be in the relativist position.'

38 *The Lonergan Reader*, 425ff. It appears that the classical ideal leaves the door open for conceptualist derailment inasmuch as it emphasizes propositional foundations, but that its *haute vulgarisation* actually *promotes* derailment. See Bernard Lonergan, *Philosophy of God, and Theology* (London: Darton, Long man & Todd, 1973), ix: 'By a conceptualist I mean a person that is a keen logician, that is extremely precise in his use of terms, and that never imagined that the meaning of terms varied with the acts of understanding that they expressed.'

39 Cf. Lonergan, *Method in Theology*, chap. 1, where he puts the project in these terms.

40 Ibid., 247.

41 David Konstan, *Friendship in the Classical World* (Cambridge: Cambridge University Press, 1997).

42 'If your system is right ... it may be the best available opinion. To go beyond that, you need a basis for being certain that the meaning of your basic terms is what you say it is, so you have to go into *les données immédiates de la conscience*.' See the interview in *Caring about Meaning*, ed. Pierrot Lambert, Charlotte Tansey, and Cathleen Going (Montreal: Thomas More Institute, 1982), 256. Again: 'But the point to the statement that the [infrastructural] pattern itself is conscious is that, once the relations are formulated, they are not found to express surprising novelties but simply prove to be objectifications of the routines of our conscious living and doing.' See Lonergan, *Method in Theology*, 18.

43 On the neuroscientific critique, see my 'Authentication of Common Sense from Below Upwards: Mediating Self-Correcting Folk Psychology,' *Lonergan Workshop* 15 (1999), 117–39.

44 Lonergan, *Philosophy of God, and Theology*, 47ff., where Lonergan compares the logician to the mortician.

Robert M. Doran, SJ

Empirical Consciousness in *Insight*: Is Our Conception Too Narrow?

This paper turns to Bernard Lonergan's *Insight* for confirmation of a position already tentatively explored, namely, that we (the community of Lonergan's students) might want to expand the standard conception of the first, or empirical, level of consciousness so as to include in empirical consciousness received meanings and values. In this way we will be able to make our own what is salutary in Martin Heidegger's notion of *Verstehen*, in Ludwig Wittgenstein's insistence on the public meaningfulness of language, and in Hans Urs von Balthasar's aesthetic 'taking to be true' (*Wahrnehmen*) the received forms expressive of God's revelation. Let me first summarize the arguments expressed in a previous paper in support of this position.[1] I will then turn to three sources in *Insight* that would seem to provide some justification for the position. The position, again, is that among the data that occur to the attentive subject of a consciousness that is also potentially intelligent, reasonable, and responsible are the meanings and values that are included in von Balthasar's 'seeing the form,' in Heidegger's preconceptual grasp of historical facticity, and in Wittgenstein's insistence on the public meaningfulness of ordinary language.

1 A Position for Exploration

These questions arose for me from being exposed to a paper by Sean McGrath at a seminar conducted in April 2003 by the Lonergan Research Institute.[2] There is a link, McGrath argues, from Scotus's intuition of the singular through Husserl's categorial intuition to Heidegger's hermeneutical intuition of the preconceptual forms of meaning to be found in historical life itself. For each of these figures knowledge is primarily intuition, but for Heidegger the intuition is not without expression, without language, where 'language' must be taken, I believe, to include all the carriers of meaning, whether linguistic in the strict sense or found in art, in spontaneous intersubjectivity, in symbols, and in the incarnate meaning of persons, communities, and their deeds. Primal truth occurs for Heidegger only within such expressedness, and never as unmediated immediacy. We have no access to experience that is not permeated by language in this broad sense. Hermeneutical phenomenology must 'loosen up the primal words' in which life expresses itself, so as to open a free space for thinking. For Heidegger, as McGrath interprets him, there is an actually intelligible thing, individual, or irreplaceable occurrence grasped by *Verstehen* prior to any original cognitive processing on the part of the understanding subject. The historically singularized thing, individual, occurrence speaks a primal word to us that precedes and makes possible our own inner word issuing from our own insights. *History* is the domain of this preconceptual understandability. This emphasis on history represents Heidegger's original contribution to the effective history of Scotism. For Heidegger it is not the case that deconstructing the definitions of theoretical thought back to their empirically given structures leads only to mute sense data. History is the arena of actually intelligible singularity.

The position that I argued in my previous paper on this issue is that Lonergan's notions of mediated immediacy and elemental meaning refer to the same 'given intelligibility' that Heidegger is expressing in speaking of primally intelligible structures of historical facticity. I related the same notions to Lonergan's distinction of the ordinary meaningfulness of everyday language and the original meaningfulness of language that expresses new discoveries, thus attempting to link both Heidegger and Lonergan with Wittgenstein. And I argued that these links do not subvert but rather strengthen and reinforce Lonergan's intentionality analysis.

The category of elemental meaning in Lonergan's work, of course, is not limited to what he acknowledges at the first or empirical level of consciousness. For 'elemental meaning' obtains wherever subject and object are not distinct; it refers to the original knowing by identity that issues into distinction only with conceptualization, formulation, objectification, and so that obtains precisely as identity not only in sensation but also in insight. The sense in act is the sensible in act, yes, but it is also true that the intellect in act is the intelligible in act. The subject's own immanently generated insights are instances of elemental meaning, and they occur at a quite distinct level of consciousness from the empirical. 'Knowledge by identity' obtains for the preconceptual unity of knower and known, whether in sensation or in the act of insight.

Now my question is whether we may also speak of an elemental identity of 'knower' and 'known' that, because it occurs in something like that act that Heidegger calls *Verstehen*, is not simply a matter of sense in act and sensible in act, but that, because it is also not a matter of immanently generated insight arising as a release to the tension of inquiry, not a matter of 'original meaningfulness,' but rather of meaningful data in the sense of 'ordinary meaningfulness,' is a form of empirical consciousness. Is there some kind of identity of 'intellect in act' and 'intelligible in act' in the very reception of meaningful data on the part of a subject who is intelligent and potentially reasonable and responsible? Is this part of what is meant by the expression 'mediated immediacy?' In Thomist language – and this question was suggested to me by McGrath in email interchanges – is there some kind of lesser *illuminatio* that occurs prior to insight into phantasm? Lonergan speaks of the elemental meaning of the smile acting as an intersubjective determinant, of the work of art prior to its being interpreted by a critic, of the dream symbol performing an office of internal communication without help from the therapist. But is something similar not true of many received data? As the dreams of the morning are the dreams of an intelligent subject and so are already invested with meaning, may we not say that many of the data received by such a subject are already invested with a meaning that is a function of their historical facticity, of personal and communal history? Is that meaning merely potential, or is there some kind of devalued or minor formal and actual intelligibility at the very level of the givenness of meaningful data? Is there an empirical givenness of intellectually structured meaning? I think there is.

Moreover, this received meaning functions effectively and constitutively even before it has been subjected to critical examination and personal and communal appropriation. This is why I am suggesting that it possesses an intelligibility that is more than the merely potential intelligibility of sense data but also less than formal and actual intelligibility in the strict sense, where the latter emerge either as concepts from our own immanently generated acts of direct understanding, or as judgments from our own immanently generated acts of reflective understanding, or from the act of faith in the fullest sense of that term. Received meaning in large part has the intelligibility of ordinary meaningfulness, of public language, but it is also the product of the original meaningfulness of the insights, judgments, and decisions of those who have preceded us, or of their biases, their failures to be intelligent, reasonable, and responsible, or of some combination of intelligence and bias working in our historical community; and our own questions arising upon its reception are what provoke our own acts of original meaningfulness. What I am suggesting we might call 'minor formal intelligibility' and 'minor actual intelligibility' have to do with this ordinary meaningfulness of publicly sedimented expression as this expression mediates the reception of data, and what I am suggesting we might call 'major formal intelligibility' and 'major actual intelligibility' are connected with the original meaningfulness of what proceeds by intelligible emanation when the subject raises his or her own questions for intelligence, reflection, and deliberation, answers these questions in acts of understanding and in judgments of fact and of value, and formulates the answers in inner and outer words that contribute eventually to the communal fund of ordinary meaningfulness.

I suggest, then, something of an analogy between the levels of intentional consciousness as they function in everyday living and the same levels as they function in distinct functional specialties in a discipline such as theology. In particular, I suggest an analogy between empirical consciousness as it functions in everyday living and empirical consciousness as it sets the objectives of the functional specialty 'research.' The common element is that all four sets of conscious operations work together as one receives data. The difference, of course, is that work in the functional specialty 'research' is a fully deliberate, chosen set of projects whose mediated object is a carefully isolated set of data that will be subject to rigorous and methodical interpretation. The data that emerge in research are the product of immanently generated acts of insight, judgment, and decision, as, for example, in the production of a critical text. That sort of specialized application does not occur in everyday, common-sense performance. Still, many of the data received in ordinary everyday living are already invested with a meaning that functions effectively and constitutively. They are not mere data of sense or of consciousness appearing in a state of unmediated immediacy. The world is already mediated by meaning to a subject whose empirical consciousness is the empirical consciousness of someone intelligent. There is an intellectually apprehensive component that functions at the level of reception. It is not Lonergan's 'insight' as a release to the tension of inquiry. It is more like *Verstehen* in Heidegger's sense of the apprehensive component of *Da-sein*. It is already invested with meaning, with an 'already given intelligibility,' with what I am suggesting we might call 'minor formal and actual intelligibility.' More precisely, we should say that the minor formal intelligibility is a function of this *Verstehen*, whereas minor actual intelligibility, the judgmental component in this apprehension, depends on the 'always with us' quality of previous judgments, or on belief, or on a suspicious suspension of belief, where 'belief' can range all the way from comfortable embeddedness in a common-sense environment to religious belonging, and is the function proximately of the personal history of the subject within the history of his or her community or network of communities (minor authenticity or inauthenticity) and remotely of the history of those communities themselves (major authenticity or inauthenticity).

Another way of approaching the issue is in terms of the intricate symbiosis of what Lonergan calls ordinary meaningfulness and original meaningfulness.

> The ordinary meaningfulness of ordinary language is essentially public and only derivatively private ... what is true of the ordinary meaningfulness of ordinary language is not true of the original meaningfulness of any language, ordinary, literary, or technical. For all language develops and, at any time, any language consists in the sedimentation of the developments that have occurred and have not become obsolete. Now developments consist in discovering new uses for existing words, in inventing new words, and in diffusing the discoveries and inventions. All three are a matter of expressed mental acts. The discovery of a new usage is a mental act expressed by the new usage. The invention of a new word is a mental act expressed by the new word.[3]

Lonergan introduces the distinction of ordinary meaningfulness and original meaningfulness as a response to a Wittgensteinian objection to his position. But it is also applicable *mutatis mutandis* to questions that might be presented from a Heideggerian perspective. Heidegger's preconceptual or fore-theoretical or 'given' intelligibility of the temporal and contextual contingencies of life is a subspecies of Lonergan's category of ordinary meaningfulness. Lonergan's distinct contribution has to do not with the ordinary meaningfulness of historical facticity but with the original meaningfulness that is responsible for 'healing and creating in history.' There is no reason to set up an opposition between them. In different ways one flows into the other. If I may quote my earlier paper:

> The original meaningfulness of one generation or even of one period in one's own life becomes the ordinary meaningfulness of a later generation or period, and problems with regard to ordinary meaningfulness give rise to the questions that issue in original meaningfulness. There is no reason for a philosophy or a theology to feel required to choose between them. The Scotist-inspired Heideggerian tendency and the Wittgensteinian tendency, whether Scotist-inspired or not, are to emphasize the ordinary meaningfulness of the public sedimentations as what is essential, and to consider the original meaningfulness that issues from so-called mental acts as at best derivative. *That*, and not naive realism in the simple sense, would be the counterposition in these views. To appeal to Lonergan's dialectic of concept and performance, we might say that Wittgenstein and, per-

> haps to a greater degree, Heidegger display a great deal of original meaningfulness and ingenuity in their talk about ordinary meaningfulness. But Lonergan students should take care not so to stress the interior operations that give rise to original meaningfulness as to pass over in silence or even denial the fact that ordinarily, that is, in the ordinary meaningfulness of everyday life, we start from publicly sedimented expressions already invested with meaning.[4]

Another approach to the same issues is through the distinction between understanding data and understanding facts. Lonergan writes, 'The understanding of data is expressed in hypotheses, and the verification of hypotheses leads to probable assertions. The understanding of facts is a more complicated matter, for it supposes the existence of two types or orders of knowledge, where the facts of the first type supply the data for the second type.'[5] Thus the task of the functional specialty 'systematics' is not the understanding of data, except insofar as the facts established by the functional specialty 'doctrines' are taken as the data that systematics attempts to understand. But the truth of the doctrines, precisely as received truth accepted in faith, functions constitutively in Christian living, and not only insofar as it is expressed in propositions but also as it is carried in art and symbols and intersubjectivity and the incarnate meaning of persons and communities, irrespective of how well the propositions are understood. As functioning constitutively, its truth may be likened to Heidegger's *alêtheia* or unconcealment. And unless it so functions constitutively, precisely accepted as true in faith, one is not prepared to subject it to systematic understanding. The facts of the first type of knowledge, functioning in the realm of ordinary meaningfulness in the faith community, are supplying data for a second, systematic type of knowledge, which, if it succeeds in elaborating any new synthesis, would be an instance of original meaningfulness. Through genuine communication, doctrinal truth can function as a linguistic expression of a primal truth disclosed to believers, a truth that in systematics is submitted to further scrutiny by theologians attempting to understand it in an explanatory fashion. Thus, when Aquinas spoke of procession in God, he was employing what had become ordinary language in his faith tradition. But when he explained procession in God as *emanatio intelligibilis*, he was exhibiting the original meaningfulness of language, where that meaningfulness is entirely a function of his own understanding of what procession in God had to be, and of course of what it could not be.

Another application has to do with revelation and the theology of reception. God's revelation is a matter of meaning, God's entering into the world of human meaning. But this means God's entry into human *reality* as constituted by meaning. Meaning *is*, it is real. Acts of meaning as cognitive are instances of reality intending reality. As constitutive, meaning 'constitutes part of the reality of the one that means': one's horizon, one's assimilative powers, one's knowledge, one's values, one's character. As communicative, meaning 'induces in the hearer some share in the cognitive, constitutive, or effective meaning of the speaker.' And as effective, meaning 'persuades or commands others or it directs [our] control over nature.'[6] These ontological aspects pertain to meaning at any stage of cultural development, in any of the differentiations of consciousness, and in the presence and absence of conversion. And they pertain to meaning no matter what its carrier might be: intersubjectivity, art, symbol, personal conduct, everyday or literary or technical language.

Moreover, the relative dominance of the dialectics of community and culture vis-à-vis the dialectic of the subject means that the horizon of the subject in the world, and the world correlative to that horizon are, prior to critical reflection on the part of the subject, largely a function of what Heidegger calls temporal and historical facticity, 'being thrown' into existence in the world at this particular time and with these particular people, with their own horizons similarly determined and limited for them by historical dialectics over which at the outset they have no control. These dialectics are what give rise to the situations that stimulate our neural demands for psychic representation and conscious integration and that mold the orientation of the intelligence and imagination that spontaneously exercise a censorship with respect to what is going to be allowed into consciousness. Thus the very reception of data invested with meaning is itself constitutive of the subject's horizon. It is precisely at this level of primordial receptivity that God's entrance into the world of human reality and meaning takes place. A theology of revelation, of God's entry into the world of human meaning, must ponder especially the level of elemental meaning, of the already given intelligibility of received data. God's entry into the world of human meaning is God's effecting transformations in that already given intelligibility of the world that is correlative to our horizons, and doing so through the cognitive, constitutive, communicative, and effective functions of God's own meaning, God's own original meaningfulness, and ultimately God's incarnate meaning, incarnate Logos, incarnate Word, the Son of the eternal Father, crucified, dead, and risen from the dead.

The formal constituent of the community, whose dialectic exerts a relative dominance over the dialectic of the subject, is common meaning. That common meaning is constitutive of the individual as a member of this community, and it is constitutive of the community itself. Its genesis occurs through an ongoing process of communication, where people share the same cognitive, constitutive, and effective meanings. The really serious divisions in the community are those that arise from the presence and absence of intellectual, moral, religious, and (I would add) psychic conversion. For then radical dialectical opposition can affect the community and its actions and the situations that arise from these actions. And these situations are precisely what stimulate neural demands in subjects, so that if the situation is not some intelligible whole but a set of 'misshapen, poorly proportioned, and incoherent fragments,'[7] this will have an effect on the subject's own emergence into selfhood. The state of the community affects the receptivity of both individuals and groups to God's entry into the world of human meaning through God's symbolic self-communication. The state of grace is an intersubjective and social situation, a communion of the three divine subjects with a community of human subjects. The dominance of the dialectic of community over the dialectic of the subject means that the relations of the present of the subject to the past are relations not only to the subject's own past but also to the past of his or her community or network of communities. These relations decisively affect the orientation or habitual context within which the reception of data occurs. They decisively affect the 'ordinary meaningfulness' of the subject's everyday life, an ordinary meaningfulness that may be more or less sinful, more or less under the influence of grace. Revelation as God's entrance into the human world of meaning shifts the probabilities in favour of graced ordinary meaningfulness, and that shift in probabilities affects the potential of subjects in community to receive the divine meaning intended by God when God enters our world of meaning.

The question of truth, then, becomes by and large the question of the validity or objectivity of the system of meanings and values by which the community, and individuals within the community, structure their lives. In particular, 'how can one tell whether one's appropriation of religion is genuine or unauthentic and, more radically, how can one tell one is not appropriating a religious tradition that has become unauthentic?'[8] That is a question that must be asked, I believe, by every Catholic at the present time, when there has been such an overlay of ecclesiastical baggage heaped upon the message of the gospel that many official authorities of the religion no longer carry genuine authority but are more concerned with their own influence and power than with the gospel's message of unconditional love. The question can be generalized, to extend to the other components of one's historically and culturally inherited symbol system. There may be no more significant question in the whole of human life than this: how can I tell whether the convictions that I have been taught to live by are a function of a tradition or set of traditions that have become unauthentic? Or to use language that we found useful earlier, how can I judge whether the ordinary meaningfulness that constitutes my present horizon, historically and culturally conditioned as it is, is a function of an unauthentic or an authentic tradition? And the answer can be discovered only by the release of the original meaningfulness by which we submit our beliefs and convictions to an immanent critique, in order to ascertain their genuineness. The answer is found in the self-transcendence that is the criterion of authenticity or genuineness, a self-transcendence that, in the stage of cultural development that is advanced by a Lonergan, can be submitted to self-appropriation. Once again, Heidegger is speaking mainly about the ordinary meaningfulness that constitutes present horizons, and Lonergan about the original meaningfulness that submits ordinary meaningfulness to critique and, probably, to transformation: to 'healing and creating.' The operations that constitute original meaningfulness, then, alone are able to pass judgment on the truth of the ordinary meaningfulness of present horizons. The immanently generated affirmation that emanates from the grasp of the virtually unconditioned is alone capable of ascertaining the truth of the unconcealedness of the mediated immediacy with which the process towards original meaningfulness begins. Heidegger's unconcealedness alone will not do, nor will von Balthasar's *Wahrnehmen*. Both must be confirmed by some sort of process that leads either to immanently generated knowledge or to the reflective understanding that grasps as virtually unconditioned the value of deciding to believe. If they cannot be so confirmed, they must be subjected to the process of transformation that is best succinctly summed up in the wonderful expression 'healing and creating in history.' The 'minor formal or actual intelligibility' of mediated immediacy must be either confirmed or corrected by the 'major formal or actual intelligibility' attained by the operations that Lonergan has clarified. It is not the case, in the last analysis, that the truth of judgment is merely a derivative of a primal unconcealedness. It is rather the case that the truth of the primal unconcealedness of mediated immediacy is a function of the major authenticity of the cultural and religious traditions that have bequeathed us this heritage. If that is lacking, then our responsibility is to correct the major unauthenticity of the received tradition; and the only way we can do that is by exercising the original meaningfulness that, under God's gift of grace, is the sole source and guarantee of such healing and creating in history: inquiry, insight, conceptualization and formulation, reflection, reflective understanding, judgment, questions for evaluation and deliberation, judgments of value, decision.

Still, Heidegger's notion of truth as unconcealment is about something essential to this exercise. It is about the first transcendental precept, 'Be attentive,' or in other words, 'Focus.' Insights are only as good as the images in which they grasp intelligibility. Forgetfulness of the images reduces and in the limit eliminates the probability that we will have the insights we need, not only to get on with our individual lives, but also to fulfil our historical responsibilities. Insight into image is infallible, but if the images are distorted, so too will be the insights. And until the forgetfulness of the data is overcome, the marshalling of the evidence for a reasonable judgment will be lacking essential components. This is what psychic conversion is all about. Whether it is defined from 'below,' as it were, as the transformation of the censorship over neural demands from a repressive to a constructive functioning, or explained from 'above' in language that appeals to a healing of what Heidegger calls the forgetfulness of Being, it is a transformation that effects a renewed link between the creative, inquiring human spirit and the materials, the elemental meaning, the mediated immediacy that at any given time constitute the starting point of the creative process.

2 Sources in *Insight*

Having summarized the position that I would like the Lonergan community to explore, let me now mention some possible corroborating material in *Insight* for this 'take' on the meaning of 'empirical consciousness.'

2.1 'Experience' in 'Patterns of Experience'

The first such source lies in the meaning of the word 'experience' as this word functions in the expression 'patterns of experience.' Lonergan writes, 'The notion of the pattern of experience may best be approached by remarking how abstract it is to speak of a sensation.' Acts of seeing, hearing, touching, tasting, smelling 'never occur in isolation both from one another and from all other events.' What is the meaning of 'all other events?' Well, acts of sensation 'have a bodily basis; they are functionally related to bodily movements; and they occur in some dynamic context that somehow unifies a manifold of sensed contents and of acts of sensing.' It is in the dynamic context that we find our first clue. A few lines later it is spoken of as 'an organizing control,' and it is described as follows: 'Besides the systematic links between senses and sense organs, there is, immanent in experience, a factor variously named conation, interest, attention, purpose. We speak of consciousness as a stream, but the stream involves not only the temporal succession of different contents but also direction, striving, effort. Moreover, this direction of the stream is variable ... There are ... different dynamic patterns of experience,' and the patterns organize the 'various elements in the experience.'[9] Those 'various elements' are spoken of as 'sequences of sensations, memories, images, conations, emotions, and bodily movements,'[10] but such sequences can exhibit not only biological purposiveness, as when they 'converge upon terminal activities of intussusception or reproduction, or, when negative in scope, self-preservation,'[11] but also 'ever novel forms that unify and relate the contents and acts of aesthetic experience.'[12] While it is true that the discovery of such forms and their establishment in the artistic deed are spoken of as acts of insight in Lonergan's sense of that term, still the artistic deed itself serves to show forth a 'deep-set wonder ... in its elemental sweep' and to 'exhibit the reality of the primary object for that wonder,' namely, the wonderer, *Da-sein*, as a question to itself. 'Art may offer attractive or repellent answers to these questions, but in its subtler forms it is content to communicate any of the moods in which such questions arise, to convey any of the tones in which they may be answered or ignored.'[13] And as those moods and tones as communicated and conveyed are Heidegger's *Befindlichkeit*, so the apprehensive component in the reception of the artistic forms is the equiprimordial *Verstehen*, which, while it is not Lonergan's 'insight' as a release to the tension of inquiry, has to be accounted more than merely sensitive receptivity.

Again, the pattern may be governed by the spirit of inquiry itself, and then it is what Lonergan calls the intellectual pattern of experience. Here intelligence so governs the sensitive process that this process is said to contract 'to an unruffled sequence of symbolic notations and schematic images.' The pattern controls what will appear in consciousness in the first place as 'the suggestive images of clues and missing links, of patterns and perspectives, that evoke the desiderated insight and the delighted cry "Eureka!"'[14] Now, while that cry is, of course, the cry of insight as a release to the tension of inquiry, the clues, links, patterns, and perspectives that are organized experientially in such a way as to evoke the cry are themselves already under the governing and organizing control of intellectual purposiveness, and so they emerge into consciousness already mediated by meaning. And that is all that I desire to maintain at the present: experience, the first level of consciousness, when organized by the intellectual pattern, is already constituted by meaningful expectations and anticipations.

The point I wish to make is probably clearest in Lonergan's discussion of the dramatic pattern, which, I think, is also the pattern that most occupies Heidegger in *Being and Time*. We, the characters in the drama of living, 'are molded by the drama itself.' While it is true that each of us discovers and develops by insight the possible roles we might play and selects and adapts those roles with some deliberation, still, prior to reflection and criticism, evaluation and decision, 'our imaginations and intelligence must collaborate in representing the projected course of action that is to be submitted to reflection and criticism, to evaluation and decision,' and the dramatic pattern is operative in that prior collaboration, 'outlining how we might behave before others and charging the outline with an artistic transformation of a more elementary aggressivity and affectivity.'[15] Some of that 'outlining' and affective 'charging' (*Verstehen* and *Befindlichkeit*) are under the influence not only of our own past behaviour, which is what is emphasized in this precise discussion in chapter 6 of *Insight*, but also, as becomes clear in chapter 7, of the dialectic of the community, which 'gives rise to the situations that stimulate neural demands, and ... molds the orientation of intelligence that preconsciously exercises the censorship' over these demands and how they will find their way into consciousness.[16] Thus, even in chapter 6 Lonergan writes, 'in ordinary living there are not first the materials and then the pattern, nor first the role and then the feelings. On the contrary, the materials that emerge in consciousness are already patterned, and the pattern is already charged emotionally and conatively.'[17] Moreover, the emotional and conative 'charging' may introduce a 'dramatic bias' into the pattern, and so exclude precisely those meaningful presentations that could release the process of inquiry towards the 'original meaningfulness' by which the subject finds his or her own way to truth and value. 'The dramatic pattern of experience penetrates below the surface of consciousness to exercise its own domination and control, and to effect, prior to conscious discrimination, its own selections and arrangements.' Those selections and arrangements that are prior to our own conscious discrimination are precisely the sort of 'meaningful data' that I am trying to call to our attention.

2.2 *Free Images and Utterances*

A second source is found in the following schematic representation:

I	Data. Perceptual Images	Free Images	Utterances
II	Questions for Intelligence	Insights	Formulations
III	Questions for Reflection	Reflection	Judgment

Lonergan says, 'The second level presupposes and complements the first. The third level presupposes and complements the second. The exception lies in free images and utterances, *which commonly are under the influence of the higher levels before they provide a basis for inquiry and reflection*.'[18] This quotation alone is probably all that is needed for me to make my point. There are presentations that occur to the conscious subject on the empirical level of consciousness that are already infused with intelligence and rationality and, we may add, with ethical overtones. These occur, I want to say, to a

Verstehen that is empirical, that receives meaningful data before these data provide a basis for one's own inquiry and reflection. May it not be said that the basis for a potential and fruitful dialogue with both Heideggerian and Wittgensteinian strands in philosophy and with von Balthasar in theology is already contained in this brief selection? In many ways, we need little or nothing more than this to establish the point that I am trying to make.

2.3 The Contextual Aspect of Judgment

The final source that I would like to call upon in this paper is found in the same chapter of *Insight*. It has to do with the contextual aspect of judgment. It was an important part of my earlier paper on this same material, and I am doing little more here than quoting once again what I said there.

The contextual aspect of judgment exhibits something of the temporality that is to the fore in *Being and Time* – not Heidegger's radical temporalizing, which will remain always problematic for anyone schooled in Lonergan's thought, but at least the dimensions of memory, presence, and anticipation. The contextual aspect of judgment is discussed in terms of 'the relation of the present to the past,' 'the relations within the present,' and 'the relations of the present to the future.' It is principally, though not exclusively, the relation of the present to the past that affects the point I am trying to make. Lonergan writes:

> Past judgments remain with us. They form a habitual orientation, present and operative, but only from behind the scenes. They govern the direction of attention, evaluate insights, guide formulations, and influence the acceptance or rejection of new judgments. Previous insights remain with us. They facilitate the occurrence of fresh insights, exert their influence on new formulations, provide presuppositions that underlie new judgments whether in the same or in connected or in merely analogous fields of inquiry. Hence, when a new judgment is made, there is within us a habitual context of insights and other judgments, and it stands ready to elucidate the judgment just made, to complement it, to balance it, to draw distinctions, to add qualifications, to provide defence, to offer evidence or proof, to attempt persuasion.[19]

I would like to adopt and adapt some of Heidegger's language at this point, and affirm that the habitual orientation formed by previous judgments and the habitual context of insights and other judgments help to constitute the intelligent and dispositional components of *Dasein* that constitute the horizon that functions in the very reception of data. And I want to emphasize that the judgments and insights that function in this way may be, not our own, but handed onto us, in the movement from above, by the community. At the same time, I would suggest that Heidegger can benefit from Lonergan's contribution especially to the discussion of the relations within the present and of the relations of the present to the future. The relations of the present to the past have to do by and large with what has become what Lonergan calls 'ordinary meaningfulness,' or what Wittgenstein would call the public meaningfulness of language, while the relations within the present and the relations of the present to the future may release the processes that exhibit original meaningfulness. Heidegger and Wittgenstein, in quite different ways, illuminate the realm of ordinary meaningfulness, and Lonergan the realm of original meaningfulness, and all three exhibit a great deal of original meaningfulness no matter what it is that they are illuminating. Moreover, it may be that original meaningfulness may be the set of elements needed to transcend the radical temporalizing in accord with which Heidegger places Being 'within' time rather than time 'within' Being.

The relations within the present, then, may be such as to show either mutual dependence and other connections or even conflicts among exist ing judgments. The connections stimulate logical efforts for 'organized coherence,' while conflicts 'release the dialectical process.' Again, the relations of the present to the future call attention to the dynamic structure of knowledge, something on which, it may safely be argued, Heidegger, at times associating or correlating Being with the transcendental imagination, does not lay sufficient stress. In brief, Lonergan says, 'All we know is somehow with us; it is present and operative within our knowing; but it lurks behind the scenes, and it reveals itself only in the exactitude with which each minor increment to our knowing is effected.'[20] But the same is true of all that we have received in the order of meaning and value. And I am asking whether all we know and all we have received reveals itself in the further reception of data, and whether those data include meanings and values. Is this not part of what is meant by the expression 'mediated immediacy'?

Notes

This paper was first composed for the April 2004 West Coast Methods Institute, Loyola Marymount University, Los Angeles. I thought it appropriate for this *Festschrift* for Michael Vertin because in a conversation prior to my delivering a summary of the paper, he had indicated that he thought what I was doing was an instance of complicating the basic structure of experience-understanding-judgment-decision. That comment led to a deeper understanding on my part of precisely what I am about in this and related recent papers. It also nicely fits the overall theme of the *Festschrift* in that it highlights the distinctive character of insight as Lonergan presents it as contrasted with, for example, Heidegger's *Verstehen*.

1 'Reception and Elemental Meaning: An Expansion of the Notion of Psychic Conversion,' *Toronto Journal of Theology* 20, no. 1 (Fall 2004), 133–57.
2 McGrath's paper has been published in a slightly revised form: Sean J. McGrath, 'Heidegger and Duns Scotus on Truth and Language,' *The Review of Metaphysics* 57, no. 2 (2003), 339–58.
3 Bernard Lonergan, *Method in Theology* (Toronto: University of Toronto Press, 2003), 255.
4 See Doran, 'Reception and Elemental Meaning,' 147 (slightly modified).
5 Lonergan, *Method in Theology*, 348.
6 Ibid., 356.
7 Ibid., 358.
8 Bernard Lonergan, 'Religious Knowledge,' in *A Third Collection*, ed. Frederick E. Crowe (New York: Paulist Press, 1985), 130.
9 Bernard Lonergan, *Insight: A Study of Human Understanding*, vol. 3 of *Collected Works of Bernard Lonergan*, ed. Frederick E. Crowe and Robert M. Doran (Toronto: University of Toronto Press, 2000), 204–5.
10 Ibid., 206.
11 Ibid.
12 Ibid., 208.
13 Ibid., 209.
14 Ibid.
15 Ibid., 211–12.
16 Ibid., 243.
17 Ibid., 212.
18 Ibid., 299, italics added.
19 Ibid., 302.
20 Ibid., 303.

S.J. McGrath

The Excessive Meaning of the Imaginal and Indirect Communication in Methodical Philosophy

The following is an effort to amplify the significance of the image in methodical philosophy. I question Lonergan's distinction between 'the sphere of the ulterior unknown, of the unexplored and strange, of the undefined surplus of significance,' from 'the sphere of reality that is domesticated, familiar, common.'[1] Is a surplus of significance not in fact constitutive of everyday living? Does this distinction of 'two spheres of reality' conceal a more original unity of the strange and the familiar? My thesis is that everyday images are horizoned by an excess of meaning, an infinite mysteriousness, which makes any talk of distinct spheres of reality artificial. An exposure of the imaginal in this new light precludes the creeping conceptualism that, even in methodical philosophy, threatens to reduce the image to a mere occasion for the insight and to conceal the primordial richness of life prior to objectification. Such exposure calls for a freer use of indirect communication in methodical philosophy; rhetoric, metaphor, and symbol, unlike technical uses of univocal language, leave the image free to signify in multiple ways. Without an explicit acknowledgment of the poverty of the univocal concept and a more generous use of indirection and exhortation, methodical philosophy remains vulnerable to the conceptualist reduction. I find evidence for this amplification of the significance of the imaginal in an admittedly Heideggerian retrieval of Aquinas on images. The Thomistic doctrine of *illuminatio* stipulates that before images become the matter for an abstraction of form, they are 'made fit' for intellection, that is, they are pre-conceptually lit up by the intellect.[2] Is the *illuminatio* not Aquinas's notion of a fore-conceptual intelligibility in the image, an intelligibility that not only precedes but also infinitely exceeds formative and apprehensive abstraction?[3]

Lonergan and the Imaginal

Aristotle's association of the imaginal with the contingent has engendered a tendency towards conceptualism in the Aristotelian-Scholastic tradition. This is somewhat surprising, given the Aristotelian premise that thinking begins with the image and returns to the image. Yet the image is associated with matter, the half-real, and the obscurity and quasi-intelligibility of things that can be otherwise. Lonergan's great contribution has been in part to purge Aristotelian-Scholastic philosophy of conceptualism by thematizing the act of insight, showing the provisionality and derivative nature of the concept. In this sense he is allied with other twentieth-century thinkers who have inaugurated a contemporary return to the imaginal (Heidegger, Ricoeur, Adorno, Benjamin, to name a few). However, Lonergan rightly sees a 'counterposition' in much nineteenth- and twentieth-century anticonceptualism, a reversion to 'mythic consciousness,' 'the refusal to move from description into explanation.'[4] In this paper I am not primarily interested in the counterposition; I *am* interested in the position coming forward in anticonceptualists such as Kierkegaard and Heidegger. The position resonates with scattered passages in *Insight.* 'Some sensitive awareness and response, symbolic of the known unknown, must be regarded as a generally and permanently recurring feature of human living,' Lonergan writes.[5] Lonergan's otherwise relentlessly theoretical philosophy ends in an acknowledgment of the inevitable breakdown of theory. As *Insight* progresses from phenomenology to metaphysics, to ethics, and crescendoes in the philosophy of God, explanations become less and less adequate to the subject matter, until the climactic question that cannot be answered by philosophy, the question about evil. For the solution Lonergan gestures to the imaginal, 'that strange dynamic component of sensitive living.' The solution will not be an explanation but 'a mystery in the threefold sense of psychic force, of sign, and of symbol.'[6] The world of nature, whose clear lines disappear in infinity, fails to explain itself. The world of spirit, ostensibly *logos* ruled, suffers shipwreck on the surd of sin. The mystical finale of *Insight* signifies the inevitability of returning from explanation to description, from concept to image.

Robert Doran's important early work *Subject and Psyche* opens a dialogue between Lonergan and imaginally oriented philosophy. Citing Gilbert Durand, Doran speaks of a 'fateful' and necessary moment in Western civilization when we moved away from the body, the image, and the anima and turned towards the intellect, the concept, and the animus.[7] Lonergan's work is the fullest appropriation of the turn to *logos,* as such, an unprecedented opportunity to fully evaluate its significance. The evolutionary trajectory of *logos* from *mythos* reaches its *telos* in the differentiation of interiority, *methodos*. The third stage is the threshold of a return to the beginning, a self-appropriated retrieval of image and feeling:

> Archetypally, this [move from myth to theory] was an option for *animus* rather than for *anima*, for spirit, *logos*, word, idea, intellect, principle, abstraction, meaning, *ratio*, *nous*, rather than for *psyche*, *mythos*, image, symbol, atmosphere, feeling, relation, earth, nature, rhythm. This option has given rise to what we have come to know as Western civilization. The archetypal significance of Lonergan's achievement, then, would be that, for the first time in the history of the unfolding of this radical option, the very structure of the option itself is laid bare and rendered capable of appropriation by those who have succeeded its makers. But today there would seem to be a cultural exigence, manifested throughout the Western world, to retrieve the option not taken at our origins. In most instances, this exigence is being responded to blindly, on the basis of a repudiation of the option that is our heritage. The cultural significance of Lonergan's achievement, then, at least from this archetypal point of view, is that the appropriation to which he invites us also renders possible a heeding of this new cultural exigence for the retrieval of *anima*, a heeding that is not blind, that does not involve a repudiation of our archetypally masculine heritage, that is attentive, intelligent, reasonable, and responsibly discriminating.[8]

The appropriation of the *logos*-option presumably includes a critique of a one-sided tendency to inflate the significance of the concept at the expense of the image. Properly interpreted, interiority includes the existential, and within that, the imaginal. Lonergan's method begins and ends with that which can never be replaced by an explanation, the incommunicably personal experience that he calls 'self-appropriation.' Without it the explanations dissolve like insights that overshoot the experiences that engender them. One would expect a sympathetic hermeneutic of myth and symbol. However, the topic is not the psyche but the intellect, not feeling but knowledge. This easily overlooked detail accounts for Lonergan's sometimes tiresome preference for technical terms, explanations, and univocal language. As Lonergan himself pointed out in 1970, *Insight* was not intended as an account of living, but as an analytic of understanding. To read it as an incomplete phenomenology, or as a one-sided anthropology, is to misread it.[9] Doran sees a development in the later Lonergan in this regard, a new sensitivity for the imaginal. He attributes it to the emergence of the good as a distinct notion apprehended in feeling. On the level of decision, where values are at issue, the affectivity, which was marginal to the intellectual conversion, becomes significant. The good is primarily disclosed in feeling, which is mediated by image and symbol. With this cue, Doran develops *Method in Theology*'s 'differentiations of consciousness,' which can only be precipitated by a conversion, into an appropriation of the symbolically mediated affective life of the soul, the 'psychic-conversion.' The 'sublation of the imaginal' is the inescapable prolegomena to moral self-transcendence. Psychic conversion entails an 'attentive, intelligent, reasonable and responsible appropriation and negotiation of one's psychic spontaneity and irrationality.'[10]

The image is the currency of common sense, of things in relation to us; the concept is the currency of explanations, of things in relation to other things. For Lonergan common sense is as foundational to knowledge as the presentation is foundational to insight.[11] But common sense is not properly concerned with knowledge; it is practical, 'knowledge not for the sake of the pleasure of contemplation, but to use knowledge in making and doing.'[12] In its normal operations, common sense is satisfied with an incomplete set of insights to be completed as the occasion requires. Common sense is Heidegger's 'average everydayness,' being-in-the-world, the mode of being nearest to us, but most elusive to theory, *Existenz,* which is determined and driven by care.[13] Where Heidegger regards common sense/everydayness as the site of the unveiling of the meaning of being, Lonergan emphasizes its epistemic limitations. Common sense 'is incapable of analyzing itself.'[14] The way swings off from Heidegger when Lonergan insists that common sense must be sublated by explanation if philosophy is to occur. Yet even for Lonergan, philosophy never overcomes the need for description. Explanation must at some point resort to image and symbol. This is so because, first, every explanation leaves us homeless. We cannot be satisfied with a disinterested account of the truth about things. To paraphrase Kierkegaard, we need to know that which is true for us. Lonergan writes: 'So fine a detachment, so rigorous a disinterestedness, is a sheer leap into the void for the existential subject. His concern is for things as related to him. He is quite intelligent; he is eager for insight; but the insight he wants is not at all the grasp of a system of terms defined by their intelligible relations to one another, but the grasp of intelligibility in the concrete presentations of his own experience.'[15] Second, the application of theory to practice requires concrete exhortative language. Without the image, there is no direct application. Explanation becomes effective in concrete living through the use of symbols, which 'release feeling and emotion and flow spontaneously into deeds no less than words.'[16] Third, mystery, however much it might be contracted by the advance of knowledge, is never eliminated from human living.[17] Lonergan sums up the need for the turn to the imaginal in the last chapter of *Insight*:

'All exercise of human intelligence presupposes a suitable flow of sensitive and imaginative presentations, and again, inasmuch as intelligence and reasonableness and will issue into words matched by deeds, they need at their disposal images so charged with affects that they succeed both in guiding and in propelling action.'[18]

Illuminatio and Excessive Meaning

The word 'image' is from the Latin, *imago*, related to *imitor*. An *imago* is an imitation, a copy of a thing, a likeness. Although it is colloquially associated with vision, etymologically 'image' has no ostensive ocular associations. Lonergan's terms 'presentation' (the sensitive image) and 'representation' (the subjectively generated image) have the advantage of explicitly avoiding ocular associations. A photograph is an image, but so is the song of a hermit thrush, the feel of a warm breeze, or the taste of red wine. The image or presentation need not be understood in a phenomenal sense, as an appearance, behind which there lurks the unknowable reality; the presentation is the self-showing of the thing, the thing as it exists for us. Through a scientific investigation we may come to know the thing as it is in-itself, but it will be *through* the presentation. Further, the concepts by which we transcend the level of presentations must be verified by a return to the presentation (the *conversio ad phantasma*). In Michael Vertin's words, a presentation is 'a sensible or imaginable content of my awareness.'[19] The presentation mediates the essence of the thing, the *species intelligibilis*, to the sense-dependent intellect via the insight. However, prior to insight, presentations are not opaque; they are luminous, the self-showing of distinct, understandable identities. Insight is not a grasp of form in undifferentiated sense data; it is a grasp of form in a datum that has already revealed itself as understandable. 'Objective abstraction is the illumination of phantasm, the imagined object,' Lonergan writes in *Verbum*. 'It consists in treating the imagined object as something to be understood as far as its specific nature goes.'[20] I do not engage an undifferentiated manifold of data in my questions; rather, I reflect on a unity within the whole of my experience at a given moment that manifestly has a specific, yet unidentified, nature. The world is not a chaotic swirl of sights and sounds; it is a coherent order of recurring patterns.

Illuminatio denotes a primordial lighting up prior to concept formation; it references the always already illuminated fore-conceptual structures of our everyday world. *Illuminatio* is what the scribe does who decorates and illustrates a manuscript with gilded letters, fantastic designs and symbols. The term is primarily active, something that is done to the data, as it is done to the manuscript. In the *Prima Pars, illuminatio* is treated in the context of a discussion of the Aristotelian middle way between Socratic naive realism and Platonic idealism.[21] The sensible phantasm cannot be directly received by the passive intellect, Aquinas tells us; it needs to be prepared, transformed. Aquinas relates how Democritus held that the sensible thing is an efficient cause of intellectual knowledge. Phantasms were erroneously believed to be 'discharged' from things and received directly by the intellect, which was, therefore, primordially passive. Plato correctly observed the incommensurability between the singular phantasm and the universal idea. He went too far in the opposite direction, however, denying the sensible thing any causal role in knowledge. Aquinas carves out a middle way by retrieving the Aristotelian distinction between the mode of being of the essence outside the soul and its mode of being within the soul. The sensible thing remains a material cause of knowledge. However, something happens to it when it enters the care of the intellect. Its essence is released from matter and universalized. For this to happen, the thing must be seen in a different light: its potential intelligibility must be released, that is, it must be illuminated by the intellect. The sensible phantasm is transformed, illuminated, made 'fit' for the abstraction of the form. In the illumination, the thing first shows itself as an *understandable* (not an *under stood*) whole. The illuminated thing possesses the unity and distinctness of that which can be the mediator of an idea. Aquinas writes: 'Not only does the active intellect throw light on the phantasm: it does more; by its own power it abstracts the intelligible species from the phantasm. It throws light on the phantasm, because, just as the sensitive part acquires a greater power by its conjunction with the intellectual part, so by the power of the active intellect the phantasms are made more fit for the abstraction therefrom of intelligible intentions.'[22] In medieval optics, vision is the effect of a light irradiating from the eye and touching the thing. The analogy with cognition suggests that the intellect is a source of light, which, touching upon things, illuminates them. The illuminated things are understandable images, neither wholly intelligible nor wholly unintelligible. They are not sunk into an undifferentiated chaos of sense data; they have the partial intelligibility of imaging distinct things. A state of fore-conceptual intelligibility, midway between the darkness of sense data prior to any consideration by the intellect, and the fully actual intelligibility of the intellected thing after the abstraction of form, is implied by the processual nature of intellection. Aquinas writes:

> We must consider that our intellect proceeds from a state of potentiality to a state of actuality; and every power thus proceeding from potentiality to actuality comes first to an incomplete act, which is the medium between potentiality and actuality, before accomplishing the

> perfect act. The perfect act of the intellect is complete knowledge, when the object is distinctly and determinately known; whereas the incomplete act is imperfect knowledge, when the object is known indistinctly, and as it were confusedly. A thing thus imperfectly known, is known partly in act and partly in potentiality.'[23]

The intellect does not pass from potentiality to act instantly, but gradually. The intelligibility of the thing develops in the intellect, like a thing that grows. 'For since the intellect passes from potentiality to act, it has a likeness to things which are generated, which do not attain to perfection all at once but acquire it by degrees.'[24] Vertin distinguishes five stages in the gradual process by which things enter into awareness: (1) sensing; (2) consideration of the phantasm as an intelligible whole and a possible content for understanding, which precipitates a direct insight; (3) (in the theoretical mode) descriptive or explanatory formulation of the grasped intelligibility; (4) verification of the formulation, reflective insight, which culminates in the judgment; (5) consideration of the value of the intelligibility, and deliberative insight.[25] Vertin does not use the term 'illumination.' However, it is implicit in (2): the illumination of the data is its consideration by the intellect as a possible content for understanding.

The epistemological point of Aquinas's doctrine of *illuminatio*, that a state of pre-conceptual intelligibility must precede apprehensive and formative abstraction, is corroborated by phenomenology. We do not ordinarily experience formless colours, unintelligible sounds, and nameless tactile sensations; we see 'the pines on the edge of the clearing'; we hear 'the wind in their branches'; we feel 'the shining sun.' Between the presentation and the insight are varying degrees of intelligibility, adumbrations of immateriality. The imaginal is a realm of twilight intelligibility, partaking both of the darkness, indistinctness, and singularity of matter, on the one hand, and the luminosity, unity, and universality of the immaterial, on the other. We dwell for the most part in this twilight between sensation and understanding. Here the soul and the body are one, the subject and the object are not yet distinguished, and the self is a being-in-the-world. We experience things as understandable, even if they are not yet understood.

Aquinas's *illuminatio* has an analogy in Edmund Husserl's important notion of 'categorial intuition.'[26] This oxymoronic composite of two terms that are usually opposed describes a dimension of experience, that is more than undifferentiated sensation, but less than categorial knowledge. Husserl discovered that the neo-Kantian disjunction between intuited contents of consciousness (sense data) and spontaneously generated formal structures (the categories) has no warrant in experience. The subjectivism that assumes that categories are imposed on the given by a synthesizing consciousness is phenomenologically unjustified. We have no intuition of raw data. Rather, we 'intuit' pre-categorially structured data, which elicit categorical expressions. The point as Heidegger understands it is that categories are not filters imposed upon the data of sensation; they do not constitute the 'hard wiring' of subjectivity. Instead, categories express fore-theoretical structures integral to the given. In other words, the fore-theoretical world is always already categorially illuminated. The *lumen naturale* is not so much a spotlight that singles out one dimension of the sensible after another; rather, to use Heidegger's metaphor, it is a clearing (*Lichtung*), an opening, a place of light, such as we encounter in a forest where the trees thin out. In this clearing, beings present themselves. This reading of *illuminatio* is suggested by a passing comment in *Being and Time*: 'When we talk in an ontically figurative way about the *lumen naturale* in human being, we mean nothing other than the existential-ontological structure of this being, the fact that it *is* in the mode of being its there. To say that it is "illuminated" means that it is cleared in itself *as* being-in-the-world, not by another being, but in such a way that it *is* itself the clearing. Only for a being thus existentially cleared do objectively present things become accessible in the light or concealed in darkness.'[27]

Lonergan's 'patterns of experience' disengage a similar structure, formal, categorially pregnant, yet prior to the abstraction of form.[28] The presentation shows itself in a context of related presentations, selected from the total field of experience according to varying criteria of subjective relevance. Presentations are always already related to one another in recurring patterns. The total field of the imaginal at any given moment would overload the subject who had no principle of selection, arrangement, and exclusion.[29] The subjective principles determining the pre-conscious selection and arrangement, rejection and exclusion of presentations in any given pattern are teleological. In the biological pattern, the principle is the animal's desire to survive and reproduce. Whatever presentations are relevant to this project are assimilated into the pattern (they are illuminated); the surplus of biologically irrelevant presentations are excluded (left in the darkness). In the aesthetic pattern the concern is the enjoyment of experience. Consequently, the aesthetic is the most open of all patterns. In the dramatic pattern, the principle is 'the desire to get things done,' the concerns of the moment, the pressures of daily life. The intellectual pattern is driven to answer certain theoretical questions; it systematically excludes all that is not relevant to the inquiry. Patterns of experience are by nature reductive; they reduce the imaginal to a manageable structure, a modicum suited to the needs of the subject in his or her situation. The pattern is both an illumination and a darkening of the imaginal. It is at once 'subjective,' that is, originating in the subject, and 'objective,' that is, received by the subject. We never have the whole field of the imaginal available to us for a survey; an *a priori* selection has always already occurred. Without the limiting schema, the presentations would be incomprehensible – not because they are unintelligible but, on the contrary, because they are excessively intelligible.

The Image as Icon

Illuminatio, categorial intuition, patterns of experience – these analogous structures underscore the pre-conceptual richness of the imaginal. As the whole of the understandable as such, the imaginal exceeds the powers of the finite intellect. The first excess of the imaginal is the sheer over-abundance of understandable experience. A second excess appears on a microcosmic scale in the understanding of particular presentations. The insight grasps the intelligibility in the presentation, but it does not comprehend the intelligibility of the thing. As Aquinas puts it, 'the essences of things are unknown to us.'[30] Where Descartes revels in his indubitable possession of clear and distinct ideas, Aquinas says, *formae substantiales per se ipsas sunt ignota,* 'We do not know substantial forms as they are in themselves.'[31] The concept is an interpretation of the insight, a fragment of the original light pouring out from the presentation. The insight is also an interpretation (it has what Heidegger calls the structure of taking something 'as' something). To fully understand the thing is to understand the mind of God, for created things are a likeness of the Creator. Hence one possible interpretation of the Latin etymology of *imago,* in Aquinas's words: 'All creatures are images of the first agent, namely God, since the agent produces its like.'[32] The essential intelligibility of the presentation reflects the absolute intelligibility of God; things 'look' like God. Josef Pieper describes this participation of creatures in divine intelligibility as 'the emergence of things from "the eye of God."'[33] To understand how an image images, how one thing can be *like* another, we need to understand both the image and the imaged. Yet we do not understand God in this life. The presentation images (*imitare*) God in ways that we cannot comprehend without the beatific vision. As Lonergan puts it, 'The world of sense is, more than all else, a mystery that signifies God as we know him and symbolizes the further depths that lie beyond our comprehension.'[34]

Karl Rahner has demonstrated that the notion of *excessus* is not only central to Aquinas's philosophical theology, it is foundational for his theory of knowledge.[35] Rahner interprets *excessus* as the pre-conceptual fore-grasp (*Vorgriff*) of being, which not only makes possible our analogous knowledge of God, but makes possible our finite knowledge of things. The operation of the agent intellect presupposes a 'transcendental experience' of the infinite, a pre-thematic, non-objective fore-grasp of the unlimited expanse of all possible reality.[36] *Excessus* is the principle of all the intellect's operations. In *Spirit in the World* Rahner looks at Aquinas's answer to the question, How is knowledge of a sensible singular possible? How does the *conversio ad phantasm* work? How exactly do we apply universal concepts to presentations?[37] The apprehended form of a concrete thing is profiled against the possible, grasped as limited to the presentations in which it is first encountered, yet simultaneously extending to further possible instantiations. This halo of understandability horizoning the concrete thing is itself profiled against the whole of being.[38] The infinity manifest in *excessus* is not an object, but the horizon of all possible objects. The *excessus* is not originally conceptual, although it makes possible the concept, nor is it ever adequately objectified. As the horizon of our average everyday existence, it is experienced but never comprehended, indicated through words that point to it, but never defined. As the illuminated arena of human understanding, the imaginal indicates an excessive intelligibility, which, in the insight, is grasped as contracted to a finite form, although also understood in the same act as infinitely exceeding it.[39]

The *excessus* of the imaginal is a consequence of the emergence of things from the divine mind. 'Every existing thing possesses the truth of its nature to the degree in which it imitates the knowledge of God.'[40] The thing's resemblance to God is the ground of its intelligibility. The thing is intelligible to the degree that it participates in absolute intelligibility. This Platonic dimension in Aquinas's thought need not be interpreted according to a confrontational model of knowing. On the one hand, we must affirm that in intellection the thing comes to the fullness of a certain modality of its intelligibility; the insight surpasses and sublates the presentation. On the other hand, the intelligibility of the presentation has an origin and destiny that is disproportionate to human cognitive faculties. Actual infinite intelligibility is not *given* in the presentation; to say so is to fall into extraversion. But the insight is more than a grasp of the finite intelligibility of the thing; it is also a glimpse of the concrete mysteriousness of the thing. At the moment that we reduce the potentially understood to an actual understanding, a higher level of potential intelligibility opens before us, the actualization of which is not in our power. Transcendental intelligibility, which is actual for God, will become actual for us when we grasp in the *visio beatifica* precisely how things image God.

The excessive intelligibility of the image is not eliminated by the insight but exposed. To understand the excess in insight we must distinguish two ways in which a thing can be mysterious: (1) the mysteriousness of the thing whose *species intelligibilis* is hidden from us in the presentation; in this sense, any presentation that is not yet understood is a mystery to the intellect; (2) the mysteriousness of the thing whose likeness to God is hidden from us; in this sense, all understood presentations remain mysteries because they are images of the infinite. The explanatory concept never succeeds in fathoming the infinite intelligibility indicated by the thing; on the contrary, it highlights its incomprehensibility. Joseph Pieper speaks of essential knowability of created things paradoxically conjoined with an essentially unknowability.[41] 'Things can be known because they are created,'. Pieper writes, 'Things are unfathomable because they are created.'[42] 'Not only God Himself but also things have an 'eternal name' that man is unable to utter.'[43] This infinite mysteriousness of the everyday leaves its mark on all patterns of experience. It becomes a central motive of the aesthetic, the most radically open of patterns. Aesthetic experience is not limited by need, be it biological, practical, or intellectual. Its *telos* is enjoyment. Its principle of selection, arrangement, and exclusion (if it can be said to exclude anything) is aesthetic delight. This should not be understood in a hedonistic sense. Aesthetic delight is neither egoistical nor sensual; it is the highest of human pleasures. Artists delight in experience for its own sake. Everything that can be experienced is relevant to them. When we participate in the experience of art, we get a glimpse of the world without our biological, practical, or intellectual filters. In a famous study of the effects of mescaline on the mind, Aldous Huxley spoke of multiple 'doors of perception,' which were for the most part shut by ordinary consciousness and opened wide by the artist and the mystic.[44] The artist does not experience some other world; he or she experiences more of this world. The painter does not see in the object something of use or something desirable; he or she delights in the thing's colour and form. Light and shadow on the human figure, the accidental forms of folded drapery, the familiar objects of daily life, are endlessly fascinating to the artist's eye.

I am arguing that the aesthetic pattern is not unique to the artist; it is foundational in every human life. The contemplative mode of perception, the experience of the presentation as object of delight, is the source and inspiration of the intellectual life; for it awakens the curiosity that drives the intellect.[45] The mind is intrigued and seduced, not by the incomprehensibility of the unintelligible – for it would make no sense to continue to ask about that – but by the partial comprehensibility of the excessively intelligible. We are spurred on by the suggestion of unexplored landscapes of meaning, hints of ideas we have never thought, glimpses of distant vistas of truth we have never visited, even in imagination. In Aquinas's theory of knowledge, two orders of intelligibility, one finite, the other infinite, intersect in every presentation. One cannot more profoundly underscore the mysticism of everyday life.

Indirection and Exhortation

When Lonergan told David Rasmussen at the Florida Congress in 1970 that he saw 'no difficulty in finding room' for 'symbolic consciousness' or 'a hermeneutic of recollection,' he suggested, by implication, that such a hermeneutic did not yet exist in his work.[46] The more developed treatment of symbol in *Method in Theology*, especially the crucial notion of elemental meaning (the analogue to Husserl's categorial intuition?), may reflect Lonergan's effort to address this lacuna.[47] However, I would argue that further phenomenological work is needed in this area. As Doran has written elsewhere in this volume, 'empirical consciousness' must be rethought so as to include 'received meanings and values.' The primordial pattern of experience is neither wordless nor uninterpreted; it is suffused by the images and colloquialism of common sense. A phenomenological description of the primordial pattern must recognize this stratum of fore-theoretical meaning and endeavour as far as possible to do it justice by finding a non-invasive access to it. The primordial pattern cannot be cashed out into technical terms. What is required is a phenomenology that resists the pull of the abstract, the slide into theory, by the use of indirect language, a phenomenology that indicates the subject matter roughly and in outline without presuming to define. Such a phenomenology will be, by necessity, image intensive, disengaging the constellations of symbols around which our psychic lives revolve. A philosophical retrieval of the discourse of undifferentiated consciousness or ordinary language need not be a 'reversion.' It can in fact serve the movement into interior differentiation, the turn from the abstract to the concrete, from essence to existence, from life theoretically considered to life as I am living it or failing to live it right now.[48] Methodical philosophy must recognize when keeping silent is not reversion, when symbolic discourse, which withholds or frustrates concepts, is not counterpositional but, as Doran puts it, 'the move toward greater concreteness on the part of the subject.'[49]

The exploratory nature of the symbol is a function of its proximity to the primordial pattern of experience. The symbol imaginally points to the concrete fore-theoretical ground of the insight. Its non-definitional nature allows it to gesture to the whole of elemental meaningfulness that originally mediates our images. It is plurivocal and multivalent, the object of a double intentionality, on the one hand imaging a concrete thing, on the other hand indicating an indeterminate range of unimaged and unimaginable associations. Hence the symbol is irreducible to the concept. It is charged with an excess that can be censured but not captured. Symbolic thinking calls for description rather than explanation. This entails inviting an inevitable amount of ambiguity into philosophy, opening up paths for thinking that proceed in multiple directions. In the Scholastic tradition, the meaning-bearing capacity of the image was understood as a central tenet of the sacramental view of the universe. The image is potentially a divine anagogue (from the Greek, 'leading upward'). As such, it oscillates with structures that not only elude our present conceptual powers, they elude all possible concepts. The symbol is horizoned by a range of significance that encompasses the whole of intelligible human activity, thought, and language. To grasp the entire significance of this referential whole of human living would be to understand precisely how human life both images and fails to image divine life. The technical term, precisely because it is univocally defined, binds us to a certain way of thinking, what Heidegger calls the theoretical 'relational sense' (*Bezugssinn*), which has always already excised the excess. The metaphor leaves everything as it was. Indirection is dangerous, for it requires that philosophy provisionally surrender its 'control of meaning' and allow itself to be led places it does not 'know.' Against the tired argument that such language has a place in literature but none in philosophy, we might point to philosophical, even technical uses of indirection in Plato, Kierkegaard, the late Schelling, or Heidegger. In these authors the intention is not to revert to a pre-rational stage of meaning, but rather, in the recognition of the limits of the explanatory, to draw on all the resources of language in order to remain faithful to the factic.

Insofar as Lonergan does not intend to directly communicate another theoretical system but to awaken his reader to the task of self-appropriation, insofar as the point is not theory but application, and the truth of *Insight* is not to be found by any test of internal coherence or deductive validity but only through applicability in one's own incommunicably unique being-in-the-world, indirection is essential to methodical philosophy. When Lonergan insists that knowing is a tripartite process of 'experiencing, understanding, judging,' the post-modern asks, 'Whose experience?' 'Whose understanding?' 'Whose judgment?' On the force of such questions Lonergan is commonly taken to be another totalizing thinker. However, the correct answer is *your* experience, *your* understanding, *your* judgment.[50] Lonergan's claim is not to have once and for all arrived at the sufficient theoretical formulation of experience, understanding, and judgment; rather, he wishes each of us to hear in these words the incommunicable modes of being-in-the-world that correspond to our own experience, understanding, and judgment in all of their haecceity. The point is not to schematize the structure of the intellect in abstract terms, but to 'assist the reader in effecting a personal appropriation of the concrete dynamic structure immanent and recurrently operative in his own cognitional activities.'[51] 'Though I cannot recall to each reader his personal experiences, he can do so for himself and thereby pluck my general phrases from the dim world of thought to set them in the pulsing flow of life ... The point here, as elsewhere, is appropriation; the point is to discover, to identify, to become familiar with, the activities of one's own intelligence.'[52]

This exhortative dimension of methodical philosophy is lost when the excessive meaning of the imaginal is overlooked. Lonergan's technical language, his insistence on using words in univocal ways, lends itself to misreading *Insight* as a *treatise* on human understanding. The followers of Lonergan, those who would continue to exhort the age to be intelligent, reasonable, and responsible, can counteract this misreading by resisting the temptation to slavishly preserve the language of the original text. The exhortative thrust is a licence to linguistic innovation. An exhortation has all of the resources of rhetoric at its disposal. Lonergan's task is nothing less than agitating the reader into existential wakefulness. Sometimes a careful refutation of the inauthentic view, the reversal of the counter-position, is required. But at other times a deliberately deflected statement is needed. Ambiguity can stalemate thinking; but it can also incite the self-interpretive act, the return to the mysteriousness of the everyday, without which there can be no conversion.

Notes

This paper is a refinement of two papers, one presented in April 2004 at the West Coast Methods Institute, Loyola Marymount University, Los Angeles, and the other in August 2004 at the Second International Lonergan Workshop, Regis College, Toronto. I had the privilege of studying under Michael Vertin from 1995–2002 at the University of Toronto. It is a testimony to Vertin's rare sensitivity to the idiosyncracies of his students that I remain to this day something other than a Lonerganian.

1 See Bernard Lonergan, *Insight*, vol. 3 of *Collected Works of Bernard Lonergan*, ed. Frederick E. Crowe and Robert M. Doran (Toronto: University of Toronto Press, 1992), 556.
2 Thomas Aquinas, *Summa Theologiae*, 1, q. 85, a. 1, ad 4.
3 See Robert Doran's 'Empirical Consciousness in *Insight*: Is Our Conception Too Narrow?' in this volume. Doran distinguishes a 'minor intelligibility' predicable of the presentation insofar as it is the always already meaningful datum of ordinary living. Doran suggests that *illuminatio* might in fact be corporate, not an act unique to the inquiring subject, but an intersubjective act, constituting a historical and linguistically charged, preconceptual understandability. On the distinctions between objective abstraction (*illuminatio*),

apprehensive abstraction (insight), and formative abstraction (conceptualization, the formation of the inner word), see Bernard Lonergan, *Verbum: Word and Idea in Aquinas*, vol. 2 of *Collected Works of Bernard Lonergan*, ed. Frederick E. Crowe and Robert M. Doran (Toronto: University of Toronto Press, 1997), 162–3. Lonergan speaks of the *illuminatio* as the first stage of abstraction and the first level of actual intelligibility in the object. See ibid., 185: 'It is the imagined object as present to intelligent consciousness as something-to-be-understood that constitutes the intelligible in act. Further, this illumination of the imagined object, this reception of it within the field of intellectual light, has the characteristic of being abstractive; for it is not the imagined object in all respects that is regarded as something-to-be-understood.' See also ibid., 187–8.

4 Lonergan, *Insight*, 567.

5 Ibid., 557.

6 Ibid., 557, 750.

7 Robert Doran, *Subject and Psyche: Ricoeur, Jung, and the Search for Foundations* (Lanham, MD: University Press of America, 1980), 111–12. Doran cites Gilbert Durand, 'Exploration of the Imaginal,' *Spring: An Annual of Archetypal Psychology and Jungian Thought* (1971), 94.

8 Doran, *Subject and Psyche*, 111–12.

9 At the 1970 Florida congress, David Rasmussen gave an early critique of Lonergan as lacking a hermeneutic of symbol and myth. See Rasmussen, 'From Problematics to Hermeneutics: Lonergan and Ricoeur,' in *Language, Truth and Meaning*, ed. Philip McShane (Notre Dame, IN: University of Notre Dame Press, 1972), 236–71. Lonergan was present at the congress and gave a brief response to the critique: 'My purpose was not a study of human life but a study of human understanding' (ibid., 310).

10 Doran, *Subject and Psyche*, 184.

11 Lonergan, *Insight*, 323.

12 Ibid., 232.

13 See Martin Heidegger, *Being and Time*, trans. Joan Stambaugh (Albany, NY: State University of New York Press, 1996), 47: 'This indifference of the every dayness of Da-sein is not nothing; but rather, a positive phenomenal characteristic. All existing is how it is out of this kind of being and back into it. We call this everyday indifference of Da sein averageness. And because average everydayness constitutes the ontic immediacy of this being, it was and will be passed over again and again in the explication of Da-sein. What is ontically nearest and familiar is ontologically farthest, unrecognized and constantly overlooked in its ontological significance.'

14 Lonergan, *Insight*, 251.

15 Ibid., 562.

16 Ibid., 570.

17 See Lonergan's reply to Rasmussen at the 1970 Florida congress in *Language, Truth, and Meaning*, 309: 'In *Insight* there are two kinds of symbolic narratives: mysteries and myths. I did not contend that as metaphysics advances, mysteries recede, and so I see no difficulty in finding room in my position for sym-

bolic consciousness or for a hermeneutic of recollection.' Note the pejorative use of 'myth.'

18 Lonergan, *Insight*, 744.

19 Michael Vertin, 'Images, Symbols, and Signs: Concrete Mediators of Human Living,' in *Image Makers and Image Breakers*, ed. Jennifer Harris (Ottawa: Legas, 2004), 139. Vertin's is a variation on Lonergan's definition of 'image.' See *Insight*, 557.

20 Lonergan, *Verbum*, 187.

21 See Aquinas, *Summa Theologiae*, 1, q. 84.

22 Aquinas, *Summa Theologiae*, 1, q. 85, a. 1, ad 4.

23 Aquinas, *Summa Theologiae*, 1, q. 85, a. 3, c. Cf. Lonergan, *Verbum*, 184–5: 'The imagined object as merely imagined and as present to a merely sensitive consciousness (subject) is not properly speaking, intelligible in potency, but the same object present to a subject that is intelligent as well as sensitive may fairly be described as intelligible in potency. Thus pure reverie, in which image succeeds image – in the inner human cinema with never a care for the why or wherefore, illustrates the intelligible in potency. But let active intelligence intervene: there is a care for the why and wherefore; there is wonder and inquiry; there is the alertness of the scientist or technician, the mathematician or philosopher, for whom the imagined object no longer is merely given but also a something-to-be-understood.' Here Lonergan suggests a mode of human awareness not determined by care. This 'pure reverie,' I would argue, is a limit concept. In fact, no human experience is devoid of care; therefore, all experience is to some degree illuminated. Lonergan's 'care' is the theoretical interest in 'the why and wherefore.' But prior to theoretical questions there are everyday practical concerns. Are we to say that such cares do not also light up the world in a particular way? Surely not. The intellectual pattern is only one way in which experience is fore-conceptually structured.

24 Aquinas, *Summa Theologiae*, 1, q. 85, a. 5, c.

25 Vertin, 'Images, Symbols, and Signs,' 141–3.

26 See Edmund Husserl, *Logical Investigations*, trans. J.N. Findlay (London: Routledge & Kegan Paul, 1970), vol. 2, sec. 45. For Heidegger's interpretation of categorial intuition see Martin Heidegger, *History of the Concept of Time: Prolegomena*, trans. Theodore Kisiel (Bloomington: Indiana University Press, 1992), 27–75. On the significance of this concept for Heidegger, see my 'Heidegger and Duns Scotus on Truth and Language,' *Review of Metaphysics* 57 (December 2003), 353–5, and my *The Early Heidegger and Medieval Philosophy: Phenomenology for the Godforsaken* (Washington, DC: Catholic University of America Press, 2006), chap. 4.

27 Heidegger, *Being and Time*, 125.

28 Lonergan, *Insight*, 204–12.

29 Fascinating stories of the confusion and disorientation of people born blind who have been given sight through modern medicine confirm this thesis. See Oliver Sacks, 'To See and Not See,' *New Yorker*, 10 May 1993, 61–6.

30 Aquinas, *De Veritate*, 10, 1. See also his *De Anima*, I, 1, 15: 'The essential grounds of things are unknown to us.'

31 Aquinas, *Quaestio Disputata de Spiritualibus Creaturis*, II ad 3. See also *De Veri tate*, 4, 1, ad 8: 'Essential differences are not known to us.'
32 Aquinas, *Summa contra Gentiles*, Book 3, chap. XIX, trans. Anton C. Pegis, in *Introduction to St. Thomas Aquinas*, ed. Anton C. Pegis (New York: Modern Library, 1948), 439. The passage continues: 'Now the perfection of an image consists in representing the original by a likeness to it, for this is why an image is made. Therefore all things exist for the purpose of acquiring a likeness to God, as to their last end.'
33 Josef Pieper, *The Silence of St. Thomas* (South Bend, IN: St. Augustine's Press, 1999), 63.
34 Lonergan, *Insight*, 714.
35 Karl Rahner, *Spirit in the World*, trans. William Dych (New York: Continuum, 1968), 146–236.
36 Ibid., 136–45.
37 Rahner's source text is *Summa Theologiae*, 1, q. 84, a. 7: 'Whether the Intellect Can Actually Understand through the Intelligible Species of Which It Is Pos sessed without turning to the Phantasm?'
38 Rahner, *Spirit in the World*, 145.
39 In his follow up to *Spirit in the World*, *Hearer of the Word*, Rahner sums up his reading of *excessus*: 'It is an *a priori* power given with human nature. It is the dynamic movement of the spirit toward the range of all possible objects. In this movement, the single objects are grasped as single stages of this finality; thus they are known as profiled against this absolute range of all the knowable. On account of the *Vorgriff* the single object is always already known under the horizon of the absolute ideal of knowledge and posited within the conscious domain of all that which may be known. That is why it is also always known as not filling this domain completely, hence as limited. And insofar as it is thus known as limited, the quidditative determination is grasped as wider in itself, as relatively unlimited. In other words it is abstracted.' *Hearer of the Word*, trans. Joseph Donceel (New York: Continuum, 1994), 47–8.
40 Aquinas, *Summa Theologiae*, 1, q. 14, a. 12, ad 3.
41 Pieper, *The Silence of St. Thomas*, 57.
42 Ibid., 53, 57. See especially 59–60: 'This relation on which the truth of things is fundamentally based – the relation between natural reality and the archetypal creative thought of God – cannot, I insist, be known formally by us. We can of course know things; we cannot formally know their truth. We know the copy, but not the relation of the copy to the archetype, the correspondence between what has been designed and its first design. To repeat, we have no power of perceiving this correspondence by which the formal truth of things is constituted. Here we can notice how truth and unknowability belong together ... It is part of the very nature of things that their knowability cannot be wholly exhausted by any finite intellect, because these things are creatures, which means that the very element which makes them capable of being known must necessarily be at the same time the reason why things are unfathomable.'
43 Ibid., 65.

44 Aldous Huxley, *The Doors of Perception* (London: Chatto & Windus, 1954).

45 Lonergan briefly acknowledges this primacy of the aesthetic in *Insight*: 'Prior to the neatly formulated questions of systematizing intelligence, there is the deep-set wonder in which all questions have their source and ground. As an expression of the subject, art would show forth that wonder in its elemental sweep' (*Insight*, 208).

46 Lonergan, in *Language, Truth, and Meaning*, 309.

47 Bernard Lonergan, *Method in Theology* (Toronto: University of Toronto Press, 2003), 64–9.

48 Cf. ibid., 275.

49 Doran, *Subject and Psyche*, 302.

50 This deflection essential to methodical philosophy is the reason for Vertin's repeated use of the first-person pronoun in his published writings.

51 Lonergan, *Insight*, 11.

52 Ibid., 13–14.

PART TWO

Insight in Theology

Frederick E. Crowe, SJ

Is God Free to Create or Not Create?

O depth of wealth, wisdom, and knowledge in God! How unsearchable his judgments, how untraceable his ways.

Romans 11:33

1 The *Festschrift*

There are various reasons for dedicating a *Festschrift* to a colleague in the academic community: his or her spread of writings, or success in public lectures, or outstanding qualities as a teacher, or generosity in sharing the chores of academe, or a milestone in life's journey, or for being a valued member of the community, a scholar and friend. It is hard to imagine one who combines all these reasons in such happy proportions as does Michael Vertin, and I am delighted to be able to contribute to this *Festschrift* in his honour. I may even boast that it is especially fitting for me to join his well-wishers, for besides sharing in the general grounds they all have, I have the additional reason that Michael three times assumed the burden of editing a book of mine. It is a very small return that I am making here.

I see a special connection too with the focus of this volume, the importance of insight, for the *Quodlibet* that concludes my essay, and indeed the whole essay, is a plea for insight, for such understanding of God's ways as is possible in our present life.

Readers will be familiar with the format Thomas Aquinas uses for the doctrines of his *Summa Theologiae*. The stage is set by a 'Whether' question (*Utrum*); in the present case, whether God is free to create or not create. This is followed by arguments against the freedom in question, 'It seems not' (*Videtur quod non*), and by arguments for that freedom, 'But on the other hand' (*Sed contra*). Finally Thomas takes up the question on his own, 'I reply as follows' (*Respondeo dicendum quod*), and provides a fundamental understanding of the whole matter, one that enables him to deal with both of the two opposed arguments.

I find it convenient to use this format, modified for my purpose, to impose some order on what may otherwise seem like scattered reflections. 'Modified' indeed, but I hope recognizable; for I do present positions for and against the liberty of the Creator; then I make my attempt at a more fundamental understanding of the whole question, my own *Respondeo dicendum quod.*

2 The Arguments For and Against

Our question, then, is whether God is free to create or not create, and for the negative side I offer one seemingly simple argument, based on the familiar Dionysian axiom, 'The good is self-diffusive.' The Leonine Index to '*bonum*' has several references to this self-diffusive aspect of the good, appealing regularly to the authority of Dionysius and using the references regularly against Thomas's own position, but there is no doubt that Thomas accepts the principle itself and explains it in a way that is meant to protect the authority of Dionysius.[1]

On this basis one might argue that God is good par excellence, that God will wish to spread this goodness around and, having no one else with whom to share it, will be obliged to create a world to receive the divine self-diffusion. One may interpret Dionysius more metaphysically, as the medievals did, or in our day invoke the power of intersubjectivity, but there is in his slogan a doctrine that is in tension with, if not opposed to, that of divine freedom in creation.

For the opposite position there is for a Catholic theologian one sufficient argument: the doctrine of Vatican I, which declared that God is perfectly free to create or not create, according to the divine will. Since I write as a Catholic theologian, I accept the Vatican declaration: the one true God, out of goodness, not for an increase in beatitude or to acquire it but to manifest the divine perfection, in a free decision, created out of nothing both spiritual and material worlds.[2] This does not seem to leave much leeway for distinctions, or for watering down the argument, but we shall see what we can do with it.

3 Learning from Experience: The Trinity

Facing the problem of reconciling two seemingly opposed positions, I look for clues in our history and ask whether the long experience of the church shows any similar problems, if so how they were handled, and whether our ancestral way of handling them provides any guidance for us today.

At once there comes to mind the history of thought on the Trinity. Here the church found itself believing in a God who was one but who was also in some way three. The solution of this conflict involved elaboration of two concepts, person and nature, and their relationship to one another. The famous use of these two concepts was their application to Christ in the Council of Chalcedon (AD 451), which declared that there was in Christ one person in two natures.[3] The full trinitarian doctrine soon followed.

The road to this solution, however, had been a long and rocky one. The church is a slow thinker, and it was more by rejecting false theories than by formulating an acceptable one that the solution was found. Very soon after the resurrection the church was able to articulate its faith in God and the Lord, as expressed in the salutations of Paul's letters: the God and Father of the Lord Jesus Christ (Romans 1:7; 1 Corinthians 1:3; etc.). Not too long after that we find the baptismal rite conferred 'in the name of the Father and of the Son and of the Holy Spirit' (Matthew 28:19). The church reflected on the implications of this practice for two or more centuries, until finally theology came to terms with it.

The first theological step to be taken on this basis was incredibly simple and incredibly difficult: namely, the use of the word 'three.' This took about a hundred and fifty years! The baptismal rite mentioned Father, Son, and Spirit, who when 'counted' do make three, but the 'counting' was the problem. To say 'three' would have enormous implications. It would presume a sameness in the three, but a sameness of what? It would predicate that sameness of the three, and call the three not natures but persons. But what was a person? Theologians were reduced to descriptions at one remove from a definition; thus Lonergan presents Augustine's formulation as follows: a 'person' is what there are three of in God![4] The simple act of 'counting' Father, Son, and Spirit turns out to be far from simple. So it was only around AD 180 that the word 'three' began to be used, and only some two or three centuries later that the formula 'In God there is one nature and three persons' became domiciled in the church.

It is not my intention to write a history of Trinitarian doctrine, but only to seek clues there on the church's way of thinking. One clue lies in the struggle to find two terms the church could use to designate what there are three of in the Trinity and what there is one of. The creative factor in this long pondering was finding the terms, giving them a fixed meaning, and having that meaning accepted for application to the Trinity.

With that I return to my own proper question. I begin where a beginning is possible: analysis of human activity as basis of the analogy of God and the human. I will consider that analogy from the divine side and from the human. I will take up the arguments with which my study began, arguments for and against divine freedom in creation. I will conclude with reflections on the mystery which God is. The arguments spoke of necessity and freedom in God, so in our study of the human side we will look for two terms that might provide an analogue for their divine counterparts, one of them applying to what is necessary in the divine activity, another to what is free – two terms, moreover, that are related to one another and so able to shed light on the divine where the essence is unity.

4 Analysis of a Human Act: Free and Not Free

The history of trinitarian thought in a slow-thinking church led us to expect a similar history in our study of necessity and freedom in the divine activity. If, however, we are to talk of divine liberty and divine necessity, our talk can be intelligible only on the analogy of the liberty and necessity we encounter as members of the human race, and that involves us in analysis of the act of human choice. We will find, in fact, that there are acts in our willing that are free and acts in our willing that are not free. The former will provide an analogy for God's freedom, the latter an analogy for what is necessary in God's activity. The term 'necessary' is unhappy, but we use it for lack of a better.

In his analysis of a human choice Aquinas would use the simple example of being sick and calling in the doctor. There is an end that is desired: say, good health. There is some deliberation about means: can I use home remedies or should I call in a doctor? My deliberations lead me to choose the second. So I call in the doctor.

The case is rarely so simple. I may, for example, because of past and ongoing history almost automatically, without deliberation, opt for calling in the doctor. We may, however, imagine the more difficult case of a democratic people holding an election in which there is a choice between two candidates. It may be a difficult choice, requiring long deliberation and perhaps some investigation – for example, the record of a candidate's voting in the previous parliament – yet the pattern of activities remains the same.

But let us return to Thomas. On the bare bones of his sickness-purpose-deliberation-choice-decision-act Thomas builds a very thorough study of human activities. Two of these are especially pertinent to our question: the acts that are not free, namely, willing the end; and the acts that are free, namely, choosing the means.

Choosing the means is more easily understood and has its importance in human living; it is, however, less in need of explanation and may be set aside for the moment. Not so the willing of the end. What is this willing of the end that is not a free act? A number of characteristics describe it. It is a habit, a general orientation; it is a built-in set of values; it is perhaps a conversion effected by grace. It is a given, a customary way of thinking and choosing, one that we did not create but received; it is a bias, perhaps for what is good, perhaps for what is evil. If for the good, it is a spontaneity, a readiness, a disposition to serve, a joy in self-sacrifice for the sake of the other, a peace in responsibility accepted – all these features apply, loosely or exactly, to our willing of the end. I grant that the traits I have described are not always so clear-cut, but generally they operate in the long run to ensure a continuity in my choices and to define my character. Now it is this pair, willing the end and choosing the means, that I suggest for an analogy to the necessity and freedom we find in God the Creator.

A pair of scholia may be mentioned. First, I have said that 'per se' willing the end is not free. That allows for disruptions in one's daily routine, when the easy continuity of a life without decisions may be broken. The example of a conversion effected by grace illustrates that. Before conversion life was simple, ends were part of the family ways, choices on important matters were rarely necessary, and on routine matters were not needed. (Do we 'decide' each morning to comb our hair?) A conversion, however, is a revolution in my way of life; it was a choice not of one means rather than another, but of one end in life rather than another. After conversion I begin a new way of life, and after a difficult period of transition, choices once again become part of that way.

So, even if the will is not free in regard to this present act of willing the end, it can be moved by God or external circumstances to conceive and to will another higher end, thus turning the present end into a new means that one freely chooses or rejects. For example, a person may make the Spiritual Exercises of St Ignatius, and be confronted in the Exercise on the Two Standards with a new end; it may be chosen or rejected, but once chosen it becomes a new orientation, a habit governing one's life and its choices.

Here I must insert a piece of history as another scholion. In the early days of the Lonergan Workshop I encountered extraordinary resistance to the idea that there are acts of willing that are not free. Now in Thomas and Lonergan the act of choosing is a compound, consisting first of willing the end, then of deliberating on the means to that end, and finally of choosing the means.[5] In that compound it is the third act that is free; but will of the end is not free unless, as just explained, that end is turned into a means and I am given by grace or destiny a higher end that becomes the governing factor in my deliberations and my choice of a new way of life.

The sharp opposition I experienced to this doctrine resulted, I think, from failure to differentiate the three activities in the compound and to assign each its proper role. Are they not all acts of willing, it may be asked? Surely they are. Then will they not surely be free acts, all of them? That difficulty is understandable. For after conversion this willing of the end is not so much an act of willing as a state of willing; there is an antecedent willingness, a habitual orientation, a way of living in which there were few if any decisions, but only the hidden intervention of God acting often through circumstances. And we do not advert to God's intervention; it is mediated to us by the home and family, by the atmosphere of the social order, the example of parents, the environment, the school in its primary grades, and so on.

There is a parallel here to the difficulty many have in regard to Lonergan's cognitional structure. They see rightly that experiencing, understanding, and judging are all cognitional acts, but then they wrongly think of them as acts of knowing. For Lonergan they are not acts of knowing: cognitional, yes, but items of knowledge, no. Only the compound can be called an act of knowing, adding to our knowledge.[6] In a somewhat similar way, three acts or activities of willing combine to reach a free decision.

I have been prolix on the will of the end in human decisions because it is not given due attention in studies of Thomas and Lonergan. We focus more on decisions, choices, the challenges of life. That, too, is understandable, for it is in the repeated willing of the means that willing the end becomes more strongly entrenched, that our character is formed, that day by day we freely and responsibly make ourselves in act what grace and environment have made us in outlook and readiness to act.[7] That free activity is our human analogue for God's free activity in our regard. But perhaps there is less need to develop a line of thought that is more generally familiar.

The element of necessity must, however, be underlined. For the chief analogy for God's self-diffusing in its interiority is the human willing of the end. And that at its base is not a free act: notwithstanding our cooperation at a second stage, the initial step is caused by God alone.[8] I described it as a habit, a general orientation, a built-in set of values, perhaps a conversion effected by grace. These at their inception we receive as gift; they are there as a willing, but not as a willing we choose; we may choose to accept them, as people respond to grace, or to repudiate them, as people resist grace, but our role is to follow or to react, not to initiate. We are at the heart of understanding God's freedom and necessity in creation: that understanding depends on the analogy we find in our human division of free and not free; if the basis of the analogy is not clear, our whole effort is useless.

We have followed the path suggested by analysis of the church's thinking on the Trinity. As our ancestors used person and nature to enlighten them on their problem, so we use human will of the end and human will of the means for entry into the mystery of divine freedom and divine necessity. Let us turn, then, to that mystery.

5 The Analogy from God's Side: Self-Diffusion *ad Intra*

The analogy that we have studied from the human side we have now to study from the divine side, beginning with the divine interiority. The three, Lonergan says, are both communicable and incommunicable, and the same reason accounts for both these claims. That is, they are distinguished from one another by real relations and so are incommunicable. For to be incommunicable means simply that they are themselves and not someone else; nor may they become someone else. But on the other hand, it is through the same real relations that they communicate, for each relation includes the opposed relation in its ratio. Thus the Father is self-diffusive towards the Son, but equally the Son is self-diffusive towards the Father. Further, the real relations are identical with the divine processions by which the Father communicates the Father's essence to the Son, and Father and Son together communicate their divine essence to the Holy Spirit.[9] (If we speak of 'self'-communication in this context, 'self' refers not to the person as person but to the person as possessing the divine essence.)

God's communication and self-diffusion *ad extra* is a freely chosen act, but God's communication *ad intra* that I am sketching is another matter. This communication is eternally full and complete. You could say, God has no future, but before that develops into heresy, add at once: God's 'future' is an already realized future, for it is always present; all that pertains to the three *ad intra* is already in act. The divine 'future' is the divine 'present.' Or, we could ask about the divine internal 'history' of the three, understanding that it is a 'history' going forwards without end or beginning; the Father is eternally begetting the Son.

This general view of God's interior life is analogous to our human willing of the end. In God it is not a free choice, nor is it in potency to a free choice. We have to conceive as potency rather than act the 'activity' in God that corresponds to our free willing, but the 'activity' that corresponds to our willing of the end is not a potency; it belongs to the divine essence and to the divine self-diffusing nature; it would remain as a divine characteristic even if there were no actual self-diffusion *ad extra*. But in fact there is potency *ad extra*, and that potency has become act. There is actual self-diffusion; God did actually become human, and *ab esse ad posse valet illatio.*

From this viewpoint any assumption of the human by the divine illustrates the potential self-diffusion. Take sacrifice as an example. For did God not become a sacrifice for us, and *ab esse ad posse valet illatio*? Or shall we speak of the humility of God? Or of the divine kenosis? All these illustrate the potential self-diffusion that belongs to the freedom of God. Whatever God actually did reveals what God is capable of doing and throws light on the divine nature. Whatever self-diffusing has actually occurred contributes to a treatise on the meaning of the self-diffusing character of God.

6 Divine Self-Diffusion *ad Extra*: God and the Human

We have studied our analogy from the human side and from the divine side. We have now to study the two together, and so we come to extrinsic denomination, an idea and way of speaking that applies to all predication to God of what is contingent. The basic point is this: there must be a correspondence of reality and predication; next, there is no contingent reality intrinsic to God; hence, predication to God of the contingent must be by extrinsic denomination; and fourthly, God is not changed by such predication.

To say, then, that God wills the created world requires a correspondence of the truth in that statement with the fact in the universe of objective reality. There is no extrinsic denomination without the reality of the extrinsic denominator. But equally there is no extrinsic denomination without the truth that corresponds to that reality. Now the reality is contingent, and nothing in God is contingent. The correspondence required for the truth to be true cannot be intrinsic to God; it has to be extrinsic.[10] Hence the important category of extrinsic denomination in such a statement as 'God created heaven and earth.'

That God can create without any change in the divine reality is apt to be a stumbling block for some, but it is not to be regarded as a singular case. There are plenty of instances of the difficulty we have in a unitary thinking of what seem conflicting attributes predicated of God. The standard example is the unitary thinking of the justice and the mercy of God; mostly we don't think the two together; we just hold both without understanding their unity.

7 The Compulsion to Self-Expression: On Argument One

Thomas concluded each article in a question by taking account of the arguments – for one side, *Videtur quod non*; for the other, *Sed contra*. Our aim in these concluding sections is to examine the arguments in the light of his *Respondeo dicendum quod*: first, the scholastic axiom that the good is self-diffusing; then, the Vatican Council on divine freedom in creating.

An easy start on self-diffusing is given in an almost daily occurrence: the simple case of expressing one's knowledge. No doubt all of us have experienced the frustration of Job's comforter: 'If one ventures to speak with you, will you lose patience? For who could hold his tongue any longer?' The frustration, the repression expressed in that 'For who could hold his tongue any longer?' reveals the power of the compulsion to speak one's mind. Closer to ordinary experience is our bent for rumour-mongering: I have heard an exciting rumour, and am bursting with the need to pass it on – not a very laudable desire, and not the highest *bonum*, but a clear case of knowledge as *diffusiva sui*.

Transfer this from the field of knowing to that of the good. Perhaps few of us can be said to be bursting with need to communicate the good, but we recognize that experience in the zeal of the saints, especially in those whose apostolate is among the poor and downtrodden. How, they ask, can I share what I have with others, the have-nots? The two aspects may combine: I am bursting with the good news of the Gospel: it is news, so we are dealing with knowledge; it is good news, so we are in the sphere of what is good for us.

The New Testament, in its overall motif as well as in particular reminders, is full of this attitude: 'Then Jesus, armed with the power of the Spirit, returned to Galilee ... He taught in their synagogues and all men sang his praises' (Luke 4:14–16). He felt the compulsion to share with others the message that urged and pressed him: 'Let us move on to the country towns in the neighborhood; I have to proclaim my message there also; that is what I came out to do' (Mark 1:38). What he would share is revolutionary: 'I have come to set fire to the earth, and how I wish it were already kindled' (Luke 12:49). After his resurrection he communicated this urge to his followers: 'Full authority in heaven and on earth has been committed to me. Go forth therefore and make all nations my disciples' (Matthew 28:18–19). In such outpourings we realize the experience of Eliphaz, Job's 'comforter,' in a setting somewhat more edifying than his.

When Jesus sent his disciples to preach and they obeyed, did they obey freely or under compulsion? Did the compulsion they experienced deprive them of their freedom? If we take Paul to the letter we might say so: 'Even if I preach the Gospel, I can claim no credit for it; I cannot help myself' (1 Corinthians 9:16). This refers to the main thrust of his ministry, for on details he surely had changes of plan and chose freely. On preaching Christ he could not help himself, but whether to go to Corinth or not was a decision he could debate. It is clear from Paul's whole history that he continually made decisions affecting his ministry, though never to the point of giving up that ministry: compulsion on the main thing, then, but freedom on details. Perhaps in this very difference we have an analogue for the divine state: a divine necessity in regard to the 'wealth, wisdom, and knowledge in God' (Romans 11:33), and a divine freedom to yield or not yield to an inner compulsion for self-diffusion in regard to all else.

It is just here that we need a Thomas Aquinas with his *Respondeo dicendum quod.* It seems irreverent to speak of God 'bursting' with the good news, but we have to ask whether God, under some divine internal pressure for self-diffusion in the infinite measure proper to God, does not actually modify the divine freedom in that experience. Surely what is a good attribute in people is somehow to be predicated also of God. It is a necessity without violence, and if this is possible in the human world, surely it is even more so in the divine. So perhaps Paul's case is instructive here; if he could combine freedom and necessity ('I cannot help myself') perhaps we have as clear a statement as we are likely to get of some such combination in the mystery that God is.

At any rate Paul's example forces us to think in a different way about necessity. God is not compelled. God deciding to enter our universe is sovereignly free in that decision. To ask whether in some possible universe God would exist through all eternity without creation, capable of creating worlds to receive the divine diffusion, yet withholding that diffusion – is this a question we must abandon here while we make a plea of mystery?

8 The Freedom of the Creator: On Argument Two

One experiences the same helpless state in trying to penetrate the divine mind in relation to Vatican I. Authority answers the *utrum* question for me as believer, an answer to which I obediently subscribe; but it leaves me dissatisfied as a theologian, with a theologian's need for understanding. It would not have satisfied Thomas, whose *Respondeo dicendum quod* would take him to deeper levels.

But there, in that reference to Thomas, we gain a hint on how we may live with what God sees fit to give us. For the same Council declared the possibility of some analogous understanding of the truths of faith. Lonergan, with all his respect for legitimate authority, loved to quote the *Quodlibet* in which Thomas insisted that authority is not enough; there must be understanding. Let us hear Thomas on this matter.

Controversy, Thomas says, can have two purposes: one purpose is to remove doubt, and here authority rules. But it can also be pedagogic (*magistralis*), not for removing error but for bringing hearers to an understanding of the truth. Here authority is not enough; it will bring students to the truth, but without science or understanding they will go away with empty heads, ignorant of the matter: *auditor ... vacuus abscedet.*[11]

Are we guilty of hubris here? Are we violating our own refusal to ask about possible worlds? Remember that Vatican I encourages the effort to understand and promises the achievement of some limited understanding,[12] but this is to be understood as applying to the actual universe, not some hypothetical one. Are we at the same impasse we encountered in regard to Argument One, so that the end of all our efforts is a stalemate in which we realize the divine mystery and simply bow our heads in adora tion?

Not quite. At least, not yet. There is still that avenue of some imperfect understanding left open by Vatican I. We are encouraged to seek understanding, and there is no understanding without the questions that seek it. Let me conclude my essay with the question that keeps nagging me: Is it possible that our thinking about freedom and necessity is blocked by a too ready application of the yes-or-no dichotomy? Philosophers study the famous question an Athenian might ask on the eve of the battle of Salamis: Is it true or is it false that such a battle will take place tomorrow? A two-valued logic will say it is true or false, one or the other, but a three-valued logic will give us a third option: true, false, or indeterminate. Philosophers again, pondering the problem of alteration from being *x* to being *y*, developed a concept of *fieri* for the movement itself: not being-*x* and not being-*y*, but a becoming. These cases are far from our problem, but they raise the question whether our tertium is not just a dream but a possibility. Does the sharp division of 'free' and 'necessary' exclude a possible third option?

Notes

1 The Leonine index gives a number of occurrences, beginning with *Summa Theologiae*, 1, q. 5, a. 4, arg. 2.
2 Denzinger-Schönmetzer (DS), *Enchiridion Symbolorum* 3002.
3 DS 302.
4 Bernard Lonergan, 'Philosophy and Theology,' in *A Second Collection*, ed. William F.J. Ryan and Bernard J. Tyrell (London: Darton, Longman & Todd, 1974), p. 199.
5 I have not noticed in either Thomas or Lonergan this use of willing as a 'compound,' but it fits easily into their thinking.
6 Bernard Lonergan, 'Cognitional Structure,' in *Spirit as Inquiry: Studies in Honor of Bernard Lonergan, S.J.* (Chicago: St Xavier College, 1964); reprinted in *Collection*, vol. 4 of *Collected Works of Bernard Lonergan*, ed. Frederick E. Crowe and Robert M. Doran (Toronto: University of Toronto Press, 1988), chap. 14.
7 Lonergan, 'The Subject,' in *A Second Collection*, 79.
8 Lonergan, 'On God and Secondary Causes,' in *Collection*, 63: 'in later Thomist doctrine ... the act of willing an end is not free.' See a plethora of references on this in Bernard Lonergan, *Grace and Freedom: Operative Grace in the Thought of St Thomas Aquinas*, vol. 1 of *Collected Works of Bernard Lonergan*, ed. Frederick E. Crowe and Robert M. Doran (Toronto: University of Toronto Press, 2000), index, under 'Will.'

9 Bernard Lonergan, *De Deo Trino*, vol. 2 (Rome: Gregorian University Press, 1964), *Questio* XVII.

10 Lonergan, *Grace and Freedom*, 105–7; see index, under 'God (predication by extrinsic denomination).'

11 Aquinas, *Quodlibetum* IV, q. 9, a. 18. Note that different editors divide this short work in different ways. For one of Lonergan's references to it, see his *De ente supernaturali* (Montreal: College of the Immaculate Conception, 1946), Introductio, 2.

12 Vatican I, DS 3016; in Lonergan's time an earlier edition made this passage number 1796 – a number his students were often to hear.

Charles Hefling

Revelation and/as Insight

A systematic theologian writing to honour a philosopher cannot help reflecting on whether systematics has anything in common with philosophy. An old question, this: 'What has Athens got to do with Jerusalem?' Plenty, I should say, when the Athenian is Michael Vertin. For the aim of systematic theology is not to prove or even to convince, but to understand. It is the theological specialty that operates on the level not of judgment but of insight. And to the promotion of insight no one has been more patiently and meticulously dedicated than Professor Vertin. Would that there were more theologians who understand as he does what it is to understand.

Having as they do this high and honourable goal in common, it might seem that my discipline and the one so ably practised by Professor Vertin are no different at all, in the long run. Yet Thomas Aquinas (who knew a lot about insight) thought otherwise, and his is the classic statement of the difference. Do we really *need* another discipline besides philosophy, taking the word in its wide original sense? Yes, Thomas replies, because of the supernatural finality of humankind. 'Eye hath not seen, nor ear heard, neither hath the human mind conceived' the ultimate end we are meant to arrive at. What this end is, and how it is reached, we cannot find out for ourselves. Somehow, we have to be informed, and since philosophy does not inform us, we have to seek elsewhere. Theology, on the position Thomas goes on to elaborate, can point the way, because it treats of knowledge that even philosophy cannot achieve – knowledge given by God, to be intellectually apprehended not by reasoning but by faith. In brief, what makes the difference between philosophy and theology is *revelation.*

So says Thomas, and theologians before and since have said much the same. The question is, How much of what they were saying survives in the third stage of meaning, when meaning is controlled not primarily by logic or metaphysics but by method? Can a methodical, historically minded, 'existential' theology that takes self-appropriation seriously claim any turf of its own? Or does Athens annex Jerusalem? In this essay I will attempt, not to answer so vast a question, but to investigate one component of an answer: the notion of revelation itself. Understanding that, we shall see, has enough complexities of its own. By understanding it, I mean what I trust Professor Vertin would mean, namely understanding it as Lonergan did, or might have done. My discussion hovers between the indirect discourse of reporting on what Lonergan himself wrote and the direct discourse of explaining how revelation can be understood as a Christian doctrine that is true. Inasmuch as these pages attempt to grasp a unity in Lonergan's thinking that he did not articulate explicitly, they belong roughly to the functional specialty he terms interpretation. Inasmuch as they aspire to shed light on what might be meant by revelation, they belong to systematics. Inasmuch as Lonergan was right, the two projects coincide: what he meant by revelation is also understanding what revelation means. But properly to ascertain whether he *was* right would require a full-scale historical, dialectical, and foundational investigation. I cannot attempt that either.

I

At the end of *Insight,* Lonergan famously extrapolates from his (philosophical) analysis of the human condition to a divine way of dealing with the problem of evil, a solution that consists in the introduction of 'some type or species' of charity, hope, and – in the eighteenth place – faith. By 'faith' he means, here, an intellectual and rational apprehension of truths that are not immanently generated – *belief,* that is, rather than faith in the later, *Method in Theology* sense. The extrapolation, however, is only heuristic. It anticipates *some* sort of belief as an element in God's solution to human decline, but it does not, cannot specify the content of what is to be believed. For that, 'it is necessary to proceed from the heuristic structure of the solution to its identification in the facts of human living and human history.'[1] Now, all solutions are religious, in that they regard God, and it is hardly too much to say that the religion Lonergan has in mind is Christian. The triad of faith, hope, and charity, after all, derives from the New Testament, even if it can also be derived philosophically, *ex post facto.* Presumably, then, it is to the history of Christianity in particular that an empirical investigator will look in order to discover the content of those beliefs that belong to the solution God has in fact provided.

What the historical investigator encounters, though, is a complex welter of a great many beliefs. Among them are beliefs taught more or less authoritatively – doctrines – some of which are doctrines *about* doctrine. The doctrine of revelation is one of these. It asserts that the object of Christian believing, the content of at least those doctrines that are of prime importance, has been divinely revealed. Thomas holds something like this second-order doctrine. It did not become the topic of a discrete tract or treatise of its own, however, until the period of baroque scholasticism, Protestant and Catholic. When it did, it served a clear function. Revelation was a 'fundamental' doctrine, logically prior to doctrines concerned with what has in fact been revealed, in that believing and accepting those doctrines presupposes believing and accepting the doctrine that revelation has occurred.

The logical priority of the doctrines that make up 'fundamental' theology in this classicist sense is what Lonergan is referring to when he speaks of 'foundations in the simple manner.'[2] Such foundations are not untrue – he insists they are as true as they ever were – but they are not adequate to the demands posed by the third stage of meaning. In a methodical theology, the doctrine of revelation is like any other doctrine. Texts that state it are subject to scholarly research and interpretation, its development is open to historical investigation, and whether the series of questions and answers in which its existence over time consists was an intelligent, reasonable, and responsible process is itself a question for dialectical analysis. There is, for example, a serious and scholarly volume that asks in its title, *Has Christianity a Revelation?* The answer it arrives at is *no:* Christianity neither has nor ever had a revelation in the sense of truths divinely authored and delivered, and the trajectory by which the doctrine of revelation developed was a mistake.[3]

But so sweeping a dismissal may itself be obtuse, hasty, and irresponsible. Let us suppose it is. Suppose that specialists in research, interpretation, and history have done their work, that the aberrations and extravagances in what has been affirmed about revelation have been sifted out, that a horizon constituted by religious, moral, and intellectual conversion has been objectified, and that finally, after all that, a notion of divinely disclosed wisdom emerges that can be apprehended and believed within such a horizon. In that case, a methodical theology would have arrived by a more complex and differentiated route at the same point that chapter 20 of *Insight* does – the point of affirming intelligently, reasonably, and responsibly that truths beyond any that human intelligence can achieve have indeed been revealed. If all this did happen, the 'purified' doctrine of revelation, so affirmed, would pass to the next functional specialty, systematics. The question then would be how best to conceive revelation so as to promote an understanding of it in relation both to other doctrines and to what we know in other disciplines, philosophy included.

That is the question of this essay. There is enough evidence in the 'later Lonergan' to warrant a probable judgment that he thought a doctrine of revelation would indeed have a place, though not a 'fundamental' place, in the constellation of Christian teachings that systematics endeavours to understand. On the other hand, there is not much evidence for how he himself understood it. Such as it is, however, the evidence I will mention points in a general way towards Christology as the zone of theology that is most relevant to understanding revelation. My proposal will be that Lonergan's own Christology sheds light on the matter.[4]

Let us begin with *Method in Theology*. Its big innovation, compared with *Insight*, is of course the role assigned to religious experience. Religion has, indeed is in some sense defined by, an *immediate*, conscious element. But Lonergan also makes it clear that only in part is Christianity a reality in the world of immediacy. It is also, in part, a reality in the world mediated by meaning.[5] Besides the 'inner word' of religious experience, there is the 'outer word' of tradition, including the propositions that mean Christian judgments of fact and value. Often, no doubt, what these mediating expressions refer to is religious experience itself.[6] 'The love of God poured into our hearts' is something people do speak and write and sing about. Nevertheless, it does not follow that this prior, inner word is all there is for outer words to express. The priority may be reversed. Religious love may be response to a divine initiative, such that 'the outer word of the religious tradition comes from God' and evokes or elicits a state of unrestricted loving. *If* this is the case, the outer word would not be just religious experience, objectified; it would be, 'in a privileged area,' God's own word. Lonergan stops short of saying this *is* the case, however, because to say so would be to shift from outlining a method to taking a stand on questions concerning such theological matters as Scripture and tradition, development and authority, inspiration – and revelation. Precisely because they are theological, he leaves such questions to the theologians.[7]

Or so he does in *Method in Theology*'s 'background' chapter on religion. Things are somewhat different in the 'foreground,' especially when Lonergan discusses the 'mediating,' direct-discourse specialties. The sequence of these four is one of successive transpositions to contexts that are more and more determinate, from the broad categories and basic orientation of 'foundations' to concrete application in 'communications.'[8] Along the way, Lonergan must at least mention the doctrines of an actual religious tradition, as provisional examples if nothing more, in order to suggest what this further determination might amount to. Among those he does mention is the second-order doctrine of revelation.

He discusses it, notably, in relation to the permanence of doctrinal meaning, a 'church doctrine' which, as formulated by the first Vatican council, has two presuppositions, both of which are church doctrines themselves: 'that there exist mysteries hidden in God that man could not know unless they were revealed' and that these mysteries have, in fact, been revealed.[9] What it means to affirm that God has 'revealed' these mysteries would seem to be a relevant question for understanding, but not one on which Lonergan has much to say. In papers written not long before *Method in Theology*, he speaks of God's having entered the human world mediated by meaning, thereby taking part in 'man's making of man,' so that 'in accepting the truths of faith we are believing not just man but ultimately God.'[10] But the only specification of this 'entry' is a brief reference to 'the handing on from generation to generation of the word first spoken in Palestine.' *Method in Theology* itself is a little more specific. There is mention in passing of 'the revelation events in which God discloses to a particular people or to all mankind the completeness of his love for them'; there is a statement that the outer word of Christianity's gospel 'announces that God has loved us first and, in the fulness of time, has revealed that love in Christ crucified, dead, and risen'; and there is a description of theology as 'reflections on the revelation given in and by Christ Jesus.'[11]

It would be irresponsible interpretation to hang too much on these faint and scattered indications. In a general way, however, they all associate revelation with Christ, while leaving open the question whether and to what extent other historical realities might qualify as 'revelation events.' Returning to *Insight*'s heuristic anticipation, we may recall that 'divinely sponsored collaboration in the transmission and application of the truths of the solution' can be expected to move 'from an initial emergent trend through a basic realization and consequent development.'[12] It would not be very audacious to identify the emergent trend with the religion of Israel, the consequent development with Christianity and more particularly with the preaching of the gospel, and the basic realization with the earthly life of Jesus. The epilogue of *Insight* invites this identification, in part, when it takes note of an 'initial message,' which is a 'divine revelation,' and which has been communicated and applied to different audiences by successive teachers.[13] Although nothing is said about the manner in which this message was initiated, we might, going a little further, ask whether the component of the solution that involves belief and the revealed object of belief is to be connected in some way with Christ as messenger, proclaimer, teacher.

To take this line of thought any further would be to enter the region of Christian theology that treats explicitly of Christ's person and work. That is what I propose to do here. Lonergan wrote a lot of Christology, nearly all of it in Latin, and though he tended to disparage these 'practical chores' of seminary teaching, he also allowed that there are parts worth preserving.

In any case, his Latin treatises remain the only samples there are of his theology as contrasted with methodology. I am going to suggest that in *De constitutione Christi,* now published in English as *The Ontological and Psychological Constitution of Christ,*[14] and especially in his much larger book *De Verbo incarnato,* there are insights that can be transplanted into *Method in Theology* soil. Briefly stated, the thesis will be that revelation is what happens in the mind of Christ.

II

I have noted so far that the 'later Lonergan' retains, but implicitly relocates, the traditional patterning of the Christian idea of revelation. On the one hand, there is *belief,* the acceptance of meanings and values mediated chiefly, though not always or necessarily, in language. On the other hand, there are mysteries, themselves 'hidden in God,' yet disclosed in such a way as to enter the world mediated by human meaning. Revelation is the passage, as it were, from hiddenness to communicability. A systematic theological account of revelation would take as its starting point the affirmation that, somehow, this transition has happened, and would go on to ask *how* it happens or might be understood to happen.

I have also culled from Lonergan's writings some gestures in the direction of Christ as a definitive 'site' of revelation. This appeal to the authority of Lonergan himself might seem unnecessary, because it might seem obvious that Christ is uniquely qualified to be the revealer of divine mystery. The doctrine of the Incarnation in its traditional sense declares that he was the eternal Word, made flesh. His utterances, then, were the Word's words, and since the Word was and is God, those words carry the authority of a divine speaker. Clearly they occupy the centre if not the whole of the 'privileged area' in which the outer word is 'not just the objectification of the gift of God's love' but rather is 'specific meaning, the word of God himself.'[15] Plausible though it appears to be, however, this line of reasoning will not do. The more differentiated explanation of the Incarnation that Lonergan presents in his Latin Christology makes it clear that the hypostatic union (to use the technical term) of humanity and divinity in Christ is not a sufficient condition of his fulfilling the role of revealer. In turn, the judgment that it is insufficient has to do with theology's relation to philosophy – with philosophy of God, the 'general transcendent knowledge' set out in chapter 19 of *Insight,* and with Lonergan's philosophy of consciousness.

As for the much-discussed chapter 19, although it cannot fulfil in a fully methodical context the function Lonergan assigns to it in *Insight* – roughly, the function of establishing *praeambula fidei* in the way classicist 'rational theology' purported to do – its philosophy of God does assume a role *within* theology and more exactly within systematics, by promoting an understanding of properly theological matters in relation to 'naturally' known truths. *Insight*'s proof of God's existence and attributes provides knowledge of what God is not that serves as a control of meaning, a tool for sorting out what could intelligibly be meant by doctrines affirmed on religious rather than philosophical grounds. It is because Lonergan holds what he does on the question of God that he construes the Chalcedonian definition, the basic Christological doctrine, in one way rather than others. And it is because he holds what he does on the question of consciousness that his construal of Chalcedon has the implications it has for understanding revelation. Four points will begin to spell this out.

(1) The essential point is that God is unrestricted. God is an act, the content of which is the idea of being. If reasonable love is the perfection of being, there is an analogy for this act in the 'higher synthesis of intellectual, rational, and moral consciousness that is the dynamic state of being in love.'[16] Because the unrestricted act that is God is necessary, it makes no intrinsic difference to God's being God whether there is or is not any being other than God. That is what divine transcendence means. No restricted being, no finite creature, is God, and every restricted being, every finite creature, is related to God in just the same way: related, namely, as one intelligible part of the contingent whole that is the emergently probable universe. All this applies to Christ's human nature, however 'nature' is conceived. Whatever Christ may be inasmuch as he is a man, it is not what he is inasmuch as he is God. Humanity and divinity remain 'unconfused, unmixed,' as Chalcedon insists.

(2) That being said, it is also true that Christ's humanity is not related to God *only* as creature to Creator, as finite to infinite, as contingent being to the unrestricted act that understands and decides for the universe within which Christ is contingent, finite, a man. For *this* humanity is the humanity of the Word who is God. To say that the Word (not the Father, not the Spirit) was made flesh is to affirm something more and other than the dependence of an intelligible unity – the life of Christ the man – on divine intelligibility. Affirming this 'more' is affirming a supernatural reality, and the only way there is for human minds to understand supernatural realities is by analogy. On Lonergan's position, the relation of Christ's humanity to the divine person who, by making it his own, became a man is such that just as God is intrinsically the same, whether or not he brings about the existence of anything else, so also the Word is intrinsically the same, whether or not he *becomes* anything else. The Word retains his own identity whether or not he has in fact become a man. But because the Word did become a man, that man's humanity is not only created: it is assumed, and consequently that man has his identity in the Word.

(3) The ontology of the Incarnation, properly understood, transposes 'quite neatly' into psychological terms and relations. The one divine person who subsists in two natures is also one divine subject of two consciousnesses. Lonergan's conception of consciousness is the key to this transposition.[17] To be conscious is not to 'do' something; it is to *be,* at a certain level of ontological completeness or perfection. What consciousness is consciousness *of,* however, is the subject; and the subject is conscious just in so far as he or she is 'doing something' – sensing, inquiring, grasping intelligibility or the virtually unconditioned, deliberating; in brief, insofar as the subject is operating psychologically. Now God is an unrestricted act analogous to the highest integration of human consciousness, the state of being in love. Add to that analogy the doctrinal affirmation that there are three who are God, and the result is Lonergan's psychological analogy for the Trinity: three divine subjects of one divine consciousness, each of whom is conscious differently from the others and so really distinct *as* subject.[18] It is one of these three, the Word, who has become a man. He is consequently the subject at once of a human consciousness and of the divine consciousness. But as the subject of humanly conscious operations Christ is like us in all things, and in this regard the first point above still applies. His human consciousness is precisely *not* divine, and the fact that it is a divine subject's human consciousness does not make it so.

(4) It follows that there exists one human consciousness by which a divine subject is present to himself: that human consciousness which is a constituent of the incarnate Word. Through conscious acts that are altogether human, the eternal Word was made aware of the selfsame eternal Word. To say this is to state the doctrine of the Incarnation itself, no more, no less, in psychological terms. The point that bears on revelation, however, is that consciousness is *only* self-presence. It is cognitive, but it is not *knowing* in the fully human sense, and in particular it is not *self*-knowing. Any conscious operation on the part of Christ the man makes the divine Word present to himself, but the fact that such an operation is conscious does not entail its being either an act of understanding what it is to be the incarnate Word, or an act of judging that the one who is performing it *is* the incarnate Word. In brief, the Incarnation gives Christ no human knowledge of himself, for the very good reason that it gives him no *knowledge* of anything at all.

The upshot of these four points is simply that *being* the incarnate Word did not provide Christ with access to knowledge that other men and women cannot achieve. If there were nothing more to say, we would be in the odd situation of having to maintain that although Christ's words *were* the words of the Word, he did not *know* they were. There is, however, more to say, but it is best said by returning to the notion of revelation and following another line of exposition.

III

Divine mysteries are mysterious not because of a defect in intelligibility but for the opposite reason: they are excessively intelligible, so to say. The reason for this disproportion is that transcendent being enters in some way into the constitution of the mystery. So, for example, created beings are intelligible, each in its own right, and the created being that is human intelligence can understand them. But the act of creation, by which God effects the existence of those beings, is a mystery. To understand it, understanding what it is to be God is required. Again, acts of charity are intelligible as threads in the fabric of 'man's making of man.' But to understand their being motivated by the love of God, by the gift of the Spirit who is God, an understanding of what it is to be God and of what it is to be 'proceeding Love' in God would be necessary. Again, Christ's human nature belongs to the universe of proportionate being, and so, in itself, it is intelligible. But to understand its being united to and by the eternal Word who is God, an understanding of what it is to be God and of what it is, in God, to be 'spoken' is required.

What it is to be God, however, is not an intelligibility we can grasp. True, our intelligence, as intelligence, is not limited in its scope. It has as its formal or adequate object *being* itself, so that our desire to know is a desire to know everything about everything. But the object of any *human* act of insight is not being itself but some limited being. For, as human, our intelligence has as its proper or proportionate object what we can imagine.[19] That is the paradox of human intelligence, to which we shall have to return presently. For the moment, note that on the Thomist position that Lonergan follows, the fulfilment of our desire to understand correctly is eschatological. The 'last end' of human becoming, what 'eye hath not seen, nor ear heard,' is an immediate knowledge of transcendent being in the life of the world to come. The traditional name for this consummate cognition is 'vision of God' or 'beatific vision.' Only by the gift (not achievement) of this 'vision' does any human mind understand what it is to be God, and only in knowing God immediately does human intelligence grasp the intelligibility of mysteries properly so called. In this life, since we cannot grasp their intelligibility, we must make do with an imperfect understanding of mysteries, and accept them on trust. By the logic of belief, however, such trust presupposes that *someone* has truly known what we can only believe. That Christ did know it – that he knew by immediate 'vision' both God and the mysteries hidden in God – is the key to understanding the Incarnation as definitive 'site' of revelation. That is the principal thesis of this essay.

The idea that Christ, in his earthly life, enjoyed the 'beatific vision' is not new. Whether it is a church doctrine, a theological doctrine, or something less authoritative, we need not inquire.[20] Lonergan accepts it, and the relevant question here is how he understood it. The six points that follow would seem to be the most important.

(1) The immediate knowledge of God with which we are concerned pertains to Jesus of Nazareth, to Christ the man, to God the Word precisely as subsisting in a human nature, to a divine subject of human consciousness just inasmuch as he is humanly conscious. On Lonergan's position, what is meant by all four phrases is the same.

(2) This knowledge is not *divine* knowledge. Inasmuch as Christ is God, he knows all that God knows – not only what it is to be God but all the mysteries hidden in God, all the universes that it is possible for God to create, and all the details, past, present, and future, of the universe that actually exists. But what Christ knows inasmuch as he is God pertains to his divine consciousness, which for reasons already discussed is not to be confused with his human consciousness, much less with knowledge that was his as humanly conscious.

(3) 'Beatific knowledge' – the term Lonergan prefers to 'beatific vision,' no doubt because the ocular metaphor can be misleading – is by contrast finite, albeit disproportionate, and it admits of degrees. Those who 'see' God see more or less of what God knows, although even Christ (according to Thomas) did not, as man, know everything that falls within the scope of God's ability. Lonergan never speaks of 'omniscience' in this connection, and the term is misleading. He does hold that Christ knew everything that pertained to his work, but also that what pertained to Christ's work has to be gathered from what that work actually was, not deduced from abstract principles.

(4) Beatific knowledge is *knowledge*. On the one hand, it is not consciousness. It is a cognitive act, whereas consciousness is a quality of certain acts, including those that are cognitive. Cognitive acts make objects present; consciousness makes its subject present. On the other hand, beatific knowledge, the adjective notwithstanding, is not an affective exhilaration. It does constitute supreme and unsurpassable happiness, but *mindful* happiness. *Eureka,* not euphoria, is the theme.[21]

(5) Although beatific knowledge is not uncreated, not infinite, not divine, it is altogether 'spiritual' in the *Insight* sense. There is no limitation by the prime potency associated with the continuum and with particular places and times. Beatific knowledge is always *in actu,* never merely potential. To know realities by beatific knowledge is to know them, not severally or sequentially, but all at once and all together. Nor has this knowing any imaginable, 'material' component. The intelligibility it grasps is not intelligibility mediated by anything sensible.

(6) For reasons the preceding points have stated, the content of beatific knowledge is inexpressible or 'ineffable.' As our ordinary acts of understanding grasp intelligibility in some presentation or representation, some 'phantasm,' so, too, they express themselves in concepts, inner words, objects of thought that retain an imaginative component. Similarly, the outer words that convey what we have understood and conceived require some vehicle such as articulate sound or discrete markings. No such multiplicity, succession, or imaginability can pertain to the expression of an intelligibility that was never so mediated in the first place. Neither concepts nor language, therefore, are capable of expressing what is known by 'seeing' God.

Before turning to how Christ's beatific vision bears on other mysteries, we may return for a moment to its bearing on his knowledge of the mystery of the Incarnation and on his self-knowledge in particular. We have seen that human consciousness, alone, does not suffice for Christ to know himself to be the incarnate Word. If, however, he also *understood* what it is to be God, what it is to be eternally begotten of the Father, and what it is to be a divine subject of human consciousness, then it was possible for him to *judge* that what he experienced consciously and what he understood intellectually were identical. But understanding what it is to be God is what beatific knowledge consists in. So, as Lonergan carefully puts it in *De constitutione Christi,* 'Christ as man, through his human consciousness *and* his beatific knowledge, clearly understands, and with certainty judges, himself to be the natural Son of God and true God.'[22] If a distant analogy may be permitted, we do not need chapter 11 of *Insight* in order to be knowers. We need it for grasping what it is to know, and so for judging that we are the knowers we are. Christ did not need beatific knowledge to be Word and Son, but without it he could not have known, humanly, the mystery of his own identity.

The point to be emphasized is that Christ's human consciousness is not the same as his immediate 'vision,' and that neither of these is the same as his self-knowledge. His psychological constitution as such does not entail knowing either God or himself. Although there is not space enough to develop it, an instructive comparison could be drawn in this regard between Lonergan's Christology and Karl Rahner's. For Rahner, the hypostatic union does suffice for Christ's knowing himself. He agrees with Lonergan that the ontological constitution of that union has its parallel in the psychological order.[23] But since the Incarnation consists in God's self-communication to a human reality by quasi-formal causality, and self-consciousness is a property of that reality, the 'ontological self-communication of God is also – and, indeed, specially and primarily – a factor in the self-consciousness of the human subjectivity of Christ.'[24] It follows, for Rahner, that in Christ the 'really existing direct vision of God is nothing other than the original unobjectified consciousness of divine sonship, which is present by the mere fact that there *is* a Hypostatic Union.'[25] In brief, for Lonergan, Christ knows the Incarnation because he has the 'vision of God'; for Rahner, Christ has this 'vision' because of the Incarnation.

Here is not the place to pursue this difference to its roots. They would almost certainly lie in different and perhaps radically opposed conceptions of consciousness. More important, at present, is a further issue that Rahner raises by asking whether the immediate vision of God is compatible with the mission and life of Jesus on earth.[26] Could Christ enjoy such knowledge and at the same time lead a genuinely human, developing life? Rahner considers that he could. So does Lonergan, but for rather different reasons, to which I now turn.

IV

To begin with, some further exposition is called for with respect to the last of the six points on the nature of Christ's beatific knowledge mentioned above: its ineffability. As such knowledge is not, in its genesis, mediated by anything sensible, so the intelligibility it grasps cannot be diagrammed, so to say, by means of visible or audible signs. There are no data on deity, and so there is no language (however broadly 'language' is understood) through which to conceive it, consider it, or think about it. From this it would appear to follow that the clarity and certainty with which Christ knows himself to be divine, the Son of God, cannot be expressed humanly, even to himself. The rest of us, if we think about ourselves in the most serious sense, do so without leaving the world mediated by meaning. We are taught how to use the word 'I,' and if later we come to know in some fashion what is meant by that word, we make use of common-sense meanings mediated by images, symbols, and stories. Even knowing oneself to be a knower in the explanatory way that Lonergan invites is a matter of applying to one's own inner experience insights produced by verbal diagrams printed in *Insight*. The intelligibility of such a self as self-appropriation appropriates can be manifested to that self by means of discourse. Can the intelligibility of such a self as Christ's? Evidently not. Moreover, this conclusion can be generalized. Not only eternal Sonship, but everything else that Christ knows by beatific knowledge, he knows not through the mediation of sensible data, but through the mediation of the divine essence. It seems, then, that the character of the knowledge that is his to share prevents him from sharing it. What he knows, he cannot think about; and what he cannot think about, he cannot deliberately communicate.

This paradox, to which the notion of Christ as mediator of divine mystery ineluctably leads, is one we have already met with. It is the paradox of human intelligence, now approached as it were from the opposite direction. An intelligence that depends on phantasms for its insight, yet grasps what it is to be God, is inconceivable, philosophically speaking. Nothing short of unrestricted intelligibility fulfils an unrestricted desire to under stand; but 'how could a creature be conceived to receive the *ipsum intelligere* that is identical with *ipsum esse*?'[27] To say, nevertheless, that human intelligence does attain the unrestricted act of understanding is thus to speak not philosophically but theologically. It is to posit a sort of transition, which Christian theology holds to be eschatological, from knowing as knowing is known to us, to knowing 'as we are known.' But what is true of human intelligence in relation to the infinitely intelligible is equally true of the conceptual objects that human intelligence generates. Inasmuch as they are generated out of the identity-in-act of such an intelligence with the intelligibility of material things, it is inconceivable that these objectifications should ever express intelligibility that is *not* the intelligibility of anything material, anything limited even extrinsically by space or time. That is the sense in which the notion of a conceptual mediation of divine mystery is paradoxical. To say, nevertheless, that humanly constituted thinking does or did express the inexpressible is again to speak theologically – of revelation. It is to posit, again, what we can think of only as a transition, a backwards eschatology as it were, moving *from* the eternal *to* the temporal, from the immediate knowledge in which the 'life of the world to come' consists, to cognitional acts of meaning such as constitute human, historical living.

To put it another way, the act or event of revelation can be thought of as a kind of 'converse insight.' It does not grasp intelligibility *in* data, or abstract form *from* phantasm. Rather, it bestows *on* phantasm, on the material component of language, an intelligibility beyond what it naturally has or intentionally mediates. Since the infinite does not change, it is only in a manner of speaking that the inexpressible intelligibility of divine mystery can be said to 'become' expressible. That it 'became' expressible within the single human consciousness of Christ as subject of his earthly life, and that his earthly life *was* its expression, is the conclusion to which this paper has been moving. For the condition of the possibility of revelation as 'converse insight' would be a consciousness through which one and the same subject knows *both* the transcendent intelligibility that is to be 'added' to language that already carries meaning, *and* the meaningful language to which this further meaningfulness will be 'added.' In Christ, that condition was fulfilled. Such was the human consciousness of the incarnate Word as the subject of both inexpressible and expressible knowing.

Since inexpressible knowledge is by definition mysterious, we can conceive its relation to expressible knowledge only by analogy, and all analogies limp. One analogy, however, that is less inadequate than others begins from that part of our own being that is inexpressible and unrestricted: wonder, the desire to know, the light of agent intellect, the intention of being. As potentially (though not actually) infinite, there is a sense in which this 'light' gives us knowledge of everything about everything. Its priority to the contents of our actual knowing accounts for its inexpressibility, since any expression would be a cognitive content. Now, even though Christ *actually* grasped by his beatific vision the unrestricted intelligibility that we (in this life) only *intend*, we do intend it, so that there is an analogy for the occurrence of revelation inasmuch as what our inexpressible intending does in us is what inexpressible 'seeing' did in Christ. To quote Lonergan's formulation of this functional analogy, 'just as we proceed from the intention of being to the acquisition of our effable knowledge, so also Christ the man proceeded from his ineffable knowing to the formation of his effable knowledge.'[28]

The analogy provides a basic answer to Rahner's question, mentioned earlier, insofar as it eliminates a common and superficially plausible objection to Christ's having known anything (except perhaps God) in an extraordinary way. The objection is that such 'extra' knowledge would be obtrusive. It could only displace or at least interfere with the normal human process of coming to know and make acquiring knowledge in the ordinary human way superfluous. Conceive beatific knowledge, however, not as a determinate content, but instead as Lonergan's analogy does, and the objection itself is superfluous. Wonder, the light of intellect, the intention of being – these are not sensations or information or insight or image or judgment. Still less is the vision of God. Nor is it the case that Christ could not in any sense learn what he did not already know. As it will be altogether new for us to know as we are known, so it was 'not without novelty,' in Lonergan's cautious phrase, for Christ to arrive at knowledge of things, not in the divine essence, but in themselves; to know them one by one, through inner and outer experience, questioning, insight, and judgment; in brief, to know them as we do.[29]

At this point it will be useful to pause for clarification by contrast. The logic of the position I am taking is that Christ, as the 'site' of revelation, needed both ineffable and effable knowledge: the former in order to know divine mysteries, the latter in order to express them. Medieval theologians argued on rather different grounds: Christ, being 'perfect in humanity' as Chalcedon has it, must have known all there is for humans to know, and his knowledge could never have been imperfect or incomplete. He was not capable of acquiring knowledge, because such a capacity is really a defect. Thomas reversed his position on this point only at the end of his career, concluding instead that being able to acquire knowledge is a positive human characteristic, which therefore belonged to Christ as truly human.

The earlier view of Christ as omniscient has by no means disappeared, but today it is more likely to go without saying that if Christ was like us in all things, his cognitive skills developed over time, and he exercised them as he did in virtue of having entered a first-century Palestinian world mediated by meanings expressed in the language of that particular place and time. Still, unless he was a Kierkegaardian 'drifter,' the meanings Christ inherited from his intellectual, moral, and religious world were only the 'material' component of his *Existenz*. What he received from others, he adapted. Like us, he had to decide what to make of himself, responsibly and therefore intelligently and reasonably, with respect to the tradition that nourished him.[30] What he was to be, he 'already' was; what he was, he 'already' knew, inexpressibly; and it was in the light of that unobtrusive certainty of purpose that he wrote 'the first and only edition of himself.'[31] At the same time, however, he 'wrote' it in others' words – words that he made his own, giving them the finitely intelligible unity of a succession of conscious acts performed over the course of thirty-some years.

Here a further analogy suggests itself. It is not one that Lonergan drew, since he did not begin to make the distinction it is based on until some years after his Christological treatises were published. I have mentioned that in *Insight* he used *faith* and *belief* interchangeably (following Thomas, who had just the single word *fides*). The two words carry different meanings in *Method in Theology*. Lonergan's statement of the difference has been found puzzling, however, and something should be said about it. Faith, he writes, is apprehensive; it is knowledge; it is 'born' of love; what it apprehends is value. Belief, on the other hand, including religious belief, is acceptance, on the ground of value apprehended and judged, of judgments that others have held and communicated. In the case of religious belief, a judgment that it would be good to accept what others have accepted is a judgment that itself rests on faith.[32] Now since beliefs, by definition, are mediated, it is possible to state their content, that is, to state what is meant by the judgments of fact or value that believing accepts. The question thus arises whether faith, as distinct from belief, has a distinct cognitive content of its own that can be stated. That is where the puzzle begins.

Certainly there are statements in *Method in Theology* referring to that which is known by faith, to what faith is knowledge *of*. These formulations are quite general. Nevertheless they belong to one stream of tradition – a broad stream, to be sure, but not the only one there is, and not the same as other streams. That being so, faith would appear to be simply a name for the basic conceptual level of some identifiable current of beliefs. On this reading, the distinction Lonergan draws turns out to be a distinction without a difference. On what I think is a better reading, however, it is true that there is no way to express the knowledge in which faith consists, except by formulating statements that, as statements, would have to be classified as statements of belief. But that is not because faith is a relatively undifferentiated type of believing. It is because faith, in itself, is inexpressible knowledge, in the sense already discussed here, whereas belief is expressible and indeed expressed. The *inexpressibility* of faith is the cognitional counterpart of the *unrestrictedness* of the love from which it is 'born.' On my interpretation, to articulate one's faith – which is arguably what Lonergan is doing at this point in *Method in Theology* – would be to effect a transition from ineffa ble to effable knowledge. Not that the expression has to be verbal. Faith is an apprehension of value, and the primary expressions of apprehended values are the judgments and decisions by which those who apprehend them constitute their living. But verbal expression is certainly not ruled out either.

To draw the analogy: what is true of faith, as *Method in Theology* defines it, is true as well of Christ's immediate apprehension of transcendent being. Just as people of faith live their lives by what they believe in the light of that faith, so Christ, who had no need of faith, lived his life by effable knowledge held in the light of his 'vision of God.' As the incarnate meaning of those who are in love with God manifests knowledge born of their being in love, so the incarnate meaning of the man Christ Jesus revealed his knowledge of the Father's love for the Son. Incarnate meaning is not mediated in words alone; it is the meaning of concrete personality, of a way of life, of deeds chosen and carried out. But for just that reason it cannot but include linguistic mediation. As faith finds its expression in formulated judgments of belief, so Christ's inexpressible knowledge manifested itself in meaningful utterance.

Such, I conclude, was the origin of Christianity's outer word. According to one of Lonergan's brief definitions, mentioned earlier, revelation is God's entry into 'man's making of man' and the cooperative human process of coming to know. My thesis has been that the entry took place as one man's making of one man, in the self-constitution of Jesus of Nazareth. As a being constituted ontologically or *metaphysically*, he was a (divine) person subsisting in a human nature. But this formulation prescinds from his psychological constitution, because a person, in the metaphysical sense, is a person whether conscious or unconscious. Secondly, then, as *psychologically* constituted, Christ was a (divine) subject of human consciousness. But this further and fuller formulation still prescinds from history, from any and all of the particular acts by which Christ was conscious, including the act of knowing of God immediately. Christ, as human, was the subject both of that inexpressible act and of all the conscious acts by which he was *self*-constituted. His constitution in this third sense was, like ours, a historical process, a becoming, a life that manifested its subject over time. For him the 'vision of God' was, as it will be for other men and women, a grace, a supernatural gift and indeed the crown of all God's gracious gifts. With it he cooperated. In its cognitional aspect, his cooperation can be thought of as the pure case of development 'from above downwards.' For Christ, it was his discovery of himself in himself. For others, it was and is the revelation of divine mystery.

V

Systematic theology does not add new articles to the creed, any more than Newton's laws put new planets into orbit. It adds only a coherent set of intelligible relations that may promote an imperfect yet fruitful understanding. What this essay has attempted to understand is revelation as occurrence, as *revelatio revelans* rather than *revelatio revelata.* In a sense, my discussion has not moved beyond the point it began from – *Insight*'s heuristic anticipation of a solution to the problem of evil – inasmuch as *revelatio revelata,* the specific meaning of the outer word that mediates that solution, still has to be identified 'in the facts of human living and human history.'

Moreover, even my explication of the 'how' of revelation, far from dispelling its mysteriousness, has reinforced it. I have emphasized, on the one hand, that there is no continuity between the infinite and the finite, between the understanding of God that is God and any understanding that outer words can express. Meanwhile, on the other hand, the whole point of my account of *revelatio revelans* has been that there is no *dis*continuity between the meaning incarnate in the man Christ Jesus and the meaning eternally uttered in God. The account may be a somewhat tidier way of stating what is stated from beginning to end of the gospel of John; but that is all it is. Tidiness is a homely virtue. But then the systematic theology that Lonergan advocates 'is really quite a homely affair.'[33]

Notes

1 Bernard Lonergan, *Insight: A Study of Human Understanding,* vol. 3 of *Collected Works of Bernard Lonergan,* ed. Frederick E. Crowe and Robert M. Doran (Toronto: University of Toronto Press, 1992), 745.

2 Bernard Lonergan, *Method in Theology* (Toronto: University of Toronto Press, 2003), 269–70; cf. 131.

3 Francis Gerald Downing, *Has Christianity a Revelation?* (Philadephia: Westminster Press, 1964).
4 A paper of mine that complements the present argument, especially on the details of development in Lonergan's Christological thinking, was delivered at the Lonergan Workshop, Boston College, in June 2004, and is to be published in the Workshop's journal with the title 'Another Perhaps Permanently Valid Achievement: Lonergan on Christ's (Self-) Knowledge.'
5 Bernard Lonergan, 'The Origins of Christian Realism,' in *A Second Collection*, ed. William F.J. Ryan and Bernard J. Tyrell (London: Darton, Longman & Todd, 1974), 245.
6 Lonergan, *Method in Theology*, 112.
7 Ibid., 119.
8 Ibid., 142.
9 Ibid., 323. A third presupposition, 'that the church has infallibly declared the meaning of what has been revealed,' is important in itself, but in the present context we are concerned only with understanding the fact of revelation, not with subsequent definitions of its meaning, infallible or otherwise.
10 Bernard Lonergan, 'Belief: Today's Issue' (1968), in *A Second Collection*, 97; 'Theology in Its New Context' (1968), in *A Second Collection*, 62; and 'The Origins of Christian Realism' (1972), in *A Second Collection*, 260.
11 Lonergan, *Method in Theology*, 283, 113, 296. The one appearance of revela tion in post–*Method in Theology* writings is ambiguous, and the context in which it appears seems to discourage taking it as evidence for what Lonergan himself held. See Bernard Lonergan, 'A Post-Hegelian Philosophy of Religion' (1980), in *A Third Collection*, ed. Frederick E. Crowe (New York: Paulist Press, 1985), 221, where Lonergan is engaged in a dialectical discussion of Eric Voegelin, who offers 'an account of revelation or inspiration' which can (help to?) meet the needs of a philosophy of religion.
12 Lonergan, *Insight*, 750.
13 Ibid., 761.
14 Bernard Lonergan, *The Ontological and Psychological Constitution of Christ*, vol. 7 of *Collected Works of Bernard Lonergan*, ed. and trans. Michael G. Shields (Toronto: University of Toronto Press, 2002). *De constitutione Christi* was first published in 1956 and reissued with only minute changes several times. See the 'General Editors' Preface,' x–xi.
15 Lonergan, *Method in Theology*, 119.
16 Bernard Lonergan, 'Christology Today: Methodological Reflections' (1975), in *A Third Collection*, 93.
17 See Lonergan, 'The Dehellenization of Dogma,' in *A Second Collection*, 25. The transposition is effected in *The Ontological and Psychological Constitution of Christ*, part 6.
18 In English, the (very brief) relevant texts are: 'Christology Today,' in *A Third Collection*, 93–4; *Topics in Education*, vol. 10 of *Collected Works of Bernard Lonergan*, ed. Frederick E. Crowe and Robert M. Doran (Toronto: University of Toronto Press, 1993), 68, n. 57; and 'Consciousness and the Trinity,' in *Philosophical and Theological Papers 1958 1964*, vol. 6 of *Collected Works of Bernard*

Lonergan, ed. Robert C. Croken, Frederick E. Crowe, and Robert M. Doran (Toronto: University of Toronto Press, 1996), 135 (in a transcribed discussion). More ample and more technical, but presupposing some familiarity with scholastic Trinitarian terminology, is *The Ontological and Psychological Constitution of Christ*, 191–7.

19 The two most succinct discussions of this crucial distinction are Bernard Lonergan, 'The Natural Desire to See God,' in *Collection*, vol. 4 of *Collected Works of Bernard Lonergan*, ed. Frederick E. Crowe and Robert M. Doran (Toronto: University of Toronto Press, 1988), 81–91, and 'Christ as Subject,' in *Collection*, 176–8. Note that Lonergan's terminology is not consistent between the two; I have conflated 'formal object' and 'adequate object,' since what he means by them is the same, and similarly with 'proper object' and 'proportional object.'

20 Relevant Roman Catholic pronouncements are the 1918 Holy Office decree *De scientia animae Christi*, Denzinger-Schönmetzer (DS) 3645–47, and Pius XII's 1943 encyclical *Mystici corporis*, DS 3812.

21 Lonergan, *Insight*, 706.

22 Lonergan, *The Ontological and Psychological Constitution of Christ*, 204–5, emphasis added.

23 Karl Rahner, 'Dogmatic Reflections on the Knowledge and Self-Consciousness of Christ,' *Theological Investigations*, vol. 5, trans. Karl-H. Kruger (Baltimore: Helicon Press/London: Darton, Longman & Todd, 1966), 205.

24 Ibid., 206.

25 Ibid., 208.

26 Ibid., 204.

27 Lonergan, 'The Natural Desire to Know God,' in *Collection*, 83.

28 Bernard Lonergan, *De Verbo incarnato* (Rome: Gregorian University, 1964), 338, emphasis added.

29 Ibid., 342.

30 See Lonergan, *Method in Theology*, 79–80.

31 Lonergan, 'The Subject' (1968), in *A Second Collection*, 83.

32 Lonergan, *Method in Theology*, 115, 118, 119.

33 Ibid., 350.

Margaret O'Gara

Two Accounts of Reception

I met Michael Vertin in a theological discussion group in 1972. In 1974 we each lectured on the topic 'The Problem of Evil' for the Lenten lecture series at the University of St. Michael's College, where we both now teach. By the time of our wedding two years later on 24 April 1976 – the Saturday after Easter – it was clear that our work in philosophy and theology would be as intertwined as our lives had become.

It is a privilege to contribute to this *Festschrift* honouring Michael Vertin, my spousal colleague, for his excellence as a teacher and a scholar. To demonstrate the intertwining of our areas of research, I wish to explore how a correct epistemological position can allow theologians to explain and appreciate the nature of reception.

I first wrote on this topic in my 1988 book about the French minority bishops at Vatican I. The French minority bishops thought that truth is recognized discursively, I argued. In particular, they believed that evidence is necessary in order to arrive at a judgment of whether or not infallibility has been exercised.[1] In 1996, Michael Vertin and I presented further reflections on this topic in a talk delivered to the Catholic Theological Society of America about the correct understanding of the Holy Spirit's assistance to the magisterium in teaching. There we argued that different philosophical positions on knowing would lead to different understandings of how the Holy Spirit assists the magisterium in its teaching. In particular, we maintained that 'the experience of searching, questioning, weighing the evidence, and communal discussion is part of the process by which the Holy Spirit assists the Church.'[2]

1 An Apparent Contradiction

In this article I want to focus on how Bernard Lonergan's discussion of knowing can correct false understandings of reception and provide a basis for the correct one. This is a significant issue for ecumenical dialogue, which increasingly recognizes the necessity of reception for the discernment of authoritative teaching. Yves Congar defines reception as the process by which one group truly takes as its own rule the thought or decision of another, and he notes that reception has often been overlooked in the church.[3] So understanding reception correctly is an important task as well for Roman Catholic theology today.

The Congregation for the Doctrine of the Faith (CDF) of the Roman Catholic Church, however, has expressed its unease with the concept of reception in its response to *The Final Report* of the Anglican-Roman Catholic International Commission (ARCIC).[4] In a preliminary response to that report in 1982, the CDF complains that ARCIC makes 'reception by the faithful a factor which must contribute, under the heading of an "ultimate" or "final indication," to the recognition of the authority and value of the definition as a genuine expression of the faith.'[5] But such an understanding, argues the CDF, is opposed by *Pastor aeternus* of Vatican I, which notes that Christ wishes his Church to be endowed with infallibility in defining; by *Lumen gentium* of Vatican II, which attributes this infallibility to bishops assembled in council; and by *Dei verbum* of Vatican II, which teaches that the task of authentically interpreting the Word of God is entrusted exclusively to the teaching office of the church.

In its 1991 response to *The Final Report*, the Vatican continues to raise questions about ARCIC's view of reception. In this response, written by both the Congregation for the Doctrine of the Faith and the Pontifical Council for Promoting Christian Unity, the Vatican notes with approval ARCIC's recognition that reception 'does not create truth nor legitimize the decision.' But, the response adds, 'it would seem that elsewhere *The Final Report* sees "the assent of the faithful" as required for the recognition that a doctrinal decision of the pope or of an ecumenical council is immune from error.'[6] The Vatican continues, 'For the Catholic Church, the certain knowledge of any defined truth is not guaranteed by the reception of the faithful that such is in conformity with Scripture and tradition, but by the authoritative definition itself on the part of the authentic teachers.'[7]

To explore this criticism further, we must first examine the position on reception taken by ARCIC.

2 ARCIC's Understanding of Reception

How does ARCIC approach reception? Its discussion of reception is set within *The Final Report*'s wider picture of conciliarity and primacy as complementary modes of the exercise of authority within the church.[8] This approach is emphasized a final time in the *Report*'s last paragraph, which evokes the complementarity of 'both a multiple, dispersed authority, with which all God's people are actively involved, and also a universal primate.'[9]

In its first statement on authority, ARCIC introduces reception within a discussion of normative conciliar decisions. When councils reach decisions on controversial questions affecting the whole church, criteria for their evaluation become especially important.[10] 'A substantial part in the process of reception is played by the subject matter of the definitions and by the response of the faithful. This process is often gradual, as the decisions come to be seen in perspective through the Spirit's continuing guidance of the whole Church.'[11] Recognition by the see of Rome and by other principal sees was one of the factors that contributed to the recognition of conciliar decisions, ARCIC notes.[12]

In its 'Elucidations,' ARCIC responds to questions about its understanding of reception. 'By "reception" we mean the fact that the people of God acknowledge such a decision or statement because they recognize in it the apostolic faith. They accept it because they discern a harmony between what is proposed to them and the *sensus fidelium* of the whole church,' ARCIC writes.[13] Reception neither creates truth nor legitimizes the decision reached; rather, 'it is the final indication that such a decision has fulfilled the necessary conditions for it to be a true expression of the faith.'[14] The whole church is involved in this acceptance, ARCIC believes, 'in a continuous process of discernment and response.'[15] In this view on reception, ARCIC states its intention to avoid two extremes. 'On the one hand it rejects the view that a definition has no authority until it is accepted by the whole church or even derives its authority solely from that acceptance. Equally, the Commission denies that a council is so evidently self-sufficient that its definitions owe nothing to reception.'[16]

The centrality of the concept of reception for ARCIC becomes clear when its treatment of infallibility is examined. On the one hand, ARCIC underlines the importance of authoritative teaching. The church at certain times 'can in a matter of essential doctrine make a decisive judgment which becomes part of its permanent witness,' ARCIC believes; and it envisions that either council or primate might articulate such a decision.[17] But, on the other hand, the entire Church must assess such a decision; that assessment clarifies the decision's significance. 'Moreover,' ARCIC continues, 'although it is not through reception by the people of God that a definition first acquires authority, the assent of the faithful is the ultimate indication that the Church's authoritative decision in a matter of faith has been truly preserved from error by the Holy Spirit.'[18] Reception finally is the work of the Holy Spirit, who 'will bring its members to receive the definition as true and to assimilate it if what has been declared genuinely expounds the revelation.'[19]

3 The Vatican Response to ARCIC

When we compare ARCIC's careful exposition of reception with the Vatican response, the latter at first seems simply to have overlooked or misunderstood the ARCIC position. The Vatican acknowledges ARCIC's recognition that reception 'does not create truth nor legitimize the decision.'[20] But, the Vatican continues, 'it would seem that elsewhere *The Final Report* sees "the assent of the faithful" as required for the recognition that a doctrinal decision of the pope or of an ecumenical council is immune from error.'[21]

This Vatican response seems to overlook ARCIC's careful clarification of this point. As noted above, ARCIC writes that 'it is not through reception by the people of God that a definition first acquires authority'; it then adds that 'the assent of the faithful is the ultimate indication that the Church's authoritative decision in a matter of faith has been truly preserved from error by the Holy Spirit.'[22] The Vatican sees in ARCIC a claim that reception is a *guarantee*, but ARCIC actually claims that reception is 'the ultimate *indication*' of a teaching's preservation from error.[23]

4 Some Distinctions from Lonergan

There appears to be a contradiction, then, between the views on reception of ARCIC and of the Vatican. I suggest, however that some distinctions from Lonergan will help us to dissolve the impression of contradiction and understand the Vatican's concerns more sympathetically. Such distinctions can also contribute to the development of Roman Catholic thought on reception.

First, the Vatican seems to fear that ARCIC is operating with a view of knowing as construction. In such a view, knowing is simply what I am feeling or thinking, presented now as a position for which a truth claim is made. In this view, committed personal or communal self-expression substitutes for knowing, and there is no special role for authoritative teachers. For this view, reception certainly is important because through reception a community 'constructs' its grasp of Christian teaching, which it labels 'revelation.' The Vatican correctly fears that this view of knowing God's revelation operates with a kind of relativist basis. In fact, this 'constructionist' view seems to eliminate revelation itself and substitute communal self-expression for it – something Vatican I explicitly warned against. The Vatican is right to reject a constructionist account of our knowing with its relativist basis.

However, in rejecting relativism, the Vatican reverts to a position characteristic of Roman Catholic thought before Vatican II: a sort of classicism. In this view, knowledge is certainly not constructed. Rather, knowing is the objective grasp of reality and is achieved by a kind of looking or illumination.

Bernard Lonergan explains his use of the term 'classicism.' 'One can apprehend man abstractly through a definition that applies *omni et soli* and through properties verifiable in every man,' he writes. 'In this fashion one knows man as such; and man as such, precisely because he is an abstraction, also is unchanging.'[24] Applied to the church's knowledge of revelation, this view sees God as the primary authoritative teacher and the magisterium as the secondary authoritative teacher, the latter divinely instituted to interpret and transmit God's revelation. Explaining Lonergan's understanding of classicism, Frederick Crowe notes that this view gives priority to teaching rather than learning. In such an approach, he writes, 'there is an original teaching, and it has absolute priority. In that case, for the Church as a whole, it is not learning but teaching that has the priority.' This means that priority is given 'primarily to sources given us by God,' explains Crowe, 'and secondarily to the magisterium also given by God to interpret the sources.'[25] Crowe notes that this view in Roman Catholic theology is linked to an emphasis on the magisterium's unique access to truth, an access often described in terms of illumination and sometimes understood as an effect of the sacrament of orders for those called to the episcopate.

An extract from a letter to the editor of a national Roman Catholic newspaper can illustrate a popular summary of the classicist position I have been elaborating. In 1996, the *Catholic New Times* carried many letters to the editor that discussed the CDF's judgment about the teaching on women's ordination.[26] One writer, John D'Asti of LaSalle, Ontario, writes, 'Catholics interpret the passage [Mt 16:13–19] to mean that Peter was the first pope of an unbroken line of popes to whom Christ gave authority over His church to "bind and loose" on earth and in heaven. This authority now rests in John Paul II and will rest in each of his successors, guided by God "until the end of the world" (Mt 28:20).' He continues, 'Christ's words to St. Peter tell us that His Vicar on earth has a special relationship with His Father. If and when God wants married priests or female priests, the pope will know.'[27]

'If and when God wants married priests or female priests, the pope will know.' In this comment, the writer puts a great emphasis on the pope as a source of knowledge because, he explains, of the pope's 'special relationship' to the Father.

While Vatican I was more sophisticated than this letter writer, its teachings on the normativity of doctrine are also embedded in a largely classicist world view. The council emphasizes that 'the meaning of the sacred dogmas is perpetually to be retained which our Holy Mother Church has once declared; nor is that meaning ever to be departed from under the pretense or pretext of a deeper comprehension of them.'[28] Vatican I also defined as dogma the unique way that, under certain circumstances and because of his office, the bishop of Rome 'is possessed of that infallibility with which the divine redeemer willed that his Church should be endowed in defining doctrine regarding faith or morals' and specified that such definitions are 'irreformable in themselves, not from the consent of the Church.'[29]

Hence it is not surprising that the Vatican has first responded to ARCIC's presentation of reception with fear and has concluded that ARCIC is mistaken. The Vatican does see that ARCIC is not overtly constructionist, since ARCIC recognizes at one point that reception 'does not create truth nor legitimize the decision.' But elsewhere, the Vatican finds ARCIC requiring 'the assent of the faithful' for the recognition that a teaching is immune from error, when in fact, the Vatican explains, such a guarantee comes by means of 'the authoritative definition itself on the part of the authentic teachers.' This last phrase reveals a clearly classicist position.

But both classicism and relativism have overlooked something important about knowing, Lonergan notes. Both of them operate with the presupposition that knowing is a kind of looking, an intellectual seeing or illumination in which the eye of the mind gazes upon the truth God is revealing.

For the first position, that of classicism, such seeing is indeed possible, and God has granted the bishops of the church a special capacity for such seeing in an illumination that is then reported to the whole church. Naturally, in such a position no reception is included since none is needed: the evidence for the teaching is provided in the content of what is taught and in the authenticity of the teachers.

For the second position, that of relativism, such intellectual seeing or intuiting is not actually possible. While the constructionist viewpoint agrees with classicism in holding that knowing would be a kind of looking, it disagrees with classicism by holding that such looking – and hence knowing – can never actually be accomplished. Hence the only alternative for the church, if it wishes to affirm God's revelation, is to reflect on its own experience and articulate this as Christian teaching. In such a position reception is very important because it is the means of constructing the actual teaching; the evidence for the teaching is provided by how much the teaching includes the experience of everyone in the community.

But Bernard Lonergan argues that both positions are wrong because, in considering knowing to be a kind of intellectual seeing or illumination, they have both misunderstood knowing. In Lonergan's claim that knowing includes not only experiencing but also understanding and judging, he provides the basis for the position that he names 'historical-mindedness.' I believe that it is such historical-mindedness, not relativism, that characterizes ARCIC's view of reception.

If knowing includes the step of understanding that follows a direct insight, then knowing is no longer an illumination. If I must not only experience the data but also answer the question, 'What is this?' then obviously my knowing is more than looking and I must consider various hypotheses and the evidence for each. Such searching introduces the category of learning into the church's experience, since the church must learn how to understand the data before it can teach about them. Furthermore, such learning includes an answer to a third question, 'Is it true?', which means that the church must weigh the evidence for different hypotheses and come to a judgment about which one is correct. As with an individual human person, so also with the community of the church such learning takes time and involves the church in a process that theologians have come to call 'reception.' Reception is the communal 'aha!' that is the fruit of experiencing, understanding, and judging.

Crowe presents this position as envisioning 'the absolute priority of learning over teaching in the Church, even with regard to the sources, divinely created and divinely given, of our faith. The sources are sources that have learned.'[30] He emphasizes that this means the church must follow the ordinary cognitional processes, 'whether in the realm of nature or the realm of grace.' He continues, 'It means asking questions on matters of which we are ignorant; forming an idea of a possible answer, indeed, forming several ideas of different possible answers; weighing the pros and cons of the several alternative ideas; finally, coming to a judgment, and being able to say "I've learned something."'[31]

In the perspective of historical-mindedness, the experience of searching, questioning, weighing the evidence, and communal discussion is part of the process by which the Holy Spirit assists the church. Several features stand out in this picture. First, it is a process; this means it takes time. Secondly, because it includes discussion and search, the position of historical-mindedness more easily portrays the involvement of the whole church in an ongoing process of discovery – not construction – that eventually finds expression in magisterial doctrinal teaching.

It is such a process that ARCIC has described in its presentation of infallibility that includes reception. While ARCIC in fact uses a historically-minded framework within which to present its idea of reception, the Vatican has misinterpreted this framework to be a constructionist perspective.

Based on this misinterpretation, it has rejected the validity of any idea of reception.

Classicists often fail to distinguish between relativism and historical-mindedness because they conceive of knowing as intellectual looking. But a corrected position – one recognizing that knowing includes experiencing, understanding, and judging – will distinguish between two accounts of reception. One, a relativist account, understands reception as the construction of views that come to be labelled 'truth.' The Vatican rightly rejects this position. But the other account of reception, a historically-minded account, understands reception as the recognition of the truth, not its construction. It is precisely this historically-minded perspective ARCIC uses when it writes, 'By "reception" we mean the fact that the people of God acknowledge such a decision or statement because they *recognize* in it the apostolic faith.'[32] This historically-minded account of reception represents an important advance in Roman Catholic theology as well as ecumenical discussion. I respectfully suggest that it merits acceptance by the Vatican.

Notes

1 Margaret O'Gara, *Triumph in Defeat: Infallibility, Vatican I, and the French Minority Bishops* (Washington, DC: Catholic University of America Press, 1988), 247–55.

2 Margaret O'Gara and Michael Vertin, 'The Holy Spirit's Assistance to the Magisterium in Teaching: Theological and Philosophical Issues,' *Catholic Theological Society of America Proceedings* 51 (1996), 137.

3 Yves Congar, 'La "réception" comme réalité ecclésiologique,' *Revue des sciences philosophiques et théologiques* 56 (1972), 369–403.

4 Anglican-Roman Catholic International Commission (ARCIC), *The Final Report* (London: SPCK & Catholic Truth Society, 1982).

5 Congregation for the Doctrine of the Faith, 'Observations on *The Final Report* of ARCIC,' *The Tablet* 236 (15 May 1982), 495, no. B.III.5.

6 Congregation for the Doctrine of the Faith and Pontifical Council for Promoting Christian Unity, 'Vatican Response to *The Final Report* of the Anglican-Roman Catholic International Commission,' *Origins* 21 (1991), 444.

7 Ibid.; cf. 446.

8 ARCIC, 'Authority in the Church I,' *The Final Report*, no. 22.

9 ARCIC, 'Authority in the Church II,' *The Final Report*, no. 33.

10 ARCIC, 'Authority in the Church I,' no. 16.

11 Ibid.

12 Ibid., no. 17.

13 ARCIC, 'Authority in the Church I: Elucidation,' *The Final Report*, no. 3.

14 Ibid.

15 Ibid.
16 Ibid.
17 ARCIC, 'Authority in the Church II,' no. 24.
18 Ibid., no. 25.
19 Ibid.
20 Congregation for the Doctrine of the Faith and Pontifical Council for Promoting Christian Unity, 'Vatican Response to *The Final Report*,' 444.
21 Ibid.
22 ARCIC, 'Authority in the Church II,' no. 25.
23 Ibid., italics mine.
24 Bernard Lonergan, 'The Transition from a Classicist Worldview to Historical-Mindedness,' in *A Second Collection*, ed. William F.J. Ryan and Bernard J. Tyrell (London: Darton, Longman & Todd, 1974), 5.
25 Frederick E. Crowe, 'The Church as Learner: Two Crises, One *Kairos*,' in *Appropriating the Lonergan Idea*, ed. Michael Vertin (Washington, DC: Catholic University of America Press, 1989), 370–1.
26 Congregation for the Doctrine of the Faith, 'Reply to the *Dubium* Concerning the Teaching Contained in the Apostolic Letter *Ordinatio sacerdotalis*,' *Origins*, no. 25 (1995–6), 401, 403.
27 John D'Asti, letter to the editor, *Catholic New Times* 20 (21 January 1996), 12.
28 First Vatican Council, *Dei Filius*, in Denzinger Schönmetzer 3020; translation (Latin into German) is from Josef Neuner and Heinrich Roos, *The Teaching of the Catholic Church*, ed. Karl Rahner, trans. Geoffrey Stevens (Staten Island, NY: Alba House, 1967), 38.
29 First Vatican Council, *Pastor aeternus*, trans. in Margaret O'Gara, *Triumph in Defeat*, 269.
30 Crowe, 'The Church as Learner,' 371.
31 Ibid.
32 ARCIC, 'Authority in the Church I: Elucidation,' no. 3, italics mine.

PART THREE

Insight in Ethics and Politics

Fred Lawrence

The Ethics of Authenticity and the Human Good, in Honour of Michael Vertin, an Authentic Colleague

Social ethics and political philosophy require an idea of the common good that takes seriously the modern concern for values and the ethics of authenticity. Bernard Lonergan's notions of value and of the human good contribute to a more integral view of the meaning of being human in a world dominated by liberal individualism and consumerism. His ideas have an affinity with many postmodern endeavours to address this concern even as he avoids the pitfalls of those approaches.

I Modernity and the Ethics of Authenticity

Modernity has become a philosophical problem for a large number of important contemporary thinkers such as Martin Heidegger and both his moderate followers, Hans-Georg Gadamer and Paul Ricoeur, and his less moderate followers, Jacques Derrida and Michel Foucault. Social philosophers related to the Frankfurt School, Max Horkheimer and Theodor Adorno, along with Jürgen Habermas, have been preoccupied with the question, as have political philosophers Raymond Aron, Hannah Arendt, Eric Voegelin, and Leo Strauss and his school, especially Allan Bloom. The Catholic philosophers Alasdair MacIntyre and Charles Taylor have also addressed the issue of modernity.

Martin Heidegger was preoccupied with the consequences of the oblivion of Being that occurs when technology becomes the ontology of the age. In order to understand modernity, Adorno, Horkheimer, and Habermas fused Marxism into Max Weber's theses on the advancing rationalization and disenchantment of the world, on the replacement of substantive by formal legal structures, and on the dominance of bureaucratic over charismatic and traditional forms of legitimacy. Eric Voegelin diagnosed modernity in terms of a 'pneumopathology' whose 'closed' rather than 'open' souls posit 'egophany' in the place of 'theophany' as the characteristic social and cultural orientation. Phenomena ranging from scientism to apocalypticism are symptomatic of this closure. Hannah Arendt melded Kantian cognitive and moral idealism with nostalgia for the Greek *polis*, while Raymond Aron's positive attitude towards modern liberal democracy was marked by Tocqueville. Leo Strauss retrieved the premodern horizon shared differently by Jerusalem and Athens for his hypothesis of the three waves of modernity initiated by Machiavelli, Rousseau, and Nietzsche, respectively, with each successive wave reacting to the shortcomings of its predecessor by returning to some aspect of nature in order to radicalize the earlier wave's very own presuppositions.

Both Alasdair MacIntyre and Charles Taylor have shared Strauss's question, progress or return?[1] and have arrived at very different conclusions. MacIntyre initially formulated the option in terms of an opposition between Saint Benedict and Nietzsche;[2] he later on framed the issue in terms of three rival traditions.[3] He himself has made the Aristotelian and Thomistic tradition of moral inquiry conversant with rival traditions. Taylor, while reproving liberalism's 'political neutrality' and the deconstructionists' disdain for morality, worked out a reconciliation of Rousseau's sense of the unique self's need for recognition with Nietzsche's view of free self-determination.[4]

Taylor developed an 'ethics of authenticity' that is communitarian. It criticizes the early modern notion of 'the unencumbered self,' which is the 'disengaged rationality' proper to Hobbesian, Cartesian, and Lockean individualism.[5] Taylor traced the genesis of the modern image of the self in three key steps:[6]

(a) The person or self derives its norms from a community whose already understood and agreed-on standards and ends are derived from an ontological order considered to be objective, so that one becomes oneself by clarifying the demands of this objective order and by living up to them.

(b) Through interiority, introspection, or what Taylor calls 'reflexivity,' the person or self (epitomized by St Augustine) is grounded in an objective, ontological, cosmological, and social hierarchy.

(c) Modern individualism 'interiorizes personhood' so that the standards for living are located not in an objective cosmological or social hier archy, but in 'radical reflexivity,' which means the subject's own capacities, feelings, inclinations, thoughts, decisions, and commitments, whether in the mode of Descartes or in that of Rousseau.

For Taylor the unique 'sentiment of one's own existence' evoked by Rousseau and the Scottish philosophers offers freedom from the confines of the disengaged self: we have to get in touch with our ownmost feelings, desires, sentiments, and affinities, and express what we are in contrast with the disengaged self's making calculated choices among alternative desires. 'In articulating [my own originality],' he writes, 'I am also defining myself. I am realizing a potentiality that is properly its own.'[7] For Taylor 'we become free human agents, capable of understanding themselves, and hence of defining an identity, through our acquisition of rich human languages of expression.' Since languages are necessarily acquired socially, 'we define [our identity] always in dialogue with, sometimes in struggle against, the identities our significant others want to recognize in us.'[8] Although there is no longer any 'publicly accessible cosmic order of meaning,' Taylor is convinced that 'in order to understand ourselves we have to see ourselves as part of a larger order ... To understand ourselves expressively requires that we acknowledge that.'[9] Taylor uses Nietzsche's metaphor of an 'indispensable horizon out of which we reflect and evaluate as persons,'[10] but then gives a non-Nietzschean reason for its significance: 'things take on importance against a background of intelligibility.'[11] Taylor does not adopt a Nietzschean stance when he insists that it would be a pernicious subjectivism to suppose that either feeling alone determines significance or that choice confers worth, for on those grounds alone difference becomes insignificant.

> Even the sense that the significance of my life comes from being chosen – in the case where authenticity is actually grounded on self-determining freedom – depends on the understanding that *independent of my will* there is something noble, courageous, and hence significant in giving shape to my own life ... Self-choice as an ideal makes sense only because some *issues* are more significant than others.[12] ... Only if I exist in a world in which history, or the demands of nature, or the needs of my fellow human beings, or the duties of citizenship, or the call of God, or something else of this order *matters* crucially, can I define an identity for myself that is not trivial.[13]

In spite of his caution, Taylor's integration of Rousseau's idea of the sentiment of existence with Nietzsche's 'vocabulary of self-mastery' sets forth the modern conception of authenticity. But it does not yet yield criteria for settling which issues or values are of self-transcendent significance rather than the arbitrary positings of an ultimately alienated subject in a more or less absurd world. If Taylor is probably right that a revival of premodern cosmologies or ontologies is impracticable, then our only hope for meaningful lives might be an ethics of authenticity. We have to face that question, but must also inquire whether there is an ethics of authenticity that, while being truly modern and contemporaneous, is not completely discontinuous from valid premodern or ancient positions. How can an ethics of authenticity integrate the ancient esteem for excellence or virtue?

II Lonergan: Generalized Empirical Method

Bernard Lonergan's work *Insight*[14] transposes the basic elements of Thomas Aquinas's philosophy of knowledge into the contemporary world of discourse that is defined both by the modern sciences of human and subhuman nature and by historical consciousness. This transposition made it possible for Lonergan to develop a phenomenology of what we do when we think we know in the fields of mathematical and scientific inquiry and in our common-sense asking and answering of questions. This phenomenology revealed a startling isomorphism (i.e., a parallelism in structural relationships as distinct from an identity) between the structure of the cognitional operations in contemporary investigation and Thomas Aquinas's account of the relationships between (1) the *prima et secunda operationes* of knowing and (2) their precise correlative internal conscious utterances (*verba intus prolata*): the definition (*verbum incomplexum*) that proceeds from simple apprehension, and the judgment (*verbum complexum*) that proceeds from the reflective *reductio in principia*.[15]

According to Lonergan, any person can perform a phenomenological re-enactment of Thomas Aquinas's two cognitional operations (understanding and judging) in response to two distinct kinds of questions: What-questions seeking the intelligibility in sensible data, and Is-it-so-questions seeking the truth of any intelligible guess or hypothesis already grasped in answer to What-questions by checking against sense data or the data of consciousness. While Thomas held with Aristotle that the adequate object of human knowing is the quiddities of things as existing in sensible matter, modern science limits its inquiry to intelligible correlations that can be gathered from sense data. Again, with Aristotle, Thomas insisted that human understanding grasps the forms of things in phantasms; modern common sense apprehends similarities and modern science grasps intelligible correlations not only in sense data but in that data as represented or schematized by imagination and, in the case of the sciences, as also measured and plotted onto graphs. Finally, Thomas Aquinas developed Aristotle's account of knowledge further into an explicit concern with the *veritas* central to his Christian mentor, St Augustine; similarly, modern science requires that hypotheses be verified, that assertions be warranted, and that we truly find out what is most probably the case.

Beyond an appreciation for the empirical method of science, Lonergan says he learned from Aquinas to generalize this method,[16] which begins and ends with the data provided by the senses (either directly or indirectly through sophisticated instruments). Empirical method can also embrace the data of human consciousness and not merely the data of the senses. Generalized empirical method is applied in a process by which we appropriate our consciousnesses as intelligent, rational, and responsible. Self-appropriation is not a Cartesian procedure. For Lonergan 'a human person is not conscious through some distinct and special operation by which one intuits oneself on the side of the object. No such operation exists; nor is there any argument in its favor unless one confuses the preliminary unstructured awareness of oneself and of one's acts with subsequent intellectual inquiry into the nature and the existence of oneself and one's acts.'[17] This seems to be the mistake Descartes made. Lonergan says:

> The aim of the present work ... [is] to assist the reader in effecting a personal appropriation of the concrete dynamic structure immanent and recurrently operative in his own cognitional activities ... What on earth is meant by rational self-consciousness? What is meant by inviting it to take possession of itself? Why is such self-possession said to be so decisive and momentous? ... Though I cannot recall to each reader his personal experiences, he can do so for himself and thereby pluck my general phrases from the dim world of thought to set them in the pulsing flow of life. Again, in such fields as mathematics and natural science it is possible to delineate with some accuracy the precise content of a precise insight; but the point of the delineation is not to provide the reader with a stream of words that he can repeat to others or with a set of terms and relations from which he can proceed to draw inferences and prove conclusions. On the contrary, the point here, as elsewhere, is appropriation; the point is to discover, to identify, to become familiar with, the activities of one's own intelligence; the point is to discriminate with ease and from personal conviction between one's purely intellectual activities and the manifold of other, 'existential' concerns that invade and mix and blend with the operations of intellect to render it ambivalent and its pronouncements ambiguous.[18]

Let us explore a moment what this means. Common-sense people or mathematicians or scientists spontaneously ask and answer questions just as Aquinas did in his day. Even so, scarcely anyone ever adverts to the data of their consciousnesses in a thematic, methodical manner while actually asking and answering questions. (Lonergan described what is meant here by the terms 'conscious' and 'consciousness' with astonishing simplicity when he wrote, 'One is aware that the window is open, but conscious that one is about to sneeze.')[19] That further task will not be undertaken so long as one restricts one's inquiry to the data supplied by sense perception. In contrast, Lonergan explained how, whenever we ask what people of common sense do when they know, or whenever we wonder what modern mathematicians and natural scientists do when they know, the answers we obtain have to be checked against the inward data given by our conscious acts of intending as we actually perform these cognitional operations. This generalized empirical method made it possible for Lonergan to revolutionize Thomist studies by his argument that Thomas Aquinas himself *performed* this type of experiment in relation to his own acts of consciousness, even though, appropriately for his historical context, he *expressed* what he had discovered experientially in the metaphysical parlance of medieval philosophy and theology.[20]

To the extent that contemporary common-sense people, mathematicians, or scientists, who perform cognitional operations day in and day out, also ask even implicitly what they are doing when they know, according to Lonergan they will have to reflect upon their spontaneous, conscious acts and apply the same generalized empirical method that he used.

From Intentionality Analysis to Horizon Analysis

Generalized empirical method attends to the data of consciousness as well as to the data of sense. When we analyse operations as conscious (i.e., our tacit awareness at work in acts of perceiving, imagining, questioning, understanding, and judging), we begin with conscious operations as intentional (perceiving, wondering about, understanding, criticizing this or that object): the *noesis* is always correlative to a *noema*. Awareness is always awareness of something. But this is only part of what is involved in our ask ing and answering questions as we come to know. The expansion of our explicit awareness of both the subject-pole and the object-pole of our conscious intending will almost inevitably lead us to realize the historically conditioned character of our conscious acts. This means becoming increasingly conscious of the formative influence emotions have upon us, and of the way we are peculiarly influenced by the vagaries of our intellectual, social, cultural, aesthetic, moral, and spiritual development. In this way intentionality analysis naturally becomes horizon analysis.[21]

In *Insight* Lonergan's intentionality analysis emphasizes reflective understanding and judgment.[22] One of the most striking features of *Insight*'s phenomenology of judgment is the highlighting of the role of responsibility when, in response to an Is-it-so-question, we marshal and weigh evidence, grasp the sufficiency or insufficiency of the available evidence, and affirm or deny the *actual* relevance of what has up to that point been only a *possi-*

bly relevant answer to a What-question. Judgments are rationally warranted if, and only if, there is sufficient evidence, and if we grasp that evidence *as* sufficient. That is why Lonergan quotes the telling maxim of La Rochefoucauld that people generally complain about their memory but never about their judgment.[23] The criterion for the sufficiency of evidence is intrinsically related to how responsible we have been in attending to the data, asking all the further relevant questions, coming up with alternative hypotheses or guesses, and critically checking these alternatives against the relevant data. Intentionality analysis starts by focusing on the presence or absence of further relevant questions as the proximate criterion for the objectivity of judgment.[24] In chapter 20, it demands that we pay attention to the remote criterion of the judgment, which is the authenticity of the knowing subject.[25] Such scrutiny of our remote criteria for judgment raises issues surrounding the identity and orientation of the whole person – not just the person's own little world of immediacy, but the far larger world 'constructed by imagination and intelligence, mediated by words and meaning, and *based largely upon belief.*'[26]

Beliefs and Faith

Lonergan stresses the role of beliefs in shaping our horizons, our identities, and our orientations. He often said that ninety-nine per cent of what geniuses know they know by believing it.[27] Beliefs include judgments of both fact and value; but they are judgments made originally by someone else, and afterwards we give our assent to them: the knowledge we first attain by believing has been mediated by someone else's exercise of attentiveness, intelligence, and reasonableness, and not by our own.

In his horizon-analysis after the completion of *Insight* Lonergan went on to clarify also the role of feelings as intentional responses in our apprehension and judgment of value.[28] This caused a major reorientation of the horizon-analysis of belief. If we examine our beliefs more closely, most of them are a function of something far more profound than reasonable assent to truths not personally generated by our own acts of knowing. What are we referring to? The fact that people believe in accord with their faith, 'the eyes of being in love.' (Lonergan's beautiful metaphor might have been a revision of the title of the young French Jesuit Pierre Rousselot's famous articles, *Les yeux de la foi.*)[29]

Lonergan's later horizon-analysis outlined a philosophy of action or an existential ethics that culminated in a phenomenology of love. In his brief descriptions of love he included the domestic love of marriage and family, the patriotic love of one's neighbourhood and political community, and the religious love of the transcendent source and ground of our questions for intelligibility, our questions for truth, and our questions for value and goodness. In this way he placed the cognitional operations of the 'head' (which engages our attentiveness, our intelligence, and our reasonableness) in the context of the 'heart,' where questions for deliberation mesh with our feelings as intentional responses to values. These feelings as intentional responses in turn take on their distinct configurations in accord with whether and how we have fallen in love.[30]

In *Insight* Lonergan transposed Thomas Aquinas's metaphysical analysis of the structure of human knowing into the contemporary framework of phenomenologically ostensible intentionality analysis. In coming to terms with the genetic and dialectical dimensions of human cognitional development, this intentionality analysis took shape as a horizon-analysis of the dynamics of the hermeneutic circle: understanding in order to believe, and believing in order to understand. These dynamics show the priority of the dramatic pattern in human living over other – biological, aesthetic, and intellectual – patterns of consciousness that function as parts within the dramatic pattern as a whole.[31]

However, our dramatic pattern of human experience is beset by bias and basic sin,[32] which is our failure to choose what the spontaneous dynamism of our spirit knows to be intelligent, reasonable, and responsible courses of action. Dramatic, individual, group, and common-sense biases, combined with basic sin, distort the hermeneutic circle of understanding and believing in the measure that the spontaneous dynamism of conscious intentionality towards intelligibility, truth, and goodness becomes warped. When the impersonal forces of a cultural and social surd prevail, the gap between our natural and our effective freedom turns into a radical moral impotence that cannot be overcome by human resources alone.[33] The inevitable time-lag between living and knowing how to live leads to the short-circuiting of human genuineness by the 'reign of sin.'[34]

Hence, as a matter of integrity, Lonergan's philosophic horizon-analysis acknowledges the necessity to yield to theological horizon-analysis because, in concrete human living, the social and cultural surd of sin can only be countered adequately by a transformation due to the gift of God's love that is disproportionate to human nature's capacity to achieve.[35] After *Insight*, in essays before *Method in Theology*, in *Method in Theology* itself, and in the writings that followed, the exigencies of horizon-analysis compelled him to transpose into contemporary terms Thomas Aquinas's theology of grace and freedom that he had originally retrieved on its own terms in his doctoral dissertation in the late 1930s.[36]

Thus far, we have seen that Lonergan's dialectical analysis of horizon shows that human development is a mixture of progress and decline.[37] As he came to see, however, concrete human development unfolds within the tension of two vectors: one vector of healing that moves from above downwards and that in the highest instance is empowered by God's self-gift (in accord with the Christian interpretation of redemption); and another vector of creativity that moves from below upwards starting with attentiveness to data, through intelligent inquiry and reasonable discernment, to responsible deliberation, evaluation, decision, and action.[38]

Values

The fruit of the evolution of Lonergan's analysis of the horizon of human beings is the articulation of a universal viewpoint or total and basic horizon that is both completely general and completely concrete.[39] This total and basic horizon is grounded in the universally immanent, operative, and normative questioning-structure proper to the human consciousness of any race, class, or gender. In light of this horizon[40] it becomes evident that in order to be fully comprehensive, reflection on the human condition must take seriously, but go beyond, the *vital* values of the overall health, strength, and graceful comportment of our bodies. *Social* values are required by cooperation in institutional recurrence schemes or goods of order in order to bring about particular goods. Then reflection on the human condition motivates the move beyond social values to *cultural* values. Aims and aspirations, whether traditional or revolutionary, on the level of culture are embodied in the stories, customs, and rituals that express the terminal values of any community. Terminal values furnish the framework by which human beings engage in reflective evaluation of their way of life, which is a particular instance of the structure of the human good.[41]

A further step moves beyond values as cultural to values as *personal*. Personal values are related to the intrinsically conversational nature of the mind and heart of persons as originators of values.[42] The conversational structure of personhood is realized to the degree that people fulfil their inbuilt demand for free self-transcendence. This occurs most frequently when people belong to communities where *cor ad cor loquitur* (heart speaks to heart) regularly or normally.

The most comprehensive concreteness is reached on the level of *religious* values[43] enshrined in any culture's elaborate overarching symbolic order: e.g., the *ma'at* of ancient Egypt, the *Tao* of China, the *nomos* of Greece, the *Torah* of Judaism, or the Law of the Cross in Christianity. Secularists may be suspicious of or debunk such overarching orders, yet they, too, work out surrogates that play the role that has been called civil religion since Vico.

For Lonergan the levels of value as vital, social, cultural, personal, and religious are governed by relations of mutual presupposition and complementarity: lower levels condition but do not determine higher levels, while each higher level depends on ones lower than it. Societies and cultures handle these complex relationships in various ways. We speak of contemporary western Europe, for example, as a highly secular culture, while we regard most Latin American or even North American cultures as religious. Whatever the specific configuration of values in any given culture, that culture is regarded as more advanced the more the different levels of culture are distinguished from each other, even if not necessarily separated. Hence, the more primitive a society is, the more global and compact are its basic self-understandings and self-expressions in rituals and celebrations, dramas, lyrics and music, songs, paintings, architecture and monuments; the more advanced the society, the more differentiated these things are.

Fragmentation and Reductionism

Modernity has tended to push legitimate distinctions between levels of value to the point of destructive separations. For example, continental liberalism's reaction to the abusive alliance between altar and throne under absolutist premodern regimes provoked a separation of church and state that, in its anticlerical thrust, secularized and privatized the public sphere. In contrast, the institutional separation of church and state in the United States's First Amendment dis-establishment of every church or sect has been less concerned with the complete banishment of religious values from the public sphere. Nonetheless, the individualism and materialism presupposed by procedural liberalism favour the repression of religious values and of any cultural and social force that runs counter to the 'unencumbered self.' The ethos that stresses the 'punctual self' with its disengaged reason and its disembodied ego generates a climate that threatens, both publicly and privately, the flourishing of all but vital values.

In this way the notorious modern dichotomies between nature and reason, between reason and faith, and between fact and value have arisen. These dichotomies wreak havoc on the complex, concrete relations among vital, social, cultural, personal, and religious values. Max Weber noted that the process of modernity's rationalization and disenchantment of society and its movement from substantive (charismatic and traditional) legitimation to formal (bureaucratic-legal) legitimation creates an 'iron cage' that either eliminates from public influence the higher levels of value or subordinates the higher to the lower. Karl Marx diagnosed these phenomena in terms of commodity fetishism. The Frankfurt School's *Kulturkritik* criticizes instrumental rationality. Even more radically, Nietzschean or postmodernist genealogy exposes dominant orientations towards power.

All these criticisms of advanced industrial societies point to the need for a sufficiently differentiated account of values that can do justice to all the levels of value, ranging from vital to religious, and help solve questions that arise from social and cultural differentiation. For instance, an intelligent and legitimate de-sacralization of certain spheres or institutions of public life does not have to mean the wholesale secularization of society and culture built into modernization's drift towards separating what needs chiefly to be distinguished. We need a normative heuristic structure of values and of *the human good* such as is worked out by Lonergan in *Insight* and *Method in Theology*.

Lonergan's approach does not require a return to premodern ontologies, cosmologies, or social hierarchies on the part of anyone appropriating and applying it, especially if such a return would entail a de-differentiation and a disregard of modern science and modern historical consciousness. Any adequate contemporary approach has to go to the roots of what Charles Taylor calls 'radical reflexivity.' In this respect, modern versions of the 'turn to the subject' have miscarried in one way or another.[44] Early moderns such as Hobbes, Locke, Descartes, and Bacon have revealed only a *truncated* subject. Rousseau and Kant in the eighteenth century and the German Idealists in the nineteenth reacted to this truncation and oversimplification by uncovering an *immanentist* subject. Nietzsche, Marx, Freud, Heidegger, Sartre, and today's deconstructionist and genealogical Nietzscheans have rightly called into question and debunked both the truncated and immanentist versions of the subject to disclose the *alienated* subject.

Lonergan alone seems to have shown how 'radical reflexivity' is not a dead end. He begins with the polymorphous existential (*not* 'existentialist') subject. By generalized empirical method he lays bare the immanent and operative dynamisms of conscious intentionality. By doing a thorough and empirically verifiable phenomenology of the subject, he goes beyond the horizons of the truncated, immanentist, and alienated subjects to disclose a total viewpoint that is basic yet not 'foundationalist' precisely because it gets beyond those other foreshortened or distorted horizons. Such a viewpoint exposes the total and basic horizon of the incarnate inquirer, 'liable to mythic consciousness, in need of a critique that reveals where ... counterpositions come from'; but this incarnate inquirer also 'develops in a development that is social and historical, that stamps the stages of scientific and philosophic progress with dates, that is open to a theology that Karl Rahner has described as an *Aufhebung der Philosophie*.'[45]

III An Adequate Heuristic of Values and the Human Good

Taylor has pointed out how Rousseau stressed the need to discriminate the sentiment of one's own existence from all other, possibly interfering, feelings arising from passions within ourselves and from outside pressures.[46] In the face of the collapse of all traditional values and goods Nietzsche has shown the need to overcome the feeling of *ressentiment* through the feeling of the superman, the successor of Zarathustra, the Dionysus *redivivus*, who is capable of willing the Eternal Return of the Same.[47]

Lonergan's account of value reached its most mature stage when he developed his theory of feelings and made explicit the transcendental notion of value by which he synthesized feelings with his account of knowing. Feelings like tiredness and hunger as correlative to non-intentional states and trends (hunger, tiredness) he distinguished from feelings that are intentional responses to objects other than ourselves, whether of pleasure and pain or of our highest aspirations. Among such intentional feelings he distinguished between those that do discriminate between what is truly good and what is apparently good, and those that do not. In discriminating true from merely apparent goods, feelings as intentional responses 'put themselves in a hierarchy' of the vital, social, cultural, personal, and religious values spoken of above.[48] On what basis are these feelings as intentional responses capable of discriminating and discerning among values? What allows feelings to reveal values? In agreement with Max Scheler and Dietrich von Hildebrand, Lonergan ascribes the ability of feelings to apprehend values to whether or not, and how, we are in love.[49]

Situations demanding action or appreciative response are feeling-laden. In them the transcendental notion of value expressed by the questions, Is this worthwhile? What am I to do? is spontaneously evoked in people.[50] These are questions for deliberation. They call for insights into the intentional feelings usually already being felt and evoked by the situation. Lonergan sometimes names such acts of understanding or insight in response to questions for deliberation 'apprehensions of value';[51] and sometimes he suggests that the feelings themselves as intentional responses to values are already 'apprehensions of value.'[52] At any rate, when deliberation occurs, intelligence and feeling come together in formulating possible courses of action, or in discerning just what the feelings and values at stake might happen to be. Deliberation needs an understanding and formulation of a possible course of action in order to ask the further question, Should I/we do it? for the sake of arriving at a judgment of value, and to come to a decision.

Overwhelmingly significant is the existential orientation[53] of the person doing the evaluating and deciding in the process of discerning value fully. Lonergan holds that a person's moral conversion determines this orientation.[54] Prior to moral conversion, a person's feelings as intentional responses are insensitive to the possible difference between satisfactions and values, or between what is only apparently rather than truly good. Once a person is morally converted, his or her feelings are under the sway of the transcendental notion of value. Then the questions, Is it worthwhile? and What should I do? cannot reduce in egocentric fashion into, What's in it for me? or What's in it for our in-group? Instead they spur us on to self-transcendence. Self-transcendence beyond selfishness breaks the calculus of pleasure and pain wide open. Then feelings as intentional responses become concerned with values: with the vital values of health and strength; with the social values enshrined in family and custom, society and education, the state and the law, the economy and technology, the church or sect; with the cultural values of religion and art, language and literature, science, philosophy, history, theology; with the achieved personal values of one dedicated to realizing values in himself and promoting their realization in others;[55] and with the religious value of the transcendent mystery of love and awe.[56]

The morally converted person places feelings as intentional responses to value in the context of the notion of value, where they become part of the process of deliberation, evaluation, decision, and action. This awareness marks the emergence of ourselves as personal, as existential subjects who freely and responsibly make ourselves who we are to be whenever we consciously intend the good in asking about values, about what is worthwhile.[57]

Whenever we ask what we should do in the context of feelings as intentional responses to values, we get insights that permit us to formulate alternative courses of action. Deliberation continues as we ponder whether we should do this or that. By means of feelings as intentional responses to values, our reflective acts of understanding discern what course of action is good or better, and a judgment of value responsibly proceeds. Lonergan finds that value 'is known in judgments of value made by a virtuous or authentic person with a good conscience.'[58] These judgments arise from a deliberative process that 'sublates and thereby unifies knowing and feeling.'[59] The criterion of value is the happy or easy conscience of the good or virtuous or authentic person: 'It is, finally, only by reaching the sustained self-transcendence of the virtuous man that one becomes a good judge, not of this or that human act, but on the whole range of human goodness.'[60]

Clarification by Contrast

Key terms used in Lonergan's formulation of the ethics of authenticity – 'self,' 'authenticity' or 'sincerity,' 'commitment,' and 'values' – are liable to be misunderstood in terms of Nietzsche's meanings, which have become common currency today. As Allan Bloom put it, for Nietzsche the 'self' is 'the modern substitute of the soul, which is a rationally ordered structure and is dependent on and subordinate to the order of the *cosmos.* The self has no order and is dependent on nothing; it makes a *cosmos* out of the chaos that is really outside by imposing an order of values on it.'[61]

Not so for Lonergan. For him the term 'self' not only refers to the conscious subject as he or she exists concretely, but represents a transposition of Aquinas's conception of the order of the human soul into a framework of conscious intentionality in which a formally dynamic structure is experienced as immanent, operative, and normative.[62] Human living is a matter not of positing values but of asking and answering questions and freely living by the answers. The pattern of inquiry, reflection, and deliberation is an exigence not for self-aggrandizement but for self-transcendence.

In the Nietzschean ethos God is dead and the highest values are repudiated; when everything is permitted, 'authenticity' replaces the good. As the antithesis of the hypocrisy of being other-directed, it entails no more than the honesty or sincerity of self-expression.[63] In Lonergan's account, 'authenticity' involves fidelity to the transcendental precepts: be attentive, be intelligent, be reasonable, be responsible, and be loving.[64] Nor does Lonergan's ideal of authenticity spurn traditional, objective standards for judging a person's words or deeds; rather, it underlines how objectivity itself is the fruit of subjectivity that is authentic precisely in the measure that it lives in the light of the pure, detached, disinterested, and unrestricted desire to know and to be in affective union with the universe of being beyond itself.[65]

In the absence of any objective standard of evaluation, the Nietzschean criterion for authenticity becomes intensity of commitment.[66] This makes feelings the ultimate criterion, but it also abolishes the distinction between pre-moral feelings as arising from any appetites whatsoever, and feelings as intentional responses to the integral scale of vital, social, cultural, personal, and religious values. In contrast, Lonergan teaches that commitment is an enactment of conscious intentionality on the level of deliberation, evaluation, decision, and action. Note also that conscious intentionality becomes conscience only when the transcendental notion of value synthesizes feelings (as intentional responses to values) with knowing to reach value judgments that are right, where the criterion of rightness is specified by the extent of the virtue or self-transcendence or authenticity of the person asking, What is worthwhile? What should I do? Should I do it?[67] Only then do we have the assurance that judgments of value are not arbitrary. This is just the opposite of the Nietzschean meaning of 'value,' in which 'values' cannot be rationally evaluated because they are original creations produced by arbitrary positings of the willful self as a primordial chaos.[68] On the Nietzschean position, values come from merely arbitrary choices instead of from responsible judgments of value. In his disgust for the utilitarian and technocratic individualism that reduced values to market prices, Nietzsche transformed expressive individualism to make whatever the oracular self unpredictably posits into a value.

The Human Good

Lonergan's notion of value corresponds to the heuristic structure of the human good. This structure is itself a development of Thomas Aquinas's amplification of Aristotle on the good. Aristotle defined the good as the object of appetite, *id quod omnia appetunt.*[69] Thomas made explicit a more intellectual dimension of the good as good of order:[70]

> [It is] the objective arrangement or institution that ensures for a group of people the regular recurrence of particular goods. As appetite wants breakfast, so an economic system is to ensure breakfast every morning ... As appetite wants knowledge, so an educational system answers the imparting of knowledge to each successive generation. But beyond the particular good and the good of order, there is the good of value.[71]

Thus far Lonergan agrees with Aristotle and Thomas in equating the good with what is desired precisely insofar as it is also intelligent and reasonable. He goes beyond this to specify more clearly the notion of the good as what is intended in questions for deliberation and aspired to in the intentional response of feelings to value:[72] 'It is by appealing to value or values that we satisfy some appetites and do not satisfy others, that we approve some systems for achieving the good of order and disapprove of others, that we praise or blame human persons as good or evil and their actions as right or wrong.'[73]

On Lonergan's analysis, whenever human beings deliberate, evaluate, decide, and act, they thereby emerge as existential subjects whose very person is at stake.[74] Whenever people as individuals are sufficiently self-transcendent in their deliberating, evaluating, deciding, and acting, they realize personal values. As mentioned above, they are originators of values in themselves and in their milieus, and they inspire and invite others to be originators too.[75] As originating values, persons are authentic, choosing self-transcendence by their good choices.[76] Then, to be persons means to be principles of benevolence and beneficence, capable of genuine collaboration and of true love.[77] Particular goods are whatever satisfy needs and fulfil capacities. Goods of order are the institutions and 'all the skill and know-how, all the industry and resourcefulness, all the ambition and fellow-feeling of a whole people, adapting to each change of circumstance, meeting each new emergency, struggling against any tendency to disorder.'[78] Terminal values (as the comprehensive objective correlatives to persons as originating values) are the values that people actually choose: 'true instances of the particular good, a true good of order, a true scale of preferences regarding values and satisfactions.'[79]

It is clear that for Lonergan, maturity entails a real apprehension, judgment, and decision regarding personal values and an appreciation of liberty as an active thrust of the self towards self-determination. When one is motivated not by a calculus of pleasure and pain but by values, one is free and 'regularly opts, not for the merely apparent good, but for the true good'; then 'the self ... is achieving moral self-transcendence ... is existing authentically ... is constituting himself as an originating value, and he is bringing about terminal values, namely a good of order that is truly good and instances of the particular good that are truly good.'[80] Then, too, personal values govern cultural, social, and vital values, because when we exist as persons, we 'meet one another in a common concern for values, [and] seek to abolish the organization of human living on the basis of competing egoisms and to replace it by an organization on the basis of man's perceptiveness and intelligence, his reasonableness, and his responsible exercise of freedom.'[81]

On Lonergan's analysis of the structure of the human good, the orientation of people is shown in the personal relations implicit in their cooperation for the sake of particular goods, and in the roles they play and the tasks they fulfil in the different institutional orders of familial, educational, technological, economic, legal, political, artistic, and religious schemes of recurrence in society. People communicate recreationally and pragmatically in these relationships. Their orientation comes most centrally to the fore when personal relationships become a matter of focal concern, which happens in friendships that go beyond motives of mutual utility or pleasure, and simply exist for their own sake. Communication on this level is constitutive precisely inasmuch as people's personal identity and orientation are at stake in it.[82]

Hence, freedom for Lonergan is a matter not of indeterminacy but of self-determination; and the commitments people undertake and 'the expectations aroused in others by the commitments'[83] are what most determine any person's free self-constitution. These commitments and the expectations that go with them regard not only performance, competence, and skill but the 'qualitative values and scales of preference' determined by their free commitments.

The diverse levels of human community correspond to the three-tiered structure of the human good, comprised by particular goods, goods of order, and terminal values.[84] The *intersubjective community* integrates experiencing and desiring subjects, with their spontaneous tendencies and elemental feelings of belonging together. As Lonergan described it:

> Its schemes of recurrence are simple prolongations of prehuman attainment, too obvious to be discussed or criticized, too closely linked with more elementary processes to be sharply distinguished from them. The bond of mother and child, man and wife, father and son, reaches into a past of ancestors to give meaning and cohesion to the clan or tribe or nation. A sense of belonging together provides the dynamic premise for common enterprise, for mutual aid and succor, for the sympathy that augments joys and divides sorrows. Even after civilization is attained, intersubjective community survives in the family with its circle of relatives and its accretion of friends, in customs and folkways, in basic arts and crafts and skills, in language and song and dance, and most concretely of all in the inner psychology and radiating influence of women. Nor is the abiding significance and efficacy of the intersubjective overlooked when motley states name themselves nations, when constitutions are attributed to founding fathers, when image and symbol, anthem and assembly, emotion and sentiment are invoked to impart an elemental vigor and pitch to the vast and cold technological, economic, and political structures of human invention and convention. Finally, as intersubjective community precedes civilization and underpins it, so also it remains when civilization suffers disintegration and decay. The collapse of imperial Rome was the resurgence of family and clan, feudal dynasty and nation.[85]

Intersubjective community corresponds to particular goods.

The *civil community* is 'a complex product embracing and harmonizing material techniques, economic arrangements, and political structures.' Of it Lonergan writes:

> The discoveries of practical intelligence, which once were an incidental addition to the spontaneous fabric of human living, now penetrate and overwhelm its every aspect. For just as technology and capital formation interpose their schemes of recurrence between man and the rhythms of nature, so economics and politics are vast structures of interdependence invented by practical intelligence for the mastery not of nature but of man.[86]

Civil community corresponds to the goods of order that arise from the developments of human intelligence enabling people to 'grasp and formulate technological devices, economic arrangements, political structures.'[87]

The *cultural community* is 'the field of communication and influence of artists, scientists, and philosophers ... the bar of enlightened public opinion to which naked power can be driven to submit ... the tribunal of history that may expose successful charlatans and may restore to honor the prophets stoned by their contemporaries.'[88] Lonergan suggests the importance of cultural community in the following terms:

> The dramatic subject, as practical, originates and develops capital and technology, the economy and the state. By his intelligence he progresses, and by his bias he declines. Still, this whole unfolding of practicality constitutes no more than the setting and the incidents of the drama. Delight and suffering, laughter and tears, joy and sorrow, aspiration and frustration, achievement and failure, wit and humor, stand not within practicality but above it. Man can pause and with a smile or a forced grin ask what the drama, what he himself is about. His culture is his capacity to ask, to reflect, to reach an answer that at once satisfies his intelligence and speaks to his heart.[89]

And so cultural community corresponds to the terminal values that arise from personal judgments of value.[90]

Civilizational and Cultural Development

We can use Lonergan's structure of the human good to analyse the historical development of civilizations and cultures. In the most primitive stage of civilizational development – hunters and gatherers in a nomadic state – intersubjective community predominates over civil community, and technology, economy, and polity exist in the most rudimentary state. Here what Jane Jacobs calls the ethics of raiding dominates the modes of making a living. Raider ethics inculcates a guardian moral syndrome with its corresponding catalogue of virtues: shun trading, exert prowess, be obedient and disciplined, adhere to tradition, respect hierarchy, be loyal, take vengeance, deceive for the sake of the task, make rich use of leisure, be ostentatious, dispense largesse, be exclusive, show fortitude, be fatalistic, treasure honour.[91]

With the agrarian revolution, goods of order required for the cultivation of the land supplant the skills, roles, and tasks of hunting and gathering nomads. Technology gets more sophisticated with the development of tools, the domestication and training of animals, and the development of newly specialized skills, roles, and tasks; economy tries to attain a steady standard of living, so that although surpluses bring about great population growth, they are used chiefly for barter and for making the next round of harvesting and planting possible. Far less frequently, surpluses are used for capital formation in the sense of 'things produced and arranged not because they themselves are desired but because they expedite and accelerate the process of supplying the goods and services that are wanted by consumers.'[92] At this stage of civilizational development, polity is organized as a centralized government dominated by upper classes.

With the commercial revolution, however, the technology of commerce shifts to money as a means of exchange, thus making possible new uses of economic surplus for capital formation, along with the novel and productive purpose of lending at interest. Besides the inevitable disruption of agrarian autarky, the newly emergent commerce promotes the proliferation of artisans, professions, guilds, and other services – in short, urban life in Aristotle's sense of 'city.'

Even the economic system of mercantilism (which equated a polity's wealth with the state's hoard of gold and silver and its agricultural output protected by tariffs instead of the sum total of productive activities) makes possible a change in the good of order as political. Civil community begins to hold sway over the intersubjective communities of pre-urban villages. In Jane Jacobs's account of the ethics of making a living, the ethics of trading starts to prevail in society over the ethics of raiding. Trader ethics inculcates the commercial moral syndrome with its set of typical virtues: shun force, come to voluntary agreements, be honest, collaborate easily with strangers and aliens, compete, respect contracts, use initiative and enterprise, be open to inventiveness and novelty, be efficient, promote comfort and convenience, dissent for the sake of the task, invest for productive purposes, be industrious, be thrifty, be optimistic.[93] The building of cathedrals and universities reflects a cultural surplus, a prosperous cultural community where, for the sake of cultural, personal, and religious values, commercial guilds of artisans, professionals, and university personnel exercise legitimate influence over the freedom of markets in the name of the common good, whose scope of concern is more comprehensive than that of the public order (in John Courtney Murray's helpful term),[94] which involves chiefly matters of technology and economy.

Finally, the discovery of technologies for controlling the motor power of fire enabled the Industrial Revolution to transforms cities and the planet itself. Production and monetary exchange, in their two interacting cycles of capital formation (i.e., the production of goods for producers) and consumer goods production, are differentiated more dramatically and manifested in the booms and slumps of business cycles. The result is massive increases in productivity, heightened urbanization, and concentrations of power and economic inequalities never before dreamed of in history. The great promise for cultural community in such tremendous economic potential has remained only ambiguously realized. Although higher standards of living bring with them an unheard-of leisure from the necessities of non-liberal labour, the new distinction between labour (i.e., the workers, who 'spend what they get') and capital (the producer goods owners who 'get what they spend') has promoted the overwhelming growth of technocracy, and the degeneration of true leisure. The same contrast between promise and achievement is suggested politically, in Ferdinand Braudel's economic history of the sixteenth and seventeenth centuries. Braudel distinguishes between two kind of economies: (1) 'market' economies exemplified by the subterranean exchange economies coeval with commerce in a context of small-scale agriculture, small businesses, and small industries in cities of typically no more than ten thousand people; and (2) 'capitalist' economies based on the fateful alliance between economic and political power at the summit of the social classes for the sake of a kind of gigantic 'success,' in which guardian moral syndromes are mixed up in disastrous ways with commercial moral syndromes.[95] Braudel's sense of 'capitalist' (which does not specify the word functionally in terms of capital formation, although this function is also connoted) indicates a top-heavy, power-driven economy that dominates countries, whether they have capitalist, socialist, or so-called mixed economies, by reigning supreme over public and private sectors both nationally and transnationally. It is the phenomenon currently parading under the heading of 'globalization.' Somewhat paradoxically, this style of economy gravitates away from genuine entrepreneurial freedom in favour of vertical managerial control exercised in bureaucratic modes, together with the worldwide dichotomy between skilled, high-paying jobs for the relatively few highly educated and unskilled, low-wage jobs for the masses.[96]

Now Lonergan's notion of the human good yields a normative intelligibility for political evaluation. Accordingly, particular goods are to be subordinated to goods of order, and goods of order are to be subordinated to terminal values. For this to happen coherently in reality, however, the integral scale of values (ranging from vital to religious, sketched in above) must be preserved intact by a sufficient number of authentic people. Today's prevalent worldwide trends have taught us that technological efficiency in multiplying particular goods can verge on the elimination of cultural, personal, and religious values. When this happens, two distortions result: first, values come to be equated with needs and desires on the level of appetite; and second, social goods of order come to be conceived as efficient means to the satisfaction of self-interested covetousness. Then the end of human living is conceived as an unlimited and disoriented satisfaction of needs and capacities disguised as freedom. This turns the normative order of civil society upside down: economy becomes subordinated to technology, and polity becomes the servant of economy. Triumphant technocracy organizes human living through the competing egoisms of individuals and groups. Paradoxically, the great potential for freedom made possible by both technical innovations and the enormous formation of capital in the second half of the twentieth century enslaves liberty by heightening the chances for unauthenticity. Why? Because in the measure that 'one's decisions have their principal motives, not in the values at stake but in a calculus of pleasures and pains, one is failing in self-transcendence, in authentic human existence, in the origination of value in oneself and one's society.'[97] This is the fateful linkage in the modern crisis between the collapse of the common good and the crisis of authenticity.

Notes

1 See Leo Strauss, 'Progress or Return? The Contemporary Crisis in Western Civilization,' in *An Introduction to Political Philosophy: Ten Essays by Leo Strauss* ed. Hilail Gildin (Detroit: Wayne State University Press, 1989), 249–310.

2 Alasdair MacIntyre, *After Virtue: A Study in Moral Theory* (Notre Dame, IN: University of Notre Dame Press, 1981).

3 See *Three Rival Versions of Moral Inquiry: Encyclopedia, Genealogy, and Tradition* (Notre Dame, IN: University of Notre Dame Press, 1991).

4 Charles Taylor, *The Ethics of Authenticity* (Cambridge: Harvard University Press, 1991).

5 Michael Sandel, *Liberalism and the Limits of Justice* (Cambridge: Cambridge University Press, 1982), 62.

6 Charles Taylor, 'The Person,' in *The Category of the Person*, ed. M. Carrithers et al. (Cambridge: Cambridge University Press, 1985), cited by Jack Crittenden, *Beyond Individualism: Reconstituting the Liberal Self* (Oxford: Oxford University Press, 1992), 15–28.

7 Taylor, *The Ethics of Authenticity*, 29.

8 Ibid., 33.

9 'Lost Belonging on the Road to Progress: Ernest Gellner and Charles Taylor in Conversation,' excerpted in *The Listener*, 20 March 1986, and cited by Crittenden, *Beyond Individualism*, 14.

10 Charles Taylor, *Sources of the Self* (Cambridge: Harvard University Press, 1989), 35.

11 Taylor, *Ethics of Authenticity*, 37.

12 Ibid., 39.

13 Ibid., 41.

14 Bernard Lonergan, *Insight: A Study of Human Understanding*, vol. 3 of *Collected Works of Bernard Lonergan*, ed. Frederick E. Crowe and Robert M. Doran (Toronto: University of Toronto Press, 1992). Incidentally, this book was also a

preliminary investigative survey of methods in common sense, mathematics, science, and ethics in preparation for a treatise on method in theology.

15 Bernard Lonergan, 'Isomorphism of Thomist and Scientific Thought,' in *Collection*, vol. 4 of *Collected Works of Bernard Lonergan*, ed. Frederick E. Crowe and Robert M. Doran (Toronto: University of Toronto Press, 1988), 133–41.

16 Lonergan, *Insight*, 95–6, 268–9.

17 See Bernard Lonergan, *The Ontological and Psychological Constitution of Christ*, vol. 7 of *Collected Works of Bernard Lonergan*, ed. and trans. Michael G. Shields (Toronto: University of Toronto Press, 2002), 183.

18 Lonergan, *Insight*, 11, 13–14.

19 Bernard Lonergan, 'Prologomena to the Study of the Emerging Religious Consciousness of Our Time,' in *A Third Collection*, ed. Frederick E. Crowe (New York: Paulist Press, 1985), 55.

20 Bernard Lonergan, *Verbum: Word and Idea in Aquinas*, vol. 2 of *Collected Works of Bernard Lonergan*, ed. Frederick E. Crowe and Robert M. Doran (Toronto: University of Toronto Press, 1997).

21 On intentionality analysis versus faculty psychology, see Bernard Lonergan, 'An Interview with Bernard Lonergan, S.J., edited by Philip McShane,' in *A Second Collection*, ed. William F.J. Ryan and Bernard J. Tyrrell (London: Darton, Longman & Todd, 1974), 222–3; *Method in Theology* (Toronto: University of Toronto Press, 2003), 3–25, 96, 245–6. On horizon, see 'Metaphysics as Horizon,' in *Collection*, 188–204, esp. 198–204; *Topics in Education*, vol. 10 of *Collected Works of Bernard Lonergan*, ed. Frederick E. Crowe and Robert M. Doran (Toronto: University of Toronto Press, 1992), 85–103; *Method in Theology*, 235–7.

22 Lonergan, *Insight*, chaps. 9, 10, and 11.

23 Ibid., 297.

24 Ibid., 308–12, 573–5.

25 Ibid., 574–5, 727–8.

26 Lonergan, *A Second Collection*, 167, emphasis mine.

27 Lonergan, *Insight*, 725–39; 'Belief: Today's Issue,' in *A Second Collection*, 87–99; *Method in Theology*, 41–7.

28 Lonergan, *Method in Theology*, 30–4 on feelings; 34–41 on value.

29 *Ibid.*, 115–24. See also Pierre Rousselot, 'Les yeux de la foi,' *Recherches de Science Religieuse* 1 (1910), 241–59, 444–79.

30 Lonergan, *Method in Theology*, 115, 261, 341.

31 Lonergan, *Insight*, 204–14 on patterns of experience.

32 Ibid., 214–31 on dramatic bias; 244–7 on individual bias; 247–50 on group bias; 250–67 on general or common-sense bias; 689–91 on basic sin.

33 Ibid., 650–3.

34 Ibid., 710–15.

35 Ibid., 715–51.

36 Bernard Lonergan, *Grace and Freedom: Operative Grace in the Thought of St Thomas Aquinas*, vol. 1 of *Collected Works of Bernard Lonergan*, ed. Frederick E. Crowe and Robert M. Doran (Toronto: University of Toronto Press, 2000).

37 Lonergan, *Insight*, 8, 256–7, 763.

38 Bernard Lonergan, 'Healing and Creating in History,' in *A Third Collection*, 100–9.

39 Lonergan, *Insight*, 587–91, esp. 589–91; *Collection*, 188–204.

40 Lonergan, *Method in Theology*, 31–2 on values as vital, social, cultural, personal, and religious.

41 Lonergan, *Insight*, 261–3 on culture; see also *Topics in Education* on culture as distinct from civilization: 50, 55, 69, 255.

42 Lonergan, *Method in Theology*, 32 on value as personal; 50–1, 53, 116, 242 on persons as originating values.

43 Ibid., 32 on religious values; 101–24 on religion.

44 For what follows the main lines of interpretation are suggested by Bernard Lonergan's 'The Subject,' in *A Second Collection*, 69–86.

45 Lonergan, *Collection*, 204.

46 Taylor, *The Ethics of Authenticity*, 27–8.

47 See Jean-Luc Marion, 'L'Effondrement des idoles et l'affrontement du divin: Nietzsche,' in *L'Idole et la distance* (Paris: Grasset, 1977), 45–105.

48 Lonergan, *A Second Collection*, 221–6, esp. 222–3.

49 Lonergan, *Method in Theology*, 106, 116, 122, 243 on love and values.

50 Ibid., 34–6 on the transcendental notion of value.

51 Ibid., 37–8.

52 Lonergan, *A Second Collection*, 221.

53 Lonergan, *Method in Theology*, 48, 50–1 on orientation and value.

54 *Ibid.*, 240–3, 270, 318.

55 Lonergan, *A Second Collection*, 168–9.

56 Lonergan, *Method in Theology*, 110–12, 115–18.

57 Ibid., 10, 51, 53, 104, 116, 242.

58 Lonergan, *A Second Collection*, 277.

59 Ibid.

60 Lonergan, *Method in Theology*, 35.

61 Allan Bloom, 'The Democratization of the University,' *Giants and Dwarfs: Essays 1960–1990* (New York: Simon & Schuster, 1990), 385.

62 Bernard Lonergan, 'The Future of Thomism,' in *A Second Collection*, 51.

63 Bloom, *Giants and Dwarfs*, 385.

64 Lonergan, *Method in Theology*, 104, 110, 254; *A Second Collection*, 165–70.

65 Lonergan, *Method in Theology*, 37, 265, 292, 338.

66 Bloom, *Giants and Dwarfs*, 286.

67 Lonergan, *A Second Collection*, 83, 168, 236, 242.

68 Bloom, *Giants and Dwarfs*, 284–7.

69 Lonergan, *A Second Collection*, 84.

70 As Aquinas said, '*finis quidem universi est aliquod bonum in ipso existens, scilicet ordo ipsius universi*' (*Summa Theologiae* 1, q. 103, a. 2 ad 3m). See John Wright, SJ, *The Order of the Universe in the Theology of St. Thomas Aquinas* (Rome: Gregorian University Press, 1957).

71 Lonergan, *A Second Collection*, 81.

72 Ibid., 277.

73 Ibid., 81–2.

74 Ibid., 80.
75 Lonergan, *Method in Theology*, 32.
76 Ibid., 51.
77 Ibid., 37.
78 Ibid., 49–50.
79 Ibid., 51.
80 Ibid., 50.
81 Ibid., 10.
82 Ibid., 78, 178, 180, 306, 356, 362 on meaning as constitutive. On these different kinds of communication, see my 'Lonergan's Foundations for Constitutive Communication,' *Lonergan Workshop* 10 (1994), 229–77; 'Aiming High: Reflections on Buckley's Theorem on Higher Education,' in *Finding God in All Things: Essays in Honor of Michael J. Buckley, S.J.*, ed. Michael J. Himes and Stephen J. Pope (New York: Crossroad/Herder, 1996), 318–39.
83 Lonergan, *Method in Theology*, 50.
84 Bernard Lonergan, 'The Role of a Catholic University in the Modern World,' in *Collection*, 108–13. See also my 'The Human Good and Christian Conversation,' in *Communication and Lonergan: Common Ground for Forging the New Age*, ed. Thomas J. Farrell and Paul A. Soukup (Kansas City: Sheed & Ward, 1993), 248–68.
85 Lonergan, *Insight*, 237–8.
86 Ibid., 238.
87 Bernard Lonergan, 'The Role of a Catholic University in the Modern World,' in *Collection*, 108.
88 Ibid., 109.
89 Lonergan, *Insight*, 261.
90 Ibid.
91 Jane Jacobs, *Systems of Survival: A Dialogue on the Moral Foundations of Commerce and Politics* (New York: Random House, 1992), 215. See too *Ethics in Making a Living: The Jane Jacobs Conference*, supplementary issue of *Lonergan Workshop* 7, ed. Fred Lawrence (Atlanta, GA: Scholars Press, 1989).
92 Lonergan, *Insight*, 233.
93 Jacobs, *Systems of Survival*, 215.
94 See Robert W. McElroy, *The Search for an American Public Theology: The Contribution of John Courtney Murray* (New York: Paulist Press, 1989), 78–87.
95 Ibid., 93–157.
96 The discussion above on development as civilizational with reference to Fer dinand Braudel depends on Gabriel Zaid's essay 'Abundancia y libertad,' *Vuelta*, no. 205 (December 1993), 15–19. Besides ideas of Jane Jacobs, I have also used ideas from Bernard Lonergan's economic manuscript, *Macroeconomic Dynamics: An Essay in Circulation Analysis*, vol. 15 of *Collected Works of Ber nard Lonergan*, ed. Patrick H. Byrne, Charles C. Hefling, and Frederick G. Lawrence (Toronto: University of Toronto Press, 1999), as well as Lonergan's 'Common Sense as Object,' in *Insight*, 232–69; for strictures on modern forms of social alienation see his 'Prologomena to the Emerging Religious Consciousness of Our Time,' in *A Third Collection*, 60–3.
97 Lonergan, *Method in Theology*, 50.

Cynthia S.W. Crysdale

Risk, Gratitude, and Love: Grounding Authentic Moral Deliberation

In the tenth chapter of the Gospel of Mark we find an intriguing case study in moral deliberation. An apparently rich man approaches Jesus, concerned about his salvation, and asks what he must do to inherit eternal life. Jesus turns the question back on the man and recites the commandments, to which the prospective disciple replies, 'Teacher, all these things I have kept from my youth' (Mark 10:20). Jesus responds in love: 'One thing you lack: Go your way, sell whatever you have, give to the poor and you will have treasure in heaven; and come, take up the cross, and follow me' (Mark 10:21). Mark records that the man turned away in sorrow, for he had many possessions.

This story has often been interpreted as a lesson about wealth, poverty, and the cost of discipleship. Indeed, the author of the Gospel of Mark takes the recounting of this story as an occasion to record other sayings of Jesus about the difficulty of sacrificing wealth: it is easier for a camel to go through the eye of a needle than for a rich man to enter the Kingdom of Heaven. I would interpret this story more broadly as Jesus's challenge to moral insight and radical decision. While the enquiring disciple wants a clear formula for righteousness, Jesus challenges him to an unknown future – a future in which he will need to take on the risk of following Jesus without knowing where it will lead. It illustrates the challenge of understanding moral deliberation as a matter of risk-taking rather than control, gratitude as well as constructive collaboration for the future, and falling in love with God as the ultimate ground of authentic action.

This essay contributes to a volume focused on the contribution Michael Vertin has made to philosophy in general and the critical realism of Bernard Lonergan in particular. My intent is to follow Vertin's lead by explicating how we engage in 'deliberative insight' as a way to ground an ethic for the current situation. My general position is that a number of mis-taken views on moral deliberation serve to bolster false understandings of ourselves as moral agents. Most notably, in our culture we tend to assume that (1) we are autonomous agents in direct control of the outcomes of our actions;[1] (2) we create values at will, rather than discover existent values as given; and (3) the ultimate end of our deliberation is merely the human good, blind to any value that may exceed human striving and well-being. I will proceed through three sections: first discussing the probability-shaped nature of moral deliberation, then examining Vertin's (borrowed) insight about complacency and concern in deliberative insights, and finally alluding to religious love as transvaluing all other values in light of transcendent meaning.

An Ethic of Risk[2]

Fifteen years ago Sharon Welch wrote *A Feminist Ethic of Risk*, in which she analysed different understandings of moral action, especially with regard to U.S. nuclear arms policy.[3] Her distinction between an ethic of control and an ethic of risk remains strikingly relevant today.

An ethic of control assumes that moral action produces clear results. It leaves little room for ambiguity and involves 'controlling events and receiving a quick and predictable response.'[4] This decisive action renders one invulnerable to evil: one has a clear plan, a strategy that will not only rid the world of the current problem but protect one from further threats. This model of moral action relies on 'the equation of responsible action and control – the assumption that it is possible to guarantee the efficacy of one's actions.'[5] It also presumes a monopoly of power, pervasive when one 'defines action as the ability to attain, without substantial modification, desired results.'[6] Though risk is not unacknowledged here, it is treated as a factor that can be quantified and managed in the short term.

An ethic of control is tied not only to the politics of power, but also to a certain utopian vision. Welch's analysis focuses on the development of nuclear weapons in the 1980s, but her comments are equally applicable in the current political climate:

> A factor contributing to distortions in the calculus of risk is the construction of the aim of moral action as the attainment of final, complete victory. The aim of a final defeat of all evil forces, or the aim of finally meeting all human needs, does not appear as anything but praiseworthy on the surface. It is indeed surprising to find that such utopian goals as the defeat of evil and meeting of all needs can have,

> and often do have, highly dangerous consequences and that these constructions make peace less likely and justice seem less likely. This distortion of a seemingly positive goal operates in several ways. One is the inability to accept the prospect of long-term struggle. Seeking utopia, people turn to types of action that appear to offer immediacy and guarantees despite the dangers that may accompany these actions.[7]

Surprisingly, Welch uses this critique of utopian action against not only the deterrent-minded public and the hawk-like government administrators, but against the peace movement itself.[8] The core of an ethic of control is not the cause being advocated but the expectation that clear and direct action will eradicate evil.

In contrast, an ethic of risk is 'responsible action within the limits of bounded power' and involves 'persistent defiance and resistance in the face of repeated defeats.'[9] This ethic attends to that which may yield only partial results. The goal of moral action is not complete success but the creation of new conditions of possibility for the future. An ethic of risk is that which accepts the long-term struggle involved in oppressive situations. It is 'an ethic that begins with the recognition that we cannot guarantee decisive changes in the near future or even in our lifetime.'[10] Further, 'the ethic of risk is propelled by the equally vital recognition that to stop resisting, even when success is unimaginable, is to die,' whether that involves physical death or the death of imagination and caring.[11]

In such situations, an ethic of risk engages one in a community of risk-takers, committed to the struggle over the long haul. It involves 'strategic risk-taking' in the face of overwhelming odds, and recognizes the irreparable damage of structural evil.

> The ethic of risk is characterized by three elements, each of which is essential to maintain resistance in the face of overwhelming odds: a redefinition of responsible action, grounding in community, and strategic risk-taking. Responsible action does not mean the certain achievement of desired ends but the creation of a matrix in which further actions are possible, the creation of the conditions of possibility for desired changes.[12]

While Welch uses nuclear arms proliferation as her example of an ethic of control, she uses novels by African American women to illustrate the struggle, dignity, and defiance characteristic of an ethic of risk. The Logan family of Mildred Taylor's *Roll of Thunder, Hear My Cry* and *Let the Circle Be Unbroken* exemplifies the acceptance of ambiguity central to an ethic of risk. Cassie Logan, coming of age in the racist South during the Depression, learns from her family how to have courage in the face of bigotry, even while it is impossible to imagine its eradication.[13]

In contrast, Paule Marshall's novel *The Chosen Place, The Timeless People* depicts Harriet, a rich, white philanthropist who, despite her generosity and good will, functions with an ethic of control. While working with the poor on a Caribbean island, Harriet comes upon two starving children in a meagre hut. Their parents are off cutting cane, and Harriet cannot bear the suffering of these hungry children. Finding a half dozen eggs in the hut, and over the loud protests of the children, she breaks and scrambles the eggs over the fire. She is shocked later to discover that the eggs were meant for sale at the local market, that the children had been beaten for allowing her to cook them, and that, in fact, the children had left the cooked eggs untouched. Harriet had assumed that her quick, simple, and direct solution would solve the problem. She is out of touch with the complex systems of family and economic meaning in which she envisions herself acting as an agent of change.[14]

Thus, an ethic of control assumes that one's moral choices will 'fix' evil in a definitive way. Most often, this solution to whatever problem is at hand involves force, coercion, or violence. It is the preferred *modus operandi* of oppressors or, more benignly, any dominant cultural or political group. In contrast, an ethic of risk recognizes the limits of power, the ambiguity of moral choice, and the partiality of any attempt to eradicate evil. Relying on the solidarity of community over the long haul, an ethic of risk looks more to creating a new matrix of possibilities than to finding a single direct solution to evil and its consequences.

I have found Welch's analysis very fruitful in understanding the dynamics of moral action, but I would like to press Welch's analysis of power to a more fundamental level. The key point is simply this: while Welch unpacks 'risk' and 'control' in light of the exercise of power, in terms of *prescriptive* norms and how one ought to engage in moral action, her ethic of risk is in fact a *descriptive* category.[15] Indeed, by examining the way in which persons make value judgments and choices one discovers that 'risk' and 'conditions of possibility' are inherent in moral judgment itself. It is, thus, not that persons choose between living an ethic of risk or living an ethic of control, but that all persons live in a world of probabilities in which control is not an option but a fantasy. An ethic of control is more of a rhetorical cover story than a serious possibility. The true contrast is between the practice of risk and the rhetoric of control.

Let me develop this claim through a phenomenology of moral practice, a method based on self-appropriation rather than social science.[16] The first step may seem tangential, but it involves an examination of how we know the 'facts' in order to reveal the distinct aspects of value judgments and decisions.

Coming to a conclusion that something is true depends on both coherence and empirical evidence. Questions arise, whether complex – What causes AIDS and which drugs are most effective in treating it? – or simple – What is that beeping sound that I hear? Proposed answers to these questions are accurate to the degree that they are internally consistent and, most important, match the evidence at hand. Now, the 'evidence at hand' may come through simple perception, using our five senses, may rely on memory and previously attained knowledge, or may involve the collection of several layers of data via highly technical means. Either way, something is determined to be true, an explanation deemed correct, when the evidence sufficiently meets the conditions implicit in a proposed answer.

For example, the beeping sound is a French fry machine if: (1) we are in the proximity of a fast food restaurant, (2) the restaurant sells French fries, and (3) the restaurant uses a deep fryer that beeps when the French fries are done. If we are standing at a roadside fruit stand on a country road some other explanation, with its list of conditions, will need to be pursued. This simplistic model of determining the facts is repeated in much more elaborate forms in laboratories across the country. Much scholarly and scientific debate revolves around whether researchers have indeed verified their hypothetical claims with sufficient evidence.[17]

Now, while some judgments of fact can be made definitively because the evidence is overwhelming, many judgments of fact remain provisional. When evidence is partial we may be in a position of making probable judgments: the beeping sound is most likely a garbage truck backing up, but we are not yet certain. In this sense, judgments of fact can involve a certain kind of 'risk' in that we may be called upon to make determinations before all the evidence is in. But this kind of risk nevertheless converges on a term in the future when we expect to know something for sure. In other words, this risk is a result of incomplete knowledge and not constitutive of judgments of fact themselves.[18]

This exposition of determinations of fact is merely a building block for understanding, in contrast, the nature of judgments of value, specifically with regard to the kind of 'risk' involved. In decision-making – again both the mundane and the monumental – one determines not what *is* the case but what *might be* the case. One weighs not the sufficiency of evidence to determine what is so, but projected courses of action and their potential outcomes. Surely, weighing these options depends a good deal on getting one's facts straight. Indeed, accurate information-gathering is an essential aspect of any good decision-making. Still, there is an element of risk involved in judgments of value and decisions that will never disappear no matter how accurate and complete one's grasp of the facts is.

Let me expand on this a bit further. First, questions for deliberation – What ought I to do in this situation? – do not come out of a vacuum but arise in conjunction with concrete discoveries of fact. My car won't start in the morning – what I ought to do depends on the reasons why it isn't working. A bit more seriously, I visit my mother and find her on the floor of her apartment, not breathing. My course of action must begin with at least a rudimentary determination of what has happened to her.

So 'What am I to do?' (value judgments/decisions) and 'What is the case?' (judgments of fact) are questions that often emerge simultaneously. And the validity of my actions does rely on my accurate grasp of the facts of the situation. Still, judgments of value and decisions go beyond a mere determination of the current facts to a determination of the probable outcomes of various courses of action. This latter determination involves calculating probabilities, and such probabilities, by their very nature, involve risk.

Thus, for example, once I get my mother to a hospital I seek expert advice about her condition. A resuscitation process has got her breathing again, but it is unlikely that she will make it through the night without an artificial respirator. Intravenous medication may help her breathing but brings with it other side effects. No treatment at all, other than bed rest and vigilance from nursing staff, is also a possibility, but repeated resuscitation, if necessary, would further damage her fragile heart.

The point is to show that the choices involved here all include a consideration of probabilities. The more accurate the predications are, the more informed our choices will be. But no matter how accurate certain predictions are, it is the nature of probability to involve uncertainty and therefore risk.

Let me explain. Statistical science, which concerns itself with how often something is likely to occur, under which circumstances, derives general conclusions from a series of specific instances. But in this case, the general conclusions come in the form of averages and ratios. One can take the number of home runs hit by a baseball star throughout his career and determine the likelihood of his hitting another home run during this World Series championship. One can take a survey of people who have used a certain drug to help them with heart problems, determine how many have had which side effects under which conditions, and then predict the likelihood of a new patient's having the same side effects. But in all these cases, the actual instances revolve non-systematically around an average, and the average, however accurately calculated, will not determine which actual instances will occur in the future. Knowing that the chance of rolling a six is one in six doesn't tell you whether *this* throw of the dice will yield a six or not.

Now the average citizen, or the military strategist, or the local doctor, does not always engage in statistical science when considering what to do. Still, no matter how simple or sophisticated one's considerations, no matter how rudimentary or elaborate one's predictions, the very *nature* of decision-making will always involve the uncertainty of not knowing *exactly* what all the repercussions of one's actions will be. At some point one must make a decision and take action, accepting the risks involved in what might unfold.

So, determining facts involves risk in the sense that, at times, we make determinations that are merely provisional because our knowledge is incomplete. But decisions, and the judgments involved in them, precisely because they regard not what *is* the case but what *might be* the case, are by their very nature provisional and involve risk.

There is a further element here, and that involves the weighing of values and the willingness of the agent. Once one has assessed the likelihood of certain outcomes to particular courses of action, one also weighs the relative values at stake in such various courses of action, as well as one's own level of commitment to such values. Thus, though the likelihood of my mother surviving is greater if I agree to have her put on a respirator, the quality of her life will be severely compromised. I must weigh her quality of life with the value of her physical survival. Perhaps my mother has asked previously that I take whatever measures necessary to keep her alive, while I feel strongly that a 'good' death, even if hastened by a lack of artificial aids, is much more important. All these considerations go well beyond the mere predictions of what will happen if I take various actions. *Given* these predictions I must still weigh the values involved, as well as my own willingness to carry out certain choices, and to live with the impending consequences.

Thus, there is this deeper level of existential risk involved in value judgments and decisions. Beyond gathering information on probable outcomes, one must consider one's acceptance of responsibility for such outcomes. As Bernard Lonergan puts it:

> For the grasp of a possible course of action need not result automatically and blindly in its execution. Further questions can be raised, and commonly their number varies with our familiarity with the situation at hand, with the seriousness or the consequences of the proposed course of action, with the uncertainties and the risks it involves, with our antecedent willingness or unwillingness to assume responsibility for the consequences and to run the risks.[19]

Thus, one can come to realize that in making concrete choices one is also making oneself. As Lonergan puts it: 'Finally, the development of knowledge and the development of moral feeling head to the existential discovery, the discovery of oneself as a moral being, the realization that one not only chooses between courses of action but also thereby makes oneself an authentic human being or an unauthentic one.'[20] Cassie Logan's Mama in *Roll of Thunder, Hear My Cry* amply illustrates this. Mama teaches the black children in their district and is committed to instilling dignity and teaching them their own history. One day the white men of the local school board arrive unexpectedly to observe her teaching:

> Mama seemed startled to see the men, but when Mr. Granger said, 'Been hearing 'bout your teaching, Mary, so as members of the school board we thought we'd come by and learn something,' she merely nodded and went on with her lesson ... Mama was in the middle of history and I knew that was bad ... But Mama did not flinch; she always started her history class the first thing in the morning when the students were most alert, and I knew that the hour was not yet up. To make matters worse, her lesson for the day was slavery. She spoke on the cruelty of it; of the rich economic cycle it generated as slaves produced the raw products for the factories of the North and Europe; how the country profited and grew from the free labor of a people still not free. Before she had finished, Mr. Granger picked up a student's book, flipped it open to the pasted-over front cover, and pursed his lips ... 'I don't see all them things you're teaching in here.'
>
> 'That's because they're not in there,' Mama said.
>
> 'Well, if it ain't in here, then you got no right teaching it. This book's approved by the Board of Education and you're expected to teach what's in it.'
>
> 'I can't do that.'
>
> 'And why not?'
>
> Mama, her back straight and her eyes fixed on the men, answered, 'Because all that's in that book isn't true.'
>
> Mr. Granger stood ... 'You must be some kind of smart, Mary ... In fact ... you're so smart I expect you'd best just forget about teaching altogether ... then thataway you'll have plenty of time to write your own book.'[21]

This is a case in which, knowing with a fair amount of certainty that the outcome of carrying on her lesson as planned would not bode well for her, Mama nevertheless accepted the negative risk in order to retain her own dignity.

In sum, then, though not all choices involve life-and-death decisions nor are as dramatic as Mama's situation, there are, nevertheless, certain kinds of risk involved in all moral agency. First, there is the minor uncertainty included in getting the facts of the current situation straight. While this risk involves a perhaps incomplete knowledge of what is the case, there is the further risk involved in predicting what might be the case if certain actions are taken. This second kind of risk is inherent in probabilities and is a risk that will never be overcome. For no matter how accurate one's predictions, such predictions are merely averages from which concrete instances often diverge. Finally, there is what I will call 'existential risk' in the sense that the outcomes of one's choices affect not only the 'objective' world but, more importantly, contribute to the very making of one's own soul.

The point of all this is to show that those who functionally presume an ethic of control make assumptions that are not only morally presumptuous but factually incorrect. We may think that action *A* directly causes consequence *B*. Sometimes the probabilities are such that this seems to be the case. In fact, though, all that we do in taking moral action is to shift the probabilities of certain kinds of outcomes. Our actions are merely one set of parameters amidst many other agents and variables. We may work hard to construe our circumstances so that our actions do have the direct and intended results that we want, but such construal is itself a manipulation of probabilities designed to reduce the risks we take in our action.

Thus, to return to Welch's analysis of power, it turns out that the ethic of control is, in large part, a myth that we tell ourselves, a rhetorical and psychic flourish that protects us from the true ambiguity of choice. Furthermore, and this is the heart of Welch's contribution, those who have more economic, political, and social power are more able to perpetuate this myth for themselves. Indeed, those with such power more often experience the efficacy of their choices and are more often protected from the vicissitudes and vulnerabilities of life.[22]

An Ethic of Gratitude

Up to this point I have tried to show that an ethic of risk can serve not only as a prescriptive mandate but is, in fact, grounded in the concrete operations of moral agency. Moral deliberation by its very nature involves a consideration of probabilities, a calculation of risks, with regard to the likely outcome of certain courses of action.

Another dimension needs to be added. To the degree that an ethic of risk is meant to serve as an antidote to the hubris of control, adverting to the probability-shaped nature of decision-making is only a first step.

Indeed, many military strategists and Wall Street brokers understand the nature of risk while nevertheless assuming an overreaching power in their attempts to 'manage' such risks. To an ethic of risk we need to add, as a further move towards humility, an ethic of gratitude, a recognition that even in our attempts to change the world we are working only with what has already been given.

Michael Vertin himself provides several clues by which to ground such an ethic of gratitude. In a 1995 article in *Method: Journal of Lonergan Studies*, Vertin explicates Lonergan's analysis of judgments of value and, in the process, adds a few notable clarifications.[23] Two in particular are important with regard to my objectives here. One is his clarification of 'possible value' as Lonergan uses the term, and the other is his allusion to 'complacency' and 'concern' as two possible terms of decision once value has been discovered.[24]

The discussion of an ethic of risk in the previous section attempted to ground such an ethic in the probability-shaped nature of all moral deliberation and action. In an effort to overcome an assumption of control in moral agency, I emphasized that all decisions merely set up conditions of possibility for the creation of value. In the process, my focus was almost entirely on moral deliberation and action as the determination of *possible* values. I outlined judgments of fact as determinations of what currently *is* the case and considered judgments of value as determinations of what *might be* the case. While this served to illustrate my points about the tentative nature of value judgments and decisions, it does not do full justice to the kinds of judgments that can arise in pursuit of responsibility.

Vertin points out that Lonergan's account of judgments of fact and judgments of value can lead to a false conclusion that the former have to do with actualities while the latter determine possibilities. In fact, Vertin maintains that both fact judgments and value judgments can determine either actualities or possibilities.

> The difference between fact judgments and value judgments is a function of the difference between the respective transcendental notions that radically underlie them, between the respective questions to which they respond, and between the respective intellectual and affective cognitional elements pivotal to their emergence. The difference is *not* that fact judgments manifest actualities alone while value judgments can manifest mere possibilities as well. On the contrary, both can manifest both actualities and mere possibilities.[25]

According to Vertin, any judgment, of fact or of value, is a matter of determining that the conditions necessary to affirm a fact or value are fulfilled. But such a determination can be one of three types: (1) an affirmation that such conditions are *actually* fulfilled; (2) an affirmation that the conditions are not currently fulfilled but that their fulfilment is *concretely possible*; or (3) an affirmation that their fulfilment is just *abstractly possible*, i.e., the materials needed for such a fulfilment of conditions are not present. To use an extremely simplistic example, as I leave for work in the morning I look outside to find out if it is raining. The proposition 'It is raining' will be fulfilled if indeed I see droplets of water on the sidewalk and get wet when I step out the door. However, such conditions may not be fulfilled, but I nonetheless notice dark clouds overhead and an ominous wind blowing while the barometer is dropping. The conditions for 'It is raining' are not fulfilled, but I can come to the judgment that the fulfilment of such conditions is concretely possible. Finally, when I step out into the morning sunshine and note that there is not a cloud in the sky, I can conclude that 'It is raining' is not actually true nor concretely possible, but is abstractly possible given a shift in conditions.

How does this play out with regard to judgments of value? Again we use a simplistic example – Should I take an umbrella when I go outside? While it may appear that the answer to this question is determined merely by the former question (i.e., I should take an umbrella if it is raining), there are a number of value considerations that are involved. There is on the one hand the value of staying dry. On the other hand there is the value of traveling unencumbered. Getting where I am going as speedily as possible without worrying about misplacing an umbrella may take greater priority. There is also the possibility of simply staying at home – perhaps today is the day I should 'telecommute' from my den. There are a number of values to be considered: staying dry, getting my work done, keeping my life as simple as possible. The judgments of value involved include the current (actual) fulfilment of certain conditions: I am dry in a warm house not likely to leak, I am getting work done already at my computer – these are all good things. Possible values include: the stimulation of my work if I go to the office to work on the computer there, the possibility that I could stay dry while getting to work (if I take an umbrella; or consider other means of staying dry such as driving my car rather than walking or wearing my rain parka and leaving the umbrella at home). Staying dry and getting work done are recognized as 'goods' – both goods that are actually present and goods that are possibly present in another form. Other values may arise if I leave home and go to work – these values and their possible instigation must be weighed in a comparative value judgment against the already existing goods of the present.

Clearly, judgments about facts, their actuality or possibility, are intertwined with determinations of value – both actually existing values and the possibility of instigating the occurrence of such values. But it is not the case that judgments of fact merely determine what *is* while judgments of value consider what *is not yet.* Nor is it the case that determinations of factual possibilities (ninety per cent chance of rain today) automatically determine courses of action and the values inherent in them (I should take an umbrella in order to stay dry).

Now, this point is important because it leads to the further point about the distinction between complacency and concern. Here 'complacency' refers not to indifference but to enjoyment. The point is that not all value judgments conclude with a decision to *instigate change* in the world. Some value judgments lead one to recognize that an already existing value needs merely to be acknowledged and enjoyed. As Vertin puts it:

> A value judgment that manifests an actual value belongs to a conscious intentional process in the pattern of *complacency,* the process that properly terminates in a decision to enjoy the actual value. Any such value judgment must be preceded by a judgment of actual fact. Alternatively, a value judgment that manifests a merely possible value belongs to a conscious intentional process in the pattern of *concern,* the process that properly terminates in a decision to attempt actualization of the possible value. Any such value judgment must be preceded by a judgment of possible fact. However, in so far as the effort to actualize the possible value is successful, the process in the pattern of concern gives way in turn to a fact judgment, value judgments, and decision in the pattern of complacency.[26]

Again, to provide examples: in light of the 2004 tsunami and its effects in south Asia, I come to notice the value of the availability of clean drinking water. A judgment of fact – that the water that comes out of my tap is clean, safe, potable water (not necessarily to be taken for granted in North America) – must precede that appreciation of value. The recognition 'Clean water is a good, in my case an already existing good' leads to 'complacency,' i.e., an appreciation and enjoyment of this value. In parallel fashion, the value of clean drinking water may lead me to actions of 'concern' – over how I can help make clean water accessible to victims of the 2004 tsunami in, say, Sri Lanka. The recognition of possible value – 'Sending clean drinking water to those who do not currently have it in Sri Lanka' must be preceded by a judgment of possible fact – we can get it to them by sending kits of chemicals to decontaminate well water, via the Canadian government.[27] In this case, the value at hand is clearly recognized, as is the problem of its absence: most effort would go into determining the feasibility and best means of getting clean water to the victims.[28]

Given the modern tendency to conceive of moral deliberation as having only to do with creating something new in the world, it is worth spending some time on this notion of complacency.[29] Vertin himself borrowed the terms 'complacency' and 'concern' from the work of Frederick Crowe, who, in three articles written in 1959, analysed these as aspects of 'willing' in the work of Thomas Aquinas. While Crowe does an extensive analysis of texts from St Thomas, his main point is to insist that willing, for Thomas, is not merely a matter of striving towards an end, in the manner of *eros* or akin to the modern existentialists' insistence on *becoming* as the primordial human challenge. While willing, and loving, are indeed seen by Thomas as dynamic and oriented towards an end, Crowe ferrets out the texts from Thomas that acknowledge that will can be a term in itself, the end of a process rather than the instigation of a process. In an effort to recognize two aspects of will, Crowe focuses on complacency as well as concern:

> Complacency in English usage has connotations which are poles apart from the Thomist *complacentia*; but it has the root sense of a concept I take to be altogether basic in Thomist psychology of the will ... It indicates that will, before being the faculty of an appetite, of process to a term, is that faculty of affective consent, of acceptance of what is good, of concord with the universe of being, and that the basic act of will is to be understood only if it is regarded not as an impulse to a term, or even the principle of process to a term qua principle, but simply as itself a term. That is to say, willing basically is the end of a process, quiescence; only secondarily is it the initiation of another process.[30]

Later in the same article Crowe again insists on the receptive nature of will as a precedent to will as motion, action towards an end, relating this to the analogy of the Trinity, particularly the Holy Spirit as the analogue of will/love:

> The evidence to be uncovered will require a passive act [of willing] that is just passive, that is simply the end of a process, a coming to rest, an act that is more accurately named complacency in the good than willing an end. It is an affective response to the good that is, rather than a seeking in any form, selfish, or self-giving, of the good that is not. It is under this aspect that love corresponds to and provides an analogy for the procession of the Holy Spirit in the Trinity, where the Third Person is a term bringing the divine processions to a close and is certainly not a Love for an object good to-be-made, to-be-done, to-be-attained, or to-be in any way that involves a not-yet. It is

> attention to this aspect and to the possibility of simple acts of compla cency, removed from all notion of striving, that can supply a needed corrective to a culture almost wholly oriented towards the objects of its concern.[31]

Though Crowe was, of course, still working with the notion of the will as a faculty, his analysis of Thomist psychology can yield an insight that can be transposed to human consciousness as now understood as a set of operations. Vertin has done this in his adoption of the terms. Along with his recognition that deliberative insights may yield judgments about both actual and possible value, he points out that these judgments in turn can yield different actions – on the one hand enjoyment of values already existing (complacency), and on the other hand the impetus to create values that are currently not operative (concern). While Vertin does not expand on this transposition, I believe that he would concur with the assumption, based on both Crowe's work and self-appropriation, that complacency – the recognition and enjoyment of actual value – undergirds any further efforts of concern.[32] To return to previous examples, unless one 'enjoys' (*complacentia*) being dry, drinking clean water, and accomplishing productive work, one cannot conceive of willing these for the future or for circumstances or people in which these are absent.

What does any of this have to do with the ethic of risk as discussed above? While in the previous section I was at pains to show that all moral deliberation and action yields only provisional consequences – conditions of possibility – rather than determinate 'controlled' outcomes, here I have added another side to a perhaps imbalanced account. 'Deliberative insights,' as Vertin names them, deal not only with what might be the case, but often yield judgments about values as they already occur. Following Crowe's insight, it is important to acknowledge that there is an aspect to deliberation and decision-making that is not just striving for the 'not yet,' but is an acknowledgment of the 'already valuable.'

The foundational importance of this point is that it implies what I call an 'ethic of gratitude' that needs to be added to the ethic of risk. The basic point is that, while persons are indeed originators of value, most importantly of themselves as value-ers, human agents are first and foremost *discoverers* of value and only secondarily *creators* of value. This means that as we engage in moral deliberation and action we need to acknowledge the *givenness* of the Good, and of the concrete goods by which we know and participate in the Good. There is a critical realism involved here that on the one hand recognizes the active contribution of the agent in determining value (against a mere empiricism), that acknowledges the *affective cognition* involved in judgments of value (against either a mere emotivism on the one side or an intellectualism on the other), while at the same time insisting that values are genuinely known and exist independent of the knower (against a mere voluntarism).[33]

The point is that if, phenomenologically, knowing and choosing value involves discovering what has already been given, authentic moral deliberation must begin with gratitude. Complacency as recognition and enjoyment of the beauty, truth, love, companionship, and communion that permeates all of creation grounds a concomitant ethic of action and concern. Just as an ethic of control is a mistaken conjecture of power in spite of the limited reality of moral agency, so an ethic that assumes the autonomous creation of value *ex nihilo* is a mistaken adoption of the role of Creator in spite of the limitations of creaturehood. An ethic of gratitude, grounded as it is, concretely, empirically, in the human agent as *discoverer* and *enjoyer* of value, can thus provide both a confidence and a humility for an ethic of risk. An ethic of risk is not merely a matter of 'taking chances' or 'calculating outcomes.' Under the guise of gratitude, complacency undergirds strategic risk-taking with careful recognition of gifts handled cautiously. Such an ethic accepts the risks of an emergent world subject to probabilities without presuming a moral deliberation that leaps out into the darkness to create values where none have existed before. An ethic of risk grounded in an ethic of gratitude becomes humble discernment combined with courageous action.

An Ethic of Love

It remains to add a final aspect to this analysis of moral deliberation. This has to do with the religious dimension of ethics. However, it is not a matter of adding a set of religious mandates or moral codes to the analysis delineated above. Rather than attend to any one religious tradition with its commandments and moral practices, my aim is to note, as Lonergan does, the phenomenology of religious experience. As Lonergan describes religious experience as an 'other worldly falling-in-love,' so I have titled this an 'ethic of love.'

A preliminary point is to establish the notion of unrestricted loving as phenomenologically foundational to the further question of how such unrestricted loving might affect one's valuing. Lonergan speaks of this as a 'religious conversion,' but such 'conversion' is not, primarily or initially, a confessional allegiance. Rather, as he puts it:

> Religious conversion is being grasped by ultimate concern. It is other-worldly falling in love. It is total and permanent self-surrender without conditions, qualifications, reservations. But it is such a surrender,

> not as an act, but as a dynamic state that is prior to and principle of subsequent acts. It is revealed in retrospect as an under-tow of existential consciousness, as a fated acceptance of a vocation to holiness, as perhaps an increasing simplicity and passivity in prayer. It is interpreted differently in the context of different religious traditions. For Christians it is God's love flooding our hearts through the Holy Spirit given to us.[34]

Religious love, as thus understood, may be conscious without being known – that is, persons may pursue meaning and value out of an under-tow of passion committed to ultimate meaning and value without ever naming this, or even attending to it. As Lonergan writes:

> Because the dynamic state is conscious without being known, it is an experience of mystery. Because it is being in love, the mystery is not merely attractive but fascinating; to it one belongs; by it one is possessed. Because it is an unmeasured love, the mystery evokes awe. Of itself, then, inasmuch as it is conscious without being known, the gift of God's love is an experience of the holy, of Rudolph Otto's *mysterium fascinans et tremendum.*[35]

At the same time, such love is of a piece with the impetus to understand, to understand correctly, and to know and promote value, all of which are inherent in human consciousness as given. Religious love is not something 'added on' to the natural quest for intelligibility, truth, and value. Rather, it situates these natural quests within a larger horizon that transcends the merely human or this-worldly. It often comes as the experienced fulfillment of such yearnings prior to any accomplishment that achieves answers through human effort. Such experienced fulfilment sets the impetus to understand, know truth, and know and create value in a new horizon. Again, here is Lonergan:

> Just as unrestricted questioning is our capacity for self-transcendence, so being in love in an unrestricted fashion is the proper fulfillment of that capacity. That fulfillment is not the product of our knowledge and choice. On the contrary, it dismantles and abolishes the horizon in which our knowing and choosing went on and it sets up a new horizon in which the love of God will transvalue our values and the eyes of that love will transform our knowing.[36]

How does such an experience of the fulfilment of my yearnings impinge on my moral deliberation? It does not, as I have already suggested, provide a ready-made set of moral prescriptions. Rather, it shifts the ground of moral deliberation from a quest to know and create good to a quest for an encounter with holiness.

Let me expand in relation to the previous discussions of gratitude and risk. For those who are religiously in love, an ethic of gratitude is not only recognition of concrete goods as given, but becomes an encounter with the Giver. Concrete goods are species of a Good beyond comprehension, experienced as mystery. Complacency is not merely enjoyment of actual value as currently found, but becomes participation in Being, a resting and quiescence that amounts to abiding in God's presence. Likewise, when an ethic of transcendent love grounds an ethic of gratitude, concern – the striving to instigate value – becomes obedience to God's will.[37]

In line with this, the consideration of probabilities inherent in the ethic of risk thus becomes a discernment of God's providence – an attempt to cooperate with whatever God is doing in a particular situation. To the degree that we shift probabilities, manipulating conditions of possibility, we do so with an eye to offsetting decline and promoting self-transcendence in ourselves and in others. We are free to become created co-creators with God rather than mistakenly taking on the role of Creator. Further, faith – the knowledge born of religious love[38] – grants us hope – the trust that our limited choices, and the ambiguity of merely creating conditions of possibility without sure knowledge of all the consequences, will nevertheless become part of a larger work of God's meaning and value. In other words, faith, hope, and charity allow us to embrace an ethic of risk, not out of self-interest or fear, but out of a truly self-transcendent confidence.

In sum, an ethic of love – religious love, an ultimately transcendent passion, an undertow of Holy fascination – moves both an ethic of risk and an ethic of gratitude out of the merely human sphere. Values that are discovered and seek to be created have as their criterion not, in the end, what is best for me as an individual or even for the human race as such, but the holiness that is a quality of Being itself. The larger narrative of 'salvation history,' and the mystery of progress, decline, and redemption as they unfold concretely from one context to the next, become the horizon of discernment.

A final note can be added. To the degree that this religious love sets one in a larger horizon of faith and hope, the 'risk' inherent in moral deliberation embraces not only calculation of probabilities but also the likelihood of failure. By that I mean to say that, under the purview of love, an ethic of risk can become an ethic of sacrifice. One can recognize that the 'conditions of possibility' by which new values can be created or dis-values reversed may require consequences that are antithetical to one's own well-being. This is the sort of choice Mama Logan made in her honest stand against the bigoted educators who visited her classroom. Such risk as sacrifice is at the heart of the passion narrative of the Christian gospel – not because sacrifice is, in itself, of value, but because sacrifice may be one of the conditions of possibility necessary for redemptive healing to take place.

Conclusion

By way of conclusion let us return to the rich yet devout man of Mark's gospel. I began the paper by citing this not only as a story about wealth as an obstacle to discipleship, but as a case study in the challenge to moral deliberation and radical decision. The rich man, in approaching Jesus, had a certain model of righteous behaviour in mind. His notion of moral deliberation included a set of clear prescriptions by which he would know if his moral pursuits had been successful or not. He lived, if you like, with an ethic of control. Jesus, while initially acknowledging this approach, pushed the potential disciple further. Jesus challenged him to an ethic of risk – sell what you have and give to the poor and come follow me. *This* mandate guaranteed no clear outcomes whatsoever, since 'come follow me' involved a whole series of 'conditions of possibilities' with unforeseen consequences.

The story illustrates as well, I believe, the ethic of gratitude. In the end, the man turns away in sorrow since he has many possessions. Still, the possessions themselves are recognized as good – indeed, to give them away to the poor indicates that there are concrete goods existent here. There is an insight into 'actual' value. The prospective value question has to do with the distribution of these goods, and it is this 'concern' that the man fails to pursue.

Finally, the issue at stake in the story is not riches and their distribution *per se* but the 'ultimate concern' – to use Tillich's term – that grounds the man's decision-making in the first place. Jesus not only tells the man to sell his riches and give to the poor but gives him a reason: 'for you will have treasure in heaven.' This is not a matter of calculus – that entrance into the kingdom of heaven is a 'controlled' consequence of his sacrifice. It is not a simple trade – treasures here versus treasures in heaven. The allusion to 'heaven' or the 'kingdom of God' is a challenge to a bigger and quite different horizon. Jesus is challenging the man to a religious love that will shift the ground on which he calculates the worth of sacrifice.

Indeed, this turns out to be the case, as the remainder of the verse indicates; having told the man, 'Go, sell whatever you have and give to the poor, for you will have treasure in heaven,' Jesus adds, 'and come, take up the cross, and follow me.' Gratitude for gifts given is meant to lead to generosity within the purview of religious love. But such generosity is only the beginning of an ethic of risk that will follow Jesus – not to 'success' but to the cross. Without gratitude, calculation of moral value becomes self-serving manipulation of probabilities. Without an otherworldly falling in love, gratitude can become self-congratulation. Without an encounter with the Holy, the sacrifice of an ethic of risk is not only counter-intuitive but an instance of insanity. Within an ethic of love, the law of the cross makes of risk a moment for redemptive healing, and gratitude becomes not obligation but overflowing compassion.

Notes

1 For example, note the rhetoric of 'choice' involved in reproductive issues. The 'pro-life' lobby stands over against the 'pro-choice' lobby with regard to the legality of abortion, as if the conception and birth of children were merely a matter of a simple choice between two options rather than a statistical relation between 'conditions of possibility' and emergent events. See my article 'Risk versus Control: Grounding a Feminist Ethic for the New Millennium,' in *Themes in Feminist Theology for a New Millennium (III)*, ed. Gaile M. Pohlhaus (Villanova, PA: Villanova Press, 2006), 1–22.

2 Portions of this section of the essay have been previously published as ibid. See also Crysdale, 'Playing God? Moral Agency in an Emergent World,' *Journal of the Society of Christian Ethics* 23 (2003), 398–426.

3 Sharon D. Welch, *A Feminist Ethic of Risk* (Minneapolis: Fortress Press, 1990). A second edition of this book has been published (Fortress Press, 2000). Citations here are from the first edition.

4 Ibid., 25.

5 Ibid., 23.

6 Ibid.

7 Ibid., 33.

8 Ibid., 43–7.

9 Ibid., 19.

10 Ibid., 20.

11 Ibid.

12 Ibid.

13 Mildred Taylor, *Roll of Thunder, Hear My Cry* (New York: Bantam Books, 1984), and *Let the Circle Be Unbroken* (New York: Bantam Books, 1983). These are discussed in Welch, *A Feminist Ethic of Risk*, chap. 4.

14 Paule Marshall, *The Chosen Place, The Timeless People* (New York: Random House, 1984), 175–81. See the discussion of this in Welch, 57–8.

15 For readers familiar with Bernard Lonergan's distinction between 'description' and 'explanation' I should make it clear that this is not the distinction I am making here. My point is to contrast values (one *should* make decisions according to an ethic of risk) – *prescriptive* propositions – with the facts of the matter (one indeed *does* live by an ethic of risk since such is the nature of

moral deliberation as it is concretely operative) – a *descriptive* position. Most of my analysis of moral deliberation falls within the purview of what Lonergan would call *explanatory* categories.

16 I am indebted here to the work of Bernard Lonergan, who developed an epistemology based on the self-appropriation of the knower, which he then expanded to incorporate a method for theology. The classic statement of his method is as follows: 'Thoroughly understand what it is to understand, and not only will you understand the broad lines of all there is to be understood but also you will possess a fixed base, an invariant pattern, opening upon all further developments of understanding.' *Insight: A Study of Human Understanding,* vol. 3 of *Collected Works of Bernard Lonergan,* ed. Frederick E. Crowe and Robert M. Doran (Toronto: University of Toronto Press, 1992), 22. For more on self-appropriation see *Insight,* 'Introduction,' and *Method in Theology* (Toronto: University of Toronto Press, 2003), chap. 1.

17 Lonergan would say that judgments of fact are complete when reflection reaches a 'virtually unconditioned.' That is to say, the conditions necessary for the judgment to be true are fulfilled. See *Insight,* 280–9.

18 On probable judgments, see *Insight,* 324ff. On the self-correcting process of learning, see ibid., 197–9.

19 Lonergan, *Insight,* 633.

20 Lonergan, *Method in Theology,* 38

21 Taylor, *Roll of Thunder,* 40–1, as quoted in Welch, *A Feminist Ethic of Risk,* 72–3.

22 This is why the ethic of risk is a *feminist* ethic of risk. To the degree that feminism takes as its task the unmasking of dominance, particularly male dominance, it relies on the experiences of women from the underside of history. To the degree that women have found themselves, proportionately, in social, economic, and political roles that deny them moral agency, they are more aware of the fact that moral choice includes ambiguity, vulnerability, and risk. It is not that women have some essentially different way of making moral decisions (by risk rather than control) or that vulnerability in and of itself is a norm to be sought after. Rather, women and many others who suffer from the powerlessness of social class, race, or sexual orientation are able to be more honest about the risk inherent in all moral choice.

23 Michael Vertin, 'Judgments of Value, for the Later Lonergan,' *Method: Journal of Lonergan Studies* 13 (1995), 221–48.

24 In discussing complacency and concern Vertin is dependent upon the work of Frederick E. Crowe, most notably three articles published in *Theological Studies* in 1959. See Crowe, 'Complacency and Concern in the Thought of St. Thomas,' *Theological Studies* 20 (1959), 1–39, 198–230, 343–59. These have been edited by Michael Vertin and published recently in book form: Frederick E. Crowe, *Three Thomist Studies,* ed. Michael Vertin (Chestnut Hill, MA: Lonergan Institute of Boston College, 2000). See also Michael Vertin, 'The Two Modes of Human Love: Thomas Aquinas as Interpreted by Frederick Crowe,' *Irish Theological Quarterly* 69 (2004), 31–45. Citations to Crowe's work will be to the 1959 *Theological Studies* articles.

25 Vertin, 'Judgments of Value,' 238–9.

26 Ibid., 239.
27 Giving clean water to individuals who need it in Sri Lanka is a concrete particular good. But note that such particular goods are dependent upon a good of order that will ensure that such goods are delivered. And the creation of goods of order oriented towards justice raises further questions. See Lonergan's discussion of the particular goods, the good of order, and terminal values in *Method in Theology*, 47–52.
28 Of course, even the question of means raises value questions as well as fact questions. Which agencies are more likely to deliver clean water in a speedy manner are questions of probability that are questions of fact but that in the very posing of them imply certain values. Speed and efficiency of delivery may be the values that take priority here. However, other considerations may come in, such as whether and how such agencies distribute aid – using coercion, force, bribery, internal theft – making the initial impetus to help require a certain savvy discernment about the best way to follow through on one's concern.
29 This is Frederick Crowe's ultimate purpose in his three articles in *Theological Studies*. In the third article in particular he contrasts 'complacency' as he has elucidated it from St Thomas with modern thinkers such as Anders Nygren on *agape* and Schopenhauer, Nietzsche, and Sartre on willing as striving. See Crowe, 'Complacency and Concern,' 353–82.
30 Ibid., 4–5.
31 Ibid., 19
32 Private conversation with Vertin in June 2004 and again in January 2005.
33 See Vertin, 'Judgments of Value,' 223–7.
34 Lonergan, *Method in Theology*, 240–1.
35 Ibid., 106. Lonergan (for whom citations of others' work is rare) here cites Rudolph Otto, Paul Tillich, and Karl Rahner.
36 Ibid.
37 Because the hailing of obedience as a duty and virtue above all others has been so detrimental in Christian history to the well-being of women, I am uneasy in highlighting it here as the term of an ethic of gratitude in love. But perhaps the point is precisely this – that obedience of love is of quite a different species than obedience forced as duty. I would appeal to the transposition of 'obedience, poverty, and chastity' as expounded by John Govan, SJ, in his retreats at Loyola House, Guelph, Ontario. Obedience is 'gentleness in the face of the present moment.' This is, in turn, founded on poverty as 'putting people before things, reverencing creation, and putting God before consolation.' Chastity is 'freedom from the addiction to feelings.'
38 See Lonergan, *Method in Theology*, 115–18, 123–4.

William F. Sullivan and John Heng

Moral Education for Health Care Professionals

There is a growing awareness of the relevance and importance of ethics in the education of health care professionals. These professionals work in highly technical settings and tend to focus on the diagnosis and treatment of the biological aspects of human diseases. The study of ethics by health care professionals has been introduced in recent years as one way to promote medicine as a human art in settings where medicine tends more and more to be regarded as only a technical science.

A principal challenge in the moral education of health care professionals is the development of a framework for decision-making by them and their patients that promotes responsible value judgments and decisions. This, in turn, presupposes an adequate understanding of what is involved in making value judgments and decisions. In this paper, we first show why a framework that emphasizes only an uncritical form of patient autonomy is inadequate. We then consider the pivotal role of feelings, or affective cognitions, in apprehending values. On this issue, we will highlight some important contributions made by Michael Vertin, in whose honour this paper has been prepared. Finally, we will propose that a proper account of the role of feelings in apprehending genuine values points to the significance of spirituality in health care and in health care ethics.

Trends in Health Care

Many patients and health care professionals today have little explicit awareness of all that is involved in being responsible moral agents. This neglect of moral subjectivity can be traced, we believe, to two trends. The first trend is the dominance of technology in modern health care. The second trend is the emergence of an understanding of patient-centred care that is based on a model of decision-making that emphasizes only a certain uncritical form of patient autonomy. Both trends have been amply described in the medical and bioethical literature.[1] Although they seem to be opposite tendencies, we suggest that they stem from the same philosophical root. Both assume an unbridgeable gap between what is subjective and what is objective when it comes to knowing values. Both lead to a sense of alienation that has been described by Bernard Lonergan as the 'refusal of self-transcendence.'[2]

On the one hand, the mechanization of health care has given rise to a prevalent view that medicine involves only the discovery of facts. Often it is asserted that a 'fact' in clinical medicine is objective because its truth does not seem to depend at all on the subjectivity or the situation of the person who is asserting the fact. On this view, facts are 'out there' in the world, as it were, for everyone to discover. In medicine, as it is commonly practised, then, diagnosis, prognosis, and decisions to treat may be linked uncritically to factual objectivism, where the relevant fact judgments are assumed to be discoveries that have little to do with knowing subjects and their contexts.

On the other hand, an understanding of patient-centred care that is based only on an uncritical form of patient autonomy, namely, accepting whatever a patient wants without scrutiny, may be linked to moral subjectivism.This is the philosophical position that value judgments depend on private, individual preferences alone, and can never fully be communicated to others, let alone be open to change through discussion with others. Absolute freedom from external restrictions is often regarded as the sole goal of this form of patient autonomy. On this view, the focus is on honouring a patient's 'choice,' the outcome of a patient's decision-making in health care, rather than on exploring the process and the grounds for those choices.

Both the sort of mechanization of health care that overlooks the human needs of patients and the promotion of an understanding of patient-centred care that is based only on an uncritical form of patient autonomy assume an unbridgeable gap between what is subjective and what is objective. Both tend to distinguish between an 'objective' world outside the patient, which is accessible to everyone, and a 'subjective' world that is the private realm of the patient. For the mechanist, the objective world is more important for clinical decision-making. The patient is looked upon as a set of measurements undertaken by means of machines, e.g., blood pressure readings, electrocardiograms, X-rays, PET and CT scans. Those who emphasize only an uncritical form of patient autonomy try to correct the mechanists' neglect of the patient's 'subjective' world. In decisions about treatment and care, therefore, they hold that a person's preferences and wishes are to be accepted as *prima facie* goods for that person, without need of further discussion or justification 'objectively.'

In our view, a fundamental need in ethics in health care today is to examine the adequacy of these notions of objectivity and subjectivity, and the bifurcation between a wholly objective world of facts and a wholly subjective realm of values. Any adequate sort of public ethics in health care would have to be based on a philosophical position that recognizes both the contribution of personal factors in coming to fact and value judgments, and also the possibility that such judgments can be judged to be reasonable and responsible by some broader standard than that of the person himself or herself.

Bernard Lonergan

Such a philosophical position can be found, we believe, in the writings of Bernard Lonergan. Lonergan has proposed that objectivity in any kind of knowing is the fruit of authentic subjectivity.[3] In terms of health care decision-making, a patient's or a health care worker's acts of knowing represent the subjective pole of decision-making, the *terminus a quo*. Objectivity is the goal that is intended by a patient's or health care worker's acts of knowing, namely, what is factually true and what is genuinely valuable or worthwhile to enjoy or pursue in a particular situation. This is the other pole of decision-making, the *terminus ad quem*. 'Authentic' subjectivity refers to how well the human knower, that is, the patient or the health care worker, performs the acts of knowing.

For Lonergan, all human knowing is animated by our spontaneous capacity to wonder and to question. Wonder and questioning already relate the inquirer to what is truly real and truly good. Questions head for answers about what exists and its value, and persons are generally not satisfied until they attain those answers.

Just as a watercolour painter or baseball player needs not only to have an innate capacity but also to master a set of skills and operations, so human knowers need both a spontaneous capacity to question and also a method of inquiry. For Lonergan, there are four distinct types of skills or operations of knowing, and they follow a sequence. The first set of operations of knowing can be labelled 'experiencing.' It is what we do when we attend to any data, whether derived from our senses or from our consciousness. A second set of operations of knowing can be called 'understanding,' whereby we try to make intelligent sense of the data we experience. The third set of operations of knowing can be described as 'judging facts.' Here we check our understanding and weigh the sufficiency of evidence for it. The fourth set of operations can be grouped under the terms 'judging values' or 'evaluating.' We consider the goodness or worthwhileness of what our judgment of fact brings to light and decide to pursue or to enjoy it in the given situation.

Some philosophers claim that our desire to know reality and goodness is in vain. They hold that we can only know *appearances* of reality and act *as if* we have knowledge of what is truly good. For Lonergan, on the other hand, a person is capable of attaining more than just knowledge of what is apparently real or good. As persons give free rein to their wonder and questioning over competing desires, as they exert effort to become careful inquirers through continuous self-correction, and as they cooperate with others who hold different pieces of the puzzle, persons improve their ability to affirm what is truly real and genuinely good.

Other philosophers, particularly postmodern thinkers like Michel Foucault, contend that what we assume to be true and good is inescapably a *social and historical construction* that is based on disguised power relationships. By contrast, Lonergan's proposal is that the method of inquiry sketched out above is common to all persons, and that, in an important sense, it is transhistorical and transcultural. Any attempt to refute or to modify Lonergan's account of knowing in a fundamental way would involve a person in performing precisely the same sequence of operations that Lonergan describes. While the content of human knowing, verified understandings and meanings, is open to revision and improvement, the structure of human knowing itself is not. Thus this structure alone, and its demands for attentiveness, intelligence, reasonableness, and responsibility, can serve as a universal standard against which particular efforts to judge facts and values can be gauged.

Moral Education

The rest of this paper will outline some implications of the considerations above for the moral education of health care professionals. We will propose that there is a need for health care professionals to develop a heightened awareness and knowledge of their capacity to discover the good in concrete situations or to make evaluations. Such moral education would include knowledge of what responsible evaluations entail, particularly the role that moral feelings play in grasping values. By moral feeling is meant those affective responses to values by means of which a person apprehends connaturally what is good.[4]

To encourage conscientious and responsible evaluations in their patients, a health care professional needs to have some personal awareness and knowledge of what such evaluations entail for himself or herself. In the past, and still to a large extent today, the focus of bioethics has been on teaching health care professionals how to apply a few general philosophical or theological principles, such as beneficence or respect for autonomy or justice, to particular cases. Understanding general principles that ought to guide moral reasoning is certainly important. We believe, however, that moral education should also enable health care professionals to be aware of, to understand, and to appropriate the process by which evaluations are made, including those that may give rise to general principles. What needs to be emphasized is the view, shared by Augustine and Aquinas, that moral truth or values are discovered or grasped through personal cognitive activity. Health care professionals also need to appreciate those optimal conditions under which one is likely to be successful in making judgments of fact and evaluations.

As part of this moral self-appropriation, health care professionals should be aware of how fact judgments are distinct from and related to value judgments or evaluations. Fact judgments answer the question, 'Is it so?' (or 'Is it possibly so?') Evaluations answer the further question, 'Is this fact good?' (or 'Is this possible fact good?') In this way, evaluations follow on from reasonable judgments of concrete fact and partially depend upon the latter for their validity. The ability to appreciate both the distinctness and the specific roles of fact judgments and evaluations in health care is crucial. This is particularly important in prudential reasoning about the goals and means of treatment in technically advanced or economically limited health care settings. Often these decisions are limited by health care professionals to judgments of fact about the medical effectiveness or futility of treatments alone, without considering the values and life goals held by patients and their loved ones.

Enabling health care professionals to appreciate the role of moral feelings, and to cultivate them, are further crucial components of moral education. Values are capable of moving persons from knowledge to decision and action in a way that mere facts do not. Moral feelings, as Bernard Lonergan put it, are the mass, momentum, drive, power of our knowing.[5] The creative arts and humanities elicit affect and can often help health care professionals to kindle and to be attentive to their desire for beauty, truth, goodness, and love. Through these avenues, topics that are important in health care, such as the value and meaning of human life, suffering, death, compassion, and justice can be raised, explored, and discussed. This is an approach to moral education of health care professionals taken, for example, by the U.S. President's Commission on Bioethics' recent anthology of literary works entitled *Being Human.*[6]

Michael Vertin has made several contributions to our understanding of the importance of feelings in moral education through his nuanced interpretation of Bernard Lonergan's remark that 'values are apprehended in feelings.'[7] Understood in the context of the later Lonergan's cognitional theory and division of feelings, Vertin clarifies the manner in which certain moral feelings enter into how one makes evaluations.

First, the relevant moral feelings are 'intentional responses' to objects. These feelings are to be distinguished from feelings that are non-intentional states or trends. Non-intentional feelings have causes or goals that are not, at least initially, also intentional objects. Examples of such feelings are irritability and hunger.[8]

Second, feelings that are intentional affective responses relate one to an object that is intended and represented. Such intentional objects can be satisfactions or values.

> Some intentional objects may evoke feelings of pleasure, gratification, and fulfillment that do not necessarily derive from anything more than one's encounter with those objects themselves, feelings that are not necessarily more than self-oriented, self-centered, self-immanent. Lonergan denominates such objects 'satisfactions.' Other intentional objects evoke feelings of delight, joy and fulfillment that derive from one's encounter – *via* such objects – with what stands beyond the objects themselves, feelings that are totality oriented, universe-centred, self-transcendent. Lonergan denominates such objects 'values'; and the self-transcending feelings they evoke, 'apprehensions of value.'[9]

Vertin refers to those self-transcending feelings that partly constitute one's cognitional access to particular values as 'deliberative insights.'[10] These deliberative insights are *affective* cognitional responses, which are distinct from *intellectual* cognitional responses, such as 'direct insights' that grasp intelligible unities, or 'reflective insights' that grasp facts.

Third, the term 'value' refers to some concrete actual or possible thing or property that one judges to be genuinely good, such as 'the ontic value of persons' and 'the qualitative value of beauty, understanding, truth, virtuous acts, noble deeds.'[11] In this sense, values are contents of knowing or categorial determinations that one arrives at by means of cognitive activities. Vertin argues that for Lonergan the fundamental meaning of 'value' is given in the transcendental notion of value. The distinction between the transcendental and the categorial corresponds to Lonergan's account of the principal division of sources of meaning.

> The principal division of sources [of meaning] is into transcendental and categorial. The transcendental are the very dynamism of intentional consciousness, a capacity that consciously and unceasingly

> both heads for and recognizes data, intelligibility, truth, reality, and value. The categorial are the determinations reached through experiencing, understanding, judging, deciding. The transcendental notions ground questioning. Answers develop categorial determinations.[12]

In the dynamic of questioning and answering, the transcendental notion of value guides the moral agent in the same anticipatory manner that wondering about being orients the knower. The transcendental notion of value provides the fundamental cognitive criterion by which we recognize values. The global objective of the transcendental notion of value goes beyond any achievement of knowing concrete values. Still, it is only because certain intentional objects partly fulfil this notion of value that these intentional objects are properly labelled 'values.'[13] In other words, prior to discovering concrete values, one's capacity to wonder about the good enables one to raise questions about some actual or possible values and provides a heuristic for what would count as an adequate answer to such a question.

Fourth, Lonergan's claim that 'values are apprehended in feelings' highlights the crucially affective dimension of deliberative insights. On Vertin's account, it is important to acknowledge that there is an affectivity that is a dimension of one's transcendental intentions of intelligibility and reality. For example, there is an affectivity that is a dimension of one's acts of insight, such as the relief and joy of an 'aha' experience of a direct insight by which one grasps a possible intelligibility in data and of a reflective insight by which one grasps some prospective fact. Nevertheless, it is the affective dimension of the transcendental notion of value that provides the fundamental criterion of one's deliberative insight in a way that does not occur with these other types of insights. One's moral being is affectively satisfied by a deliberative insight, the content of which is expressed in a judgment of value. This affective satisfaction signifies a harmony or congruence between the affective dimensions of one's transcendental intending of value and one's deliberative insight.[14]

Vertin further insists that, although deliberative insights are thoroughly affective, one ought not infer from this that they are not also thoroughly cognitive. Rather, the affectivity of one's deliberative insight provides the total cognitional grounds, justification, or foundation for one's subsequent value judgment. On this account, it is a radical flaw to disjoin cognition and affectivity at any time, but especially with regard to value judgments. This position challenges the position of philosophical subjectivism that, because value judgments involve affectivity, they are never more than subjective expressions about objects that one considers to be agreeable. It also challenges the view that, in order for value judgments to be genuine or epistemically objective, one must suppress or disregard one's affective responses. In the same way that knowing a fact involves a personal insight and judgment, in and through which the fact is known, so also knowing a value involves a further personal insight and judgment in and through which the value is known. Because of this, moral education needs to promote the affective conditions for morally authentic subjectivity that enables one to grasp values that are not just satisfactions.

As well, Vertin offers some helpful clarifications of how affectivity is also relevant to decisions that follow from value judgments. Distinct from the cognitional process by means of which one discovers actual or possible values are decisional issues that involve choosing to enjoy an actual value or to actualize a possible value. In the case of a value judgment through which one discovers an actual value, the decisional issue is to choose to enjoy it. If one discovers a possible value, the decisional issue is to choose to actualize it. Decisions to enjoy some actual value are given to one in the mode of decisional complacency (*complacentia*) or contentment. A decision to actualize some possible value is a choice that is given to one in the mode of decisional unrest or concern. Decisional complacency is distinct from the cognitive satisfaction of one's moral being that arises when one makes a genuine value judgment. Similarly, decisional concern is distinct from the cognitive dissatisfaction of one's moral being that arises when one has not yet achieved an adequate answer to a question of value.

Much of health care involves executing decisions to actualize possible values, such as restoring health, which occur in the mode of decisional concern. If a health care professional's life is predominantly one of decisional concern, this can lead to excessive anxiety, stress, and care-worn weariness. Many health care professionals acknowledge such stress, which can become a health issue for themselves and their patients. In addition, such excessive decisional concern can undermine the conditions for careful deliberation and decision-making.

The analysis presented here suggests that a decision made in the mode of complacency is not a decision to do nothing. Rather, it is a choice to enjoy actual values in the mode of decisional contentment. For health care professionals and patients whose entire horizon may be dominated by a preoccupation with health problems and efforts to overcome them, there can be a failure also to advert to actual present values. This health care context may eclipse any religious notion of an ultimate good that would ground one in a mode of decisional contentment. Conversely, a basic orientation to an ultimate good provides an antidote to an excessive level of anxiety and concern, even in a health care context where one is preoccupied by many particular concerns. This is a health care issue with cultural and spiritual dimensions. The question of basic orientations leads to a consideration of the role of spirituality in the moral education of health care professionals.

Spirituality

Health care professionals need to understand something about the contexts of decisional contentment and concern within which they and their patients make moral decisions. What is the ultimate end of health care? What gives a person's health and life, including suffering and death, its deepest meaning? Such questions are inherently spiritual. Even if not all health care professionals or patients are religious, almost everyone asks spiritual questions of themselves and others at some point. This often occurs at a time of personal crisis, such as with the loss of health or personal capacities or relationships, or when one is near the end of one's life.

In discussing decisions about treatment and care with patients, health care professionals usually are comfortable with providing information about the merits, limitations, and risks of various treatment options. They generally tend to overlook, reject, or feel unprepared to discuss spiritual questions that may, to a large extent, shape patients' perceptions and decisions about treatment and care and be the affective grounds for their decisions. Attending to ultimate questions raised by spiritual issues in themselves and in their patients is an important goal in the moral education of health care professionals. They need to know what to listen for, particularly when their patients raise spiritual questions but do not use religious language. They also need to know how to connect themselves and their patients to appropriate spiritual resources. This is an integral part of enabling responsible moral decision-making.

A further consideration is the relevance of the church's long tradition of spiritual discernment and direction for moral decision-making. Health care professionals and patients who understand the pivotal role of moral feeling in judgments of value in health care may find, for example, the testing of feelings through spiritual discernment and direction illuminating. We need to find a way to incorporate the insights of this tradition of spiritual discernment and direction into the teaching of bioethics to health care professionals.

Finally, the term 'education' in English and the Romance languages is derived from the Latin words *ex* and *ducere* – to lead outside or to lead beyond. Beyond what? Beyond the horizon of our current, limited interests, knowledge, and projects. Our horizons can expand and they can also undergo fundamental shifts in orientation. When the latter happens, we undergo a conversion. Health care professionals should be attentive to the need for moral conversion and development in themselves and their patients. Moral conversion here refers specifically to a stable orientation to genuine value. Moral education for health care professionals, then, ought to mean more than learning to apply general principles to particular cases. It should also address different basic orientations to life, including one's own orientation.

The challenge of modern health care is the eclipse of personhood in both health care professionals and patients. This loss of a sense of personhood has its philosophical roots in an uncritical acceptance of a truncated understanding of objective and subjective, and in the assumption that there is an unbridgeable dichotomy between objectivity and subjectivity. What we have tried to outline are some preliminary ideas on moral education for health care professionals that might help to integrate the subjective and objective elements of health care decision-making. In recognizing themselves as persons, particularly as persons that relate to the transcendental notions of being and value, health care professionals are better able to attend to their patients as persons. This means understanding the human ends to which medical technology should be subject, and encouraging reflection, dialogue, and self-transcendence in decisions having to do with the values and life goals of their patients in the context of their concrete circumstances.

Notes

We wish to thank Sr Gill Goulding, IBVM, for her helpful insights on the third part of this paper, and Danny Monsour for his editorial suggestions.

1 On the mechanization of health care, see Henk ten Have, 'Medicine and the Cartesian Image of Man,' *Theoretical Medicine* 8 (1987), 235–46; and R. Lewinsohn, 'Medical Theories, Science, and the Practice of Medicine,' *Social Sci ences and Medicine* 46 (1998), 1261–70. On patient autonomy, see Anne Donchin, 'Understanding Autonomy Relationally: Toward a Reconfiguration of Bioethical Principles,' *Journal of Medical Philosophy* 26 (2001), 365–86.

2 Bernard Lonergan, *Method in Theology* (Toronto: University of Toronto Press, 2003), 55.

3 Ibid., 265, 292.

4 We are drawing on Jacques Maritain's analysis of moral experience in *The Range of Reason* (New York: Charles Scribner's Sons, 1952), 26–9, and Bernard Lonergan's account of feelings in *Method in Theology*, 30–41.

5 Lonergan, *Method in Theology*, 30.

6 *Being Human: Core Readings in the Humanities*, ed. Leon Kass (New York: W.W. Norton, 2004).

7 Lonergan, *Method in Theology*, 37.

8 Michael Vertin, 'Judgments of Value, for the Later Lonergan,' *Method: Journal of Lonergan Studies* 13 (1995), 231.
9 Ibid., 232.
10 Ibid., 228, 235.
11 Lonergan, *Method in Theology*, 31.
12 Ibid., 73–4.
13 Vertin, 'Judgments of Value,' 234.
14 Ibid., 234, n. 42.

Kenneth R. Melchin

Democracy, Sublation, and the Scale of Values

I am delighted to have been invited to contribute to this volume in honour of Michael Vertin.[1] Michael's work in ethics is well known among Lonergan scholars and has been influential in shaping a number of important conversations on topics both substantive and methodological. His writing invariably reflects his person: it is humble yet powerful, faithful yet innovative, meticulous yet wide sweeping in its import, and challenging while loving. Michael has been a friend and colleague for many years, and for this I am grateful.

This essay forms part of a wider set of explorations that have held my attention for nearly a decade, explorations into the challenges to ethics posed by our experiences and ideas of democracy.[2] My concern here is with the way our commitment to democratic pluralism seems to require the relativization of values. Democracy requires pluralism, and this means we must accept the conflicting values that are held by diverse cultural groups in society. As Charles Taylor points out, this democratic initiative has been animated by a high ethical commitment to authenticity, justice, and the welfare of all.[3] Yet it has also resulted in a capitulation to ethical relativism and, in the limit, to an evacuation of the meaning of ethical language itself. If pluralism requires recognizing the equal status of all values, then the content of each value can only fade in public significance. Values are pronounced private, but what is left for the public realm are freedom, equality, and toleration, values that have found themselves at the top of a hierarchy that is not supposed to exist. Given the way values are understood, as private and culturally, religiously, or ideologically relative, we are left with few resources for working together through the hosts of concrete value conflicts that threaten the foundations of public society itself.

It has seemed to me that Lonergan's insights into an integral scale of values could help sort out some of these difficulties.[4] I have taken this occasion to examine some of the tools that Lonergan developed for thinking in a historically conscious way about complex relations among values. In *Method in Theology*, chapter 2, he distinguishes among five types of values – vital, social, cultural, personal, and religious – and argues that they can be ordered in an ascending scale from 'vital' through to 'religious.' I have done some thinking about this scale in relation to his threefold analysis of the structure of the human good[5] and his references to 'sublation.'[6] My focus is on how the idea of sublation helps us understand how we can ground a hierarchical relation among values while preserving the achievements of modern democracy.

In this exploration, I have asked whether Lonergan's philosophy provides grounds for differentiating among different kinds of values, not simply on the basis of their cultural origins[7] or their fields of operation,[8] but according to more basic, generalizable criteria rooted in the structure of consciousness. We know that, in chapters 7 and 18 of *Insight* and in chapter 2 of *Method in Theology*, he sets out an analysis of three levels of the human good that correspond to the three levels of consciousness: experience, understanding, and judgment. But this is an analysis of the inner structure of value. Here, value is the term or goal that is achieved when we move through the operations of consciousness, from the experience of desires and needs for particular goods, through an understanding of the goods of order that condition their achievement, to the judgments of value that affirm our understandings to be truly good. I wanted to know whether the levels of consciousness also provided a basis for differentiating among types of values. What I found was that they do. Moreover, when we examine this relation to the operations of consciousness with a focus on 'sublation,' we discover that kinds of values can be ordered hierarchically but, interestingly, according to a novel way of understanding 'hierarchy.'

The import of this discovery for understanding the relation between ethics and democracy is, I suggest, quite profound. The challenge of democracy in our age is to reconcile our commitment to freedom, diversity, and difference with an ethical framework for affirming the priority of universal values such as those articulated in charters of rights.[9] If values could be differentiated and relations among values affirmed, not on the basis of culture or spheres of practice, but on the basis of something common to all persons, then judgments of value need not be personally or culturally discriminatory. I suggest that this is what Lonergan's analysis of the scale of values provides. Moreover, I have found that there are rich and powerful insights into the meaning of freedom and pluralism and the role of religion in democracy that flow from this analysis.

Michael Vertin's 2003 essay 'Acceptance and Actualization: The Two Phases of My Human Living'[10] has been helpful to me in this exploration. In particular, I have been inspired by his insights into the distinction between the 'acceptive' and 'actualized' phases of ethical living. His argument is that, prior to Lonergan's differentiation of the two phases of the functional specialties,[11] there is a more basic differentiation between two phases in responsible human living. In the first phase, transcendental method knows and affirms an already actual good, while in the second phase, knowing and willing are essentially innovative; they bring into being a good that, to this point, has been only a possibility. It is this insight into the innovative dimension of ethical life in the second phase that has helped shape my thinking about the relations among the levels in the scale of values.

My hunch was that there was much to be learned about the relations among levels in the scale of values from the 'below-upwards' and 'above-downwards' phases of the functional specialties. But I had always thought about the first phase as innovative and the second as what we might call 'traditional.' Michael's analysis seems to suggest this is reversed: it is the second phase that is essentially innovative. It was in puzzling through this apparent contradiction that I hit on some important insights into how the way of tradition, as understood properly in terms of the second phase of the functional specialties, is essentially and ineluctably innovative. Fidelity to foundations and doctrines, when they are correct, sets the conditions for a terrific acceleration in the capacities for innovation. This can be seen clearly in the relation between science and technology when new scientific judgments of truth pave the way for a proliferation of insights into technological possibilities. But fidelity to foundations and doctrines also introduces an ethical demand for innovation, for living differently.[12] It is this obligation and the directed capacity for ethical innovation that has helped me to begin thinking in a new way about the multiple accountabilities among the levels in the scale of values. Needless to say, I have taken these insights beyond the range of questions explicitly addressed by Michael Vertin in his essay, and for this I assume complete responsibility. Still, even if colleagues find difficulties with my arguments, I remain convinced that there are riches to be mined from Michael Vertin's work in this area.

Before proceeding, I would like to offer a comment on the topic of this volume, *The Importance of Insight.* It is not an accident that the subtitle of Michael's essay 'Acceptance and Actualization' is cast in personal terms. Throughout his work, Michael Vertin has forever turned to personal observations on his own operations of meaning for the evidential base for his arguments and analyses. This, I would say, is what is most important about 'insight' in Lonergan's work. There is an awesome integrity to a method that resolutely demands of scholars a consistency between the content of their arguments and the personal operations of meaning at work in their discovery and formulation. Achieving this consistency requires that we take up the challenge of observing and understanding ourselves in our operations of meaning in a thoroughgoing way, and this is not easy. This integrity is evident throughout Michael's work, and I have tried as best I can to follow his lead in the explorations that follow.

My strategy, then, is to work through an understanding of the five levels of the scale of values, tracing the relations to the levels of consciousness, illustrating how sublation offers a novel way of understanding the hierarchical relations among the levels, and drawing out implications for understanding the challenges of ethics and democracy.

Vital Values

I begin with the vital values, and I examine what is involved when we desire or need things that are vital to our personal lives. We pursue such things as food, water, clothing, shelter, health, and security, and generally we presume such pursuits to be ethically valid. Take hunger, for example. There is a profound sense in which hunger is a principle of motion. It shifts us out of a state of rest and sets us in motion in pursuit of food. When we eat, our hunger is satisfied and we can return to a state of rest. Yet for humans, satisfying hunger generally is not mindless or merely visceral; it is mediated by meaning. So we discover trees that bear edible fruit or animals that are easier than others to hunt. We learn to shop and cook for ourselves. We learn the difference between food that makes us sick and nutritious food that sustains health. What we glean from these discoveries is that future instances of hunger can be satisfied in similar ways, and our insights become the basis for decisions and actions. What this illustrates is that ethics is fundamentally about human motion and how acts of meaning inform and constitute this motion. What we know when we know that something is good is the vector or direction of progress that is discovered and affirmed in this motion. This is what it means to say that securing food is a value rather than merely a matter of animal instinct.

Now, on the most basic level of vital values, the central criteria for this vector are supplied by bodily experiences normally felt as desires and needs. Hunger unsettles us and mobilizes us to act, it provides the question that guides our quest, and it supplies us with the central conditions our action must fulfil if it is to satisfy. The question the value must answer is a question rooted in this physiology. But the desire is not the whole story; it is only a beginning. We need an insight and a judgment to grasp and affirm a scheme of action that will answer this question, and we need a decision to actuate the content of the insight as the form of the motion. These can happen in an instant, with little explicit reflection, yet they need to happen, otherwise nothing meaningful happens. When we eat food that makes us sick or when have to change our regime to maintain health, we discover how inadequate and misleading our desires can be.

What is interesting is that while the experience and satisfaction of hunger supply a central component of this vector of progress, they are not themselves the foundation of value. This is because the form or principle of the action is not provided simply by the experience and fulfilment of desire or need; it is achieved only by performing the complete set of operations of meaning. Here, I suggest, we see a first example of what Lonergan means by 'sublation.' Through our operations of understanding, judgment, and decision we 'sublate' our experience of hunger. We take it up and establish it on a new basis, as a question and criterion for meaningful action. We include it, preserve it, and allow it to guide our operations of meaning. But we also carry it forward to a fuller realization in a course of action that chooses from available alternatives and is integrated into a wider pattern of living.

Still, vital values do answer questions about desires and needs, and they establish bodily experiences as their central conditions or criteria. Through the operations of meaning we convert needs, desires, and satisfactions into acts of meaning, but guiding our insights and deliberations are the experiences of a vital, healthy life that play a central role in differentiating among courses of action. Sublation grasps how we take up and preserve the central import of these experiences as we set them within the wider context provided by higher operations of meaning.

One final point: Understanding sublation can help clarify some popular misconceptions about vital values. Often we speak about acquiring food as valuable *because* it satisfies hunger. What is invoked here is a form of the teleological argument, and the image created is that satisfaction is the end and acquiring food the means. Pursuing vital values is judged good because it is thought to be a means for attaining the satisfaction. This gives the appearance of endowing the satisfaction of desire with an intrinsic value that is transferred, secondarily, to the means.[13]

I would say this is a mistake, and understanding sublation helps clarify the misconception. It is not the satisfaction of desire that is the end or *telos*; rather, the end is achieved only in the performance of all the acts of meaning that inform and bring about the particular good.[14] The physiological experiences direct the quest. However, these experiences are taken up and transformed by operations of understanding, judgment, and decision, and together these operations of meaning have their own inner *telos*. I suggest that rather than imagining a teleology moving from desire to satisfaction that is based on a means-ends relationship among *contents of meaning*, we would do better to think of a teleology based on the relation of sublation among *operations of meaning*. We move from experience through insight and judgment to decision, with the bodily experiences furnishing the question and criteria for the later operations. The *telos* or end is not an inherent quality of the final result, nor is it merely the criterion of desire and its satisfaction. Rather, it is the direction of progress that unfolds as the self-transcending dynamism in and among the operations of meaning themselves. The *telos* is sublation.

Social Values

When we examine more closely the ways we normally satisfy our desires and needs in daily life, something new comes to light that provides a second instance of sublation and a basis for a hierarchical differentiation between social and vital levels of values. But understanding sublation also provides a novel and distinctive meaning for the term 'hierarchy,' an understanding that recognizes a more complex form of accountability among the levels in the scale of values. What we discover is that vital values normally are achieved through goods of order in which groups of people come together in patterns of cooperation to achieve together what none could achieve on their own.[15] The social pattern has an inner logic or intelligibility that often emerges historically without deliberate planning, yet eventually it needs to be understood to assure that the roles, contributions, and duties of all fit together into a coherently functioning whole.

What is striking about the patterns of cooperation of a family, a business, an economy, or a police force is that often they give rise to obligations that are not themselves objects of personal desire. Quite the opposite: the routines of a family assign unpleasant duties to children, workplaces entail burdensome obligations, economies require painful sacrifices, and policing imposes dangers and difficulties that we normally avoid. the meaning and value of these obligations lies in their contribution to an overall pat tern that coordinates the diverse contributions of all into a functioning whole. The pattern is not in the first instance an object of desire or need; it is an intelligible order that must be understood.

Social values assure the recurrent achievement of hosts of vital values. Yet the way they do so has a curious structure to it, and here we see a second instance of sublation that illuminates Lonergan's novel way of understanding value and the relations among values. As with vital values, the foundation of social value is not in the satisfaction of desire, but in the performance of the operations of meaning that culminate in an intelligent, reasonable, and responsible decision to act. With social values, however,

these operations are doubly removed from the experience of needs and desires. With social values, the central question is not about desires and needs; it is about the achievement and maintenance of an ordered pattern of roles and tasks that serves a common purpose. It is the intelligibility and coherence of this functioning whole that assures the common purpose, and this is the social concern. With social values, the principle question and criterion guiding our operations of meaning shifts from an object of desire or need to an object of understanding. And just as understanding sublates experience, so, too, do values rooted in a social intelligibility sublate the vital values that achieve personal satisfactions.

This relationship of sublation has five interesting features. First, social values are not reducible to vital desires and needs. They may appear to be simply means for the satisfaction of desires but, again, this is not correct. They are a different kind of value and they answer questions, not about desires and needs, but about intelligibly functioning orders. They take up the vital values and link them inextricably into new kinds of patterns, and for these patterns to function requires citizens to cultivate new skills, habits, and virtues that are irreducibly social. We can cultivate feelings for these social values, but these would be feelings of a completely different kind: they would be intentional responses to the social values.[16]

Second, social values are higher than vital values, and when conflicts arise the higher social values must prevail. Social values like those operative on a fishing boat, or a farm, or in a bank or housing construction crew ensure the routines that deliver food and housing to a society. Employees, suppliers, and clients have legitimate desires and needs for food and housing. But when opportunities arise for satisfying these needs through theft, betrayal, abuse of privilege, lying, cheating, laziness, or irresponsibility – strategies that violate the social values – it is the higher obligations to the societal organizations that must command their judgments and decisions.

Third, social values do not negate or override vital values, they affirm them. When crew members on a fishing boat live out their responsibilities and obligations, they secure and affirm the value of providing fish to feed the community. Even when conflicts arise that require them to put these obligations ahead of their own desires for food, their decisions and actions implicitly affirm the value of feeding hungry people. The difference is that with social values, what is affirmed is not simply the satisfaction of needs or desires for oneself, but the satisfaction of the needs and desires of all.

Fourth, while social values are higher, they are accountable to vital values. They must condition their sustained provision for all, and this is a principal measure of the success of the social order. The statistics associated with the wide-scale provision of vital values for all members of human society provide data for the ongoing evaluation of social and economic life. When society fails in this provision, then vital values can provide criteria for a critique of social values and a call for their transformation.

Fifth, social values must themselves submit to the higher values of culture. Thus, while they have their own internal requirements and their own tendencies to resist change, their excellence is achieved by being taken up into the higher project of culture. Here is where they are coordinated in relation to the other dimensions of human life, and here is where they are critically evaluated in terms of their longer-reaching impacts on culture and civilization.

Sublation involves all five of these relations of accountability among the levels in the scale of values. I suggest that it is in personally examining the interrelations among the levels of our own conscious operations that we get the clearest insights into these distinctive features of sublation.

Cultural Values

The significance of cultural values comes to light when we reflect on the patterns of cooperation of social life and ask, not simply about their productivity or efficiency, but about how they fit together with each other to make up an entire life for a society or civilization. Here we do not simply understand and evaluate social schemes individually; we evaluate and judge them in relation to the wider ecologies that are created by their interactions with each other and with the ecologies of biology and zoology. Here the principal question guiding our operations of meaning is not simply the intelligibility of social orders, but their contributions to the wider project of human living. Here the foundation of value moves to the third level of intentional consciousness, the level of judgment.

At this point, I suggest that an interesting differentiation arises from Lonergan's insights into historical consciousness. If we understand culture *classically*, as a relatively static completed achievement, we will ask about its component parts and its internal relations. Here, to determine cultural values we look for things like coherence and maintenance and the ordered relations of parts to a defined whole. However, if we understand cultures *historically*, as dynamic entities that begin, develop, decline, and are transformed in the interaction with other cultures, then our notions of cultural value are open-ended. They focus, not on end results, but on directions of change, on progress and decline. For Lonergan, it was clearly the latter that informed his work in *Method in Theology*. To speak of cultural values is to speak of values that have their foundation on the third level of consciousness, the level that informs the functional specialties of history and doctrines, the level of reflection and judgment. Here the principal issues are the questions of progress and decline, what is going forwards in the dynamic unfolding of history.

Again, the considerations of culture put values on a new footing, one that sublates vital and social values. And, again, we can see in the distinctive features of the idea of sublation a way of understanding and relating values that is based not in the contents but in the operations of meaning. Higher values are higher, not because they contain some higher intrinsic quality of goodness, nor because they are a means to some end that contains some such intrinsic goodness, nor because they aggregate clusters of individual desires into some majority consensus. Rather, values are higher because they represent later operations in a methodologically differentiated set of operations of meaning that, together, yield more comprehensive actuations of the self-transcending dynamism of human consciousness.

What is interesting in this discussion is the way the ethical capacities and obligations for *innovation* arise when social values submit to the critique and guidance of cultural values. For example, when social institutions fail to provide vital values amply and diversely for all, artists, poets, journalists, philosophers, and social activists rise up to proclaim cultural values like political equity and economic justice. On their own, these cultural values do not solve the problems of equity and justice, nor do they provide detailed programs for the reorganization of social schemes. What they do is provide guidance or direction for innovative thinking on the social and vital levels of value. This innovative thinking can be enhanced significantly by cultural achievements like good human science, good literature, good philosophy, good education, and charters of rights. But incorporating these achievements into the fabric of social life requires a massive project of transforming our day-to-day social routines and the values that sustain them. This work of innovation cannot be done by the artists, philosophers, or poets; it can only be done by the women and men involved in the routines of social life who have appropriated the cultural values and made them their own.[17]

Personal and Religious Values and the Challenges of Democratic Pluralism

With personal and religious values, the journey through the levels of consciousness comes to completion. The full turn to interiority that is realized on the fourth level of consciousness regards not simply the patterns of progress and decline in history, but persons as operators of human meaning whose authenticity and inauthenticity are the grounds for progress and decline. The criteria governing our deliberations here ask what we are making of ourselves in our decisions, and they call for actions that cultivate virtuous and redemptive patterns of living and relating in culture. The bases for decisions are the conversions, the transformations in human persons from inauthenticity to authenticity that give rise to sustained flows of decisions that promote progress and reverse decline.

There is a lot more that needs to be said about personal and religious values. In the space remaining, however, I would like to suggest a number of ways in which this analysis can help address some of the concerns around democracy and values relativism that prompted this exploration.

(1) Political theorists like John Rawls have sought to articulate an understanding of democracy that places the liberty, equality, dignity, and rights of persons at the centre of political life. Similarly, in international politics we have seen a growing commitment to values and institutions that uphold and protect the rights of persons, even when these persons are threatened within their own national boundaries. I suggest we can discern in these patterns of ideas and events the makings of a transformation in consciousness from a global society based on cultural values to one based on personal values. Central to the projects of the political philosophers is the commitment to cultural diversity and to the dignity and rights of persons who, alone, can choose for themselves how they will make their way through this diversity. In world politics, we have pronounced the sovereignty of nations to be qualified and circumscribed by the global requirement that, regardless of culture, basic standards of human personhood must be upheld. I think we are seeing the standards of international political consciousness shift from values rooted in cultures to values rooted in trans-cultural features of human personhood.

The challenge in this transformation, however, is understanding the relations between the values of human personhood and the other types of values that we live out diversely in social and cultural life. In most of the literature on democracy, we see these diverse values understood in relation to their cultures of origin. Consequently, the problem arises of how to reconcile the commitment to cultural difference with our universal obligations to the dignity and rights of persons. Liberal theorists like Rawls handle this problem by drawing a clear line between a small core of values that must elicit the agreement of all and those culturally diverse values on which we can neither require nor expect agreement. Critics have observed, I think correctly, that this dividing line fails to recognize the public import of values (pronounced merely cultural or private) that fall outside of the inner circle.

Lonergan's analysis offers a different way of approaching this question. The scale of values differentiates values, not according to their culture of origin, but in terms of how they relate and function within the scheme of operations of human deliberation and decision-making. This framework provides grounds for a discussion of the *public* relevance of the entire spectrum of values, and it can establish grounds for diversity in content while holding values accountable for their functional or operational contributions to the diverse projects of social and cultural life. More than this, Lonergan's analysis provides grounds for understanding how these diverse kinds of values interrelate and how they must serve each other. This, I suggest, is an important contribution to this global project of political transformation.

(2) In his *Political Liberalism*,[18] John Rawls understands democracy to be about freedom and pluralism because diverse cultures are expected to hold irreconcilably conflicting values. Rights and freedoms become the central public values because they provide grounds for cultural diversity and fair procedures for dealing with the conflicts that arise from this diversity. I suggest that this image is based on a classical understanding of cultures and cultural values. If we follow Lonergan in understanding cultures historically rather than classically, we find that cultures are not autonomous, self-contained entities; rather, they are dynamically changing entities that develop and decline, not simply in their internal relations but in their relations with each other. Here, the relevant cultural values of our age can be understood as the patterns of progress and decline that we find in the climate of globalization that has been created in the latter twentieth and the early twenty-first centuries.

The point here, I suggest, is that we are already doing what Rawls pronounces impossible: we are discerning and slowly forging agreements on transcultural values.[19] By shifting focus from the content of values to their structure and function in relation to operations of meaning, we can understand how this is possible, where it is happening, and why it makes sense. Lonergan offers tools for shifting from a descriptive to an explanatory understanding of cultural values and for differentiating between a classical and historically conscious understanding of cultures. These tools, I suggest, offer significant resources for advancing the project that was so central to Rawls's life and work.

(3) Central to recent discussions of democracy are arguments about the meaning and role of freedom, pluralism, and religion. In large measure, *freedom* tends to be conceived as the absence of constraint or the ability to choose without interference from others. Lonergan's analysis offers an alternative way of thinking that admits the role of vital, social, cultural, personal, and religious values in establishing the conditions for freedom: Freedom is the human capacity to constitute one's actions and oneself through operations of meaning.[20] These operations have a dynamic self-transcending structure that moves us through the scales of values and establishes its own immanent dynamic as the norm for differentiating and relating suc-

cessively higher levels of values. Similarly, *pluralism* is not simply the capitulation to relativism in the face of culturally diverse values, classically conceived. It is the ethical obligation to collective learning[21] that is rooted in the structure of consciousness that carries us both upwards and downwards through all the levels of value, the lower being taken up in the higher and the higher providing direction for the concrete realizations achieved in the lower. Finally, *religion* is not simply a cultural value to be relegated to the status of private opinion. It is a basic orientation of consciousness itself that establishes the highest level of value as the open-ended horizon of ultimacy and love that all other levels of value must serve. Democracy now must facilitate the exploration and cultivation of religious values on a global scale.

Conclusion

There is a lot more to be said here. My hope is that some of these ideas from Lonergan eventually find their way into significant public debates on democracy. John Haughey has written a marvellous essay on the foundations of human rights. He grounds rights in the structure of consciousness and places Lonergan's personal values at the centre of international politics for our age. This is a wonderful beginning to a very large project. My hope is that I have offered some insights on sublation and the scale of values that can help advance this work. Central to this project, however, is the method of self-appropriation itself. If our arguments are to carry weight in a fully public discourse, their evidential base cannot be a corpus of texts from a Catholic philosopher. It must be a set of activities accessible to all persons, the activities of reflecting on their own operations of meaning. The method of self-discovery is what is most important about insight. For this reason, I am pleased to be able to contribute to this volume dedicated to the importance of insight. I am doubly pleased that it is dedicated to my friend and colleague, Michael Vertin.

Notes

1 An earlier version of this paper was presented at the Second International Lonergan Workshop, Toronto, 1–7 August 2004.

2 See, e.g., Kenneth R. Melchin, 'Reaching Toward Democracy: Theology and Theory When Talk Turns to War,' *The Catholic Theological Society of America, Proceedings* 58 (2003), 41–59; 'What Is a Democracy Anyway? A Discussion between Lonergan and Rawls,' *Lonergan Workshop* 15 (1999), 99–116.

3 Charles Taylor, *The Malaise of Modernity* (Toronto: Anansi Press, 1991).

4 See Bernard Lonergan, *Method in Theology* (Toronto: University of Toronto Press, 2003), 30–2, 39, 50, 52, 111–12, 115, 240; 'Natural Right and Historical Mindedness,' in *A Third Collection*, ed. Frederick E. Crowe (New York: Paulist Press, 1985), 173. The most extensive analysis of Lonergan's scale of values is in Robert Doran, *Theology and the Dialectics of History* (Toronto: University of Toronto Press, 1989), 88–90, 93–107, 108–14, 148–9, 195–8, 209–10, 421–4, 476–8, 522–4. For other good discussions of the scale of values, see Elizabeth Morelli, *Anxiety: A Study of the Affectivity of Moral Consciousness* (Lanham, MD: University Press of America, 1985), 75–9; and Mark Doorley, *The Place of the Heart in Lonergan's Ethics* (Lanham, MD: University Press of America, 1996), 64–72. I am grateful to my friend and colleague Michael Stebbins for recommending the worth of trying to understand Lonergan's scale of values.

5 See Lonergan, *Method in Theology*, 47–52; and *Insight: A Study of Human Understanding*, vol. 3 of *Collected Works of Bernard Lonergan*, ed. Frederick E. Crowe and Robert M. Doran (Toronto: University of Toronto Press, 1992), 237–9, 619–21.

6 For Lonergan's discussions of 'sublation,' see *Method in Theology*, 241–3, 316–17, 340.

7 The analysis of values in relation to their cultures of origin is quite common. See, e.g., Seyla Benhabib, ed., *Democracy and Difference: Contesting the Boundaries of the Political* (Princeton: Princeton University Press, 1996); James Bohman and William Rehg, eds., *Deliberative Democracy: Essays on Reason and Politics* (Cambridge, MA: MIT Press, 1997); Charles Taylor et al., *Multiculturalism: Examining the Politics of Recognition*, ed. Amy Gutmann (Princeton: Princeton University Press, 1994); John Rawls, *Political Liberalism* (New York: Columbia University Press, 1996).

8 For a good analysis of the value of 'justice' in terms of its spheres of operation, see Michael Walzer, *Spheres of Justice: A Defence of Pluralism and Equality* (New York: Basic Books, 1983).

9 For an excellent analysis of human rights in terms of Lonergan's structure of consciousness, see John Haughey, 'Responsibility for Human Rights: Contributions from Bernard Lonergan,' *Theological Studies* 63 (2002), 764–85.

10 Michael Vertin, 'Acceptance and Actualization: The Two Phases of My Human Living,' *Method: Journal of Lonergan Studies* 21 (2003), 67–86.

11 Michael clarifies that this priority is methodical, not necessarily chronological; ibid., 68, n. 6.

12 This ethical demand for innovation helps to understand a great deal of work in fields like political theology, liberation theology, feminist ethics, and Catholic social thought.

13 This misunderstanding seems to be the basis for the criticism that John Finnis raises against Lonergan's ethics. See his *Fundamentals of Ethics* (Washington: Georgetown University Press, 1983), 42–50.

14 This insight could have been one of the reasons why Lonergan changed his language, between *Insight* and *Method in Theology*, in speaking about the first level of the good. In *Insight* he speaks of the first level of the good as 'the object of desire' (237, 619). However, in *Method in Theology* he speaks of the

end or object of the first level of the human good as the 'particular good' (48).

15 I am indebted to J. Michael Stebbins for the expression 'patterns of cooperation.' See 'Business, Faith and the Common Good,' *Review of Business*, no. 19 (Fall 1997), 5–8; 'Toward a Developmental Understanding of the Common Good,' in *Religion and Public Life: The Legacy of Monsignor John A. Ryan*, ed. R.G. Kennedy et al. (Lanham, MD: University Press of America, 2001), 119–31; 'The Meaning of Solidarity,' in *Labor, Solidarity and the Common Good: Essays on the Ethical Foundations of Management*, ed. S.A. Cortright (Durham, NC: Carolina Academic Press, 2001), 61–74.

16 For Lonergan's discussion of feelings as intentional responses to values, see *Method in Theology*, 30–4. See also extended discussions in Doran, *Theology and the Dialectics of History*; Doorley, *The Place of the Heart in Lonergan's Ethics*; and Morelli, *Anxiety*.

17 Michael Vertin explores the structure of this process and its relation to Lonergan's functional specialties in 'Acceptance and Actualization,' 79–86.

18 See John Rawls, *Political Liberalism*, 3–46; see also Melchin, 'What Is a Democracy?'

19 For another analysis that recognizes the possibility and worth of working towards agreements on transcultural values through the processes of public discourse and deliberation, see Charles Taylor, 'The Politics of Recognition,' in *Multiculturalism*, ed. Gutman, 66–73.

20 See Lonergan, *Insight*, 631–56.

21 See also Melchin, 'What Is a Democracy?' 105–9.

PART FOUR

Further Thoughts on Insight

Philip McShane

The Importance of Rescuing *Insight*

1 Contexts

A first context is obviously the occasion: celebrating the retirement of the bright-eyed mystery and the luminous darkness of this circumstance[1] in Mike's life. And already I have pointed to a second context in the note, one that recalls the book that has haunted his life. It has also haunted my own life, and there is a definite sense in which this article adds another expansive five years to my previous reflection on *Insight*'s fate. Further, I would note the context of the discovery, forty years ago in February 1965, of the strategy of functional specialization. That, also, I would ask you to bear in mind.

But before I add to the list of contexts I must voice my esteem and friendship for Mike. And gratitude: with Mike's help in 1974 I found an academic niche in Halifax at a time when I could not even get a job as a postman (I was rejected as overqualified!). That year I had the pleasure of reading his doctorate work, a magnificent foray into the push forward of Maréchal, and have been reading Mike's work regularly since: but I shall touch on that in section 8 below.

The eleven sections to follow add overlapping contexts. But what of the content of my essay? It is the proposed context of sections 6 and 7. I am using *context* here in a sense familiar from Lonergan: 'Actually, context is the interweaving of questions and answers.'[2] Yet it has, perhaps, an unfamiliar twist that in a later culture of linguistic feedback[3] will be familiar: the later familiarity will 'bear in mind' that context is a person. The context-content is, then, an adult poise in a position regarding adult growth (6), and (7) its retirement function.

The second section takes up the question of my title. Section 3 focuses on the logic of the rescue talked of in the title. Section 4 turns to the topic of *function,* and section 5 enlarges on that under the title '*Praxis.*' Section 8, as I mentioned already, turns to the ongoing context that is Mike Vertin. Section 9 broadens the reflection to the contexts that we all are. Section 10 seeks to identify the context that I am and that you are, and the eleventh section raises the question of a fuller response. The final section was added to fulfil the request of the gallant editors for a push for unity: to them much thanks.

Some of what I have mentioned here may sound strange, so I conclude this introductory reflection with a final context that will add familiarity: the context supplied by the recently published Volume 17 of Lonergan's *Complete Works.*[4] As the editors note in their preface, there are two significant essays here, 'among the most important pieces that Lonergan ever wrote,'[5] and I shall quote from both of them below. First, there is the context of a questionnaire on philosophy: how healthy is it now, thirty years after Lonergan's reply, among the Jesuits or in the larger culture? Are bows and arrows still facing muskets?[6] Is there still a presence of 'the arrogance of omnicompetent common sense'?[7] And even if things are improving, there is ever the need for 'a hermeneutic of suspicion and a hermeneutic of recovery.'[8] To that hermeneutics Lonergan has made – Mike and I would claim – his singular contribution. 'Investigators are urged' by both *Insight* and *Method in Theology* towards 'a projective test in which investigators reveal their own notions[9] of authenticity and unauthenticity both to others and to themselves.'[10] That projective test is brutally focused in the second half of page 250 of *Method,* certainly among the most important pieces that Lonergan wrote. This essay has its core context in the final lines of that page.

Mike and I, over the years, have talked and joked about retirement, retirement even as a beginning. I retired early, and found a new lease on life. What precisely might such a new lease be in the context, the character, of the struggle towards the third stage of meaning?

2 Rescuing *Insight*

I make these following sections as brief as possible, and here I make my claim quite simply. *Insight* is to be rescued by the gradual development of functional specialization as a dominant and differentiated pattern of global culture.

Does *Insight* need rescuing? This has been my sentiment from my first reading of it in 1957, when it struck me that 'this won't take.' That sentiment has grown to be an increasingly luminous conviction within, and

Insight's rescuing has been a topic of my writings since I grappled in 1969 with the mess of musicology and the need in it for functional collaboration.[11] The rescuing of *Insight* eventually became the central concern of what I called *Cantowers*, a retirement project cut off recently for the sake of more immediate effectiveness.[12] But I am getting ahead in contexts.

At all events, my view of the need for the rescue of *Insight* has deepened in these five decades, in these five weeks. 'This won't take'? I seemed magnificently prepared for the book through graduate studies in mathematical physics: yet those first five chapters baffled me, and I was quickly disillusioned by chapter 6 of any sense that, well, we were into common sense. Only in these last years, 2002–6, when I decided to 'repeat,' exactly fifty years later, my early studies in physics, did I sense some serious progress. So, for example, after forty-five years, I figured out the legitimacy of Lonergan's claims regarding energy.[13] Nor have I been any speedier in my struggle to mesh the two sets of canons in a fuller hermeneutics.[14] But I won't go on: each of us has our story of struggle.

Method in Theology, although a dangerously descriptive book, gives the structure of the rescuing in chapter 5 and in section 5 of chapter 10. Other sections of my essay will help towards a sense of that process, but, briefly, it is a matter of recycling the book *Insight*: and your work too, of course, and Mike's. Moreover, the recycling increasingly will be unrestrictedly multidisciplinary and omnicultural, with the process from research 'up' involving a sloping convergence to the comprehensive task of that section 5, with a different sloping 'back down' to the communication process that grounds the further recycling.[15]

All this is too compact, but a few extra doctrinal pages here would unbalance my essay's sketching. So I turn rather to issues of logic as a technique in the early stages of a science.[16]

3 A Logic of Rescuing

We can take 'logic' as given in the simple but relevant preliminary description early in *Insight*: 'Logic is the effort of knowledge to attain the coherence and organization proper to any stage of its development.'[17] Or, if you are up to it and are cool with the context of the mathematical logic lectures of 1959, you can take it as suggested by Lonergan in scribbles of 1965, where he writes of it in terms of levels of mediation: 'second level of mediation, based on the tools of meaning ... study of math, modern logic [norms as incorporated in math structures and procedures] ... third level mediation, based on operations; some operations, foundational logic; all relevant operations: method, including foundational logic – broader, more complete.'[18] In either context the parallel with the technique-logic of chemistry makes sense, a logic that emerged in the 1860s: the logic of the periodic table, with its quite complex expression. That expression controls the introduction to chemistry and it controls its progress.

I have suggested elements of a logic of method in terms of what I call metaphysical *words*, the most elementary of which, W1, is $f(p_i; c_j; b_k; z_l; u_m; r_n)$.[19] Are such *words* necessary? Best let Lonergan handle the unpopular answer: Yes.

> The aim of discursive reasoning is to understand; and it arrives at understanding not only by grasping how each conclusion follows from premises, but also by comprehending in a unified whole all the conclusions intelligibly contained in those very principles. Now this comprehension of everything in a unified whole can be either formal or virtual. It is virtual when one is habitually able to answer readily and without difficulty, or at least 'without tears,' a whole series of questions right up to the last 'why?' Formal comprehension, however, cannot take place without a construct of some sort. In this life we are able to understand something only by turning to phantasm; but in larger and more complex questions it is impossible to have a suitable phantasm unless the imagination is aided by some sort of diagram.[20]

Let me illustrate the controlling power of W1, either in initial or advanced work. Take the words 'phantasm' and 'consciousness.' The control alerts one, beginner or expert, to the reality referred to as zoological: a layered reality of physics and chemistry and botany. Without being thus alerted one could be stuck with a dangerous initial descriptive meaning, and with that meaning there is little chance of a broadened base of dialogue with modern searching. 'From such a broadened basis one can go on to a developed account of the human good.'[21] Without that shift, one remains more than 'a little breathlessly and a little late.'[22]

I cannot here enter further into the techniques of creative control – at all events, it involves an undeveloped field[23] – but perhaps the manner in which the next two sections lead to two further diagrammatic controls will be of some help in following up the pointing.

4 Function

The diagram at the end of this section, then, aims to help us get to grips with the meaning of 'function' in functional specialization. But first, muse over the treatment of function in *Method in Theology*. It is, to say the least, not very explicit. I have struggled with that meaning for forty years, since

Lonergan gave me a ten-minute sketch in 1966, with his eight fingers, of his historical metadynamics. One has to struggle in fantasy[24] towards a meaning for functional interpretation, functional systematics, etc. It is a matter of musing over the handing on of a possible or probable advance efficiently[25] to the next group in the cycle of collaboration. A comment on one aspect of that handing on should help towards appreciating the simple diagram that concludes this section. Let me go back to a troublesome piece of Lonergan's writing: *The Sketch*,[26] an incomprehensible summary of a massive book that remains to be written. There he writes of producing pure formulations in the process of interpretation. 'They are pure formulations if they proceed from an interpreter that grasps the universal viewpoint and if they are addressed to an audience that similarly grasp the universal viewpoint.'[27] Pretty hairy stuff, that. Pause now with me over the diagram (Figure 1): like a running track with lanes superimposed over the usual diagram of the eight specialties. There are in fact seven lanes, which I think of from the inside as going from red through yellow, etc., to the spectrum colour indigo on the 'outside' track. You might think of the lanes as representing different approaches to collaboration, some more compact or more confused than others.[28] For me the outside indigo track represents the contemporary best poise regarding collaboration.[29] What might that poise, shared by the group,[30] be? Here it is useful to draw on an analogy with physics: bear with me in this brush past popular talk of modern physics.

Current popular talk in physics is of GUTs, Grand Unification Theories. They don't actually exist: what are present are Tentative Unification Theories, TUTs. Similarly, UV, the universal viewpoint, is not a formulated metatheory: what can exist, in a collaborative group at any stage, is TUV. Just as, then, in physics there is in any generation a common perspective and *ethos* tracking from cyclotron research to classroom rumblings, so there is to be a TUV in theology. And in both cases the collaboration is predominantly with those who share one's perspective: one keeps 'on track.' What, then, of dialogue with other views? That is the *per se* task of the eighth functional specialty.[31] Since we have not begun operating globally and differentiatedly in this functional fashion in any discipline, all this is hard to imagine: indeed, it is stressful foundational fantasy.[32]

So I return in conclusion to the point made at the beginning of this section about function as a topic in *Method in Theology*. I recall now a remark of Fred Lawrence, made when the group of five authors – including Mike – was struggling with *Searching for Cultural Foundations*:[33] 'Lonergan didn't have time to fantasize.' The tired hero patched together as best he could a set of reflections that could contextualize his article of 1969.[34]

Figure 1

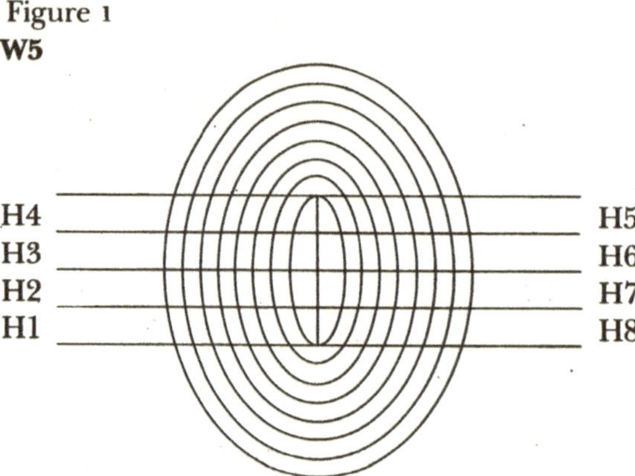

5 *Praxis*

Perhaps what comes to mind here for Lonergan students is Part 3 of *A Third Collection* with its title 'Theory and Praxis.' And that certainly is a piece of this context. But I wish here to be practical about being practical, and so I write very discomfortingly about the contrast between the effete and the practical. The contrast is not between speculation and hard-nosed doing: for speculation[35] is the key issue of the practicality I have in mind, the practicality 'that Aristotle named *phronesis* and Aquinas named *prudentia*.'[36] Think of it as a luminosity that colours function, goal-driven and end-called towards that 'final stage that ... bears fruit.'[37] Think of it as in contrast with intellectual gatherings whose function seems to centre on and end in the conference hall or in the library, effetely. Think of it as a poise of a group, an 'aesthetic apprehension of the group's origin and story which is operative whenever the group judges, evaluates, decides, or acts – and especially in a crisis,'[38] an ontological meaning of a creative minority that is bent towards larger 'common meaning and ontology.'[39] The group is luminously 'on track,' psychically dominated by its dark apprehension of the *field*[40] and of common meaning's ongoing needs, desperate in these axial times.

It seems best to move immediately to an imaging of the full genetic[41] logic of this pragmatics, but before doing so it is as well to invite *Wit*[42] to the rescue. When you steer your article to and through the publisher, or when you leave the learned conference, where does the effort end? Where was it aimed to end? Consider even the entire learned conference: what is its committed orientation? And so on. There emerges the possibility 'of marking with a chortle the chasms that divide the successive orientations of

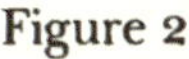

Figure 2

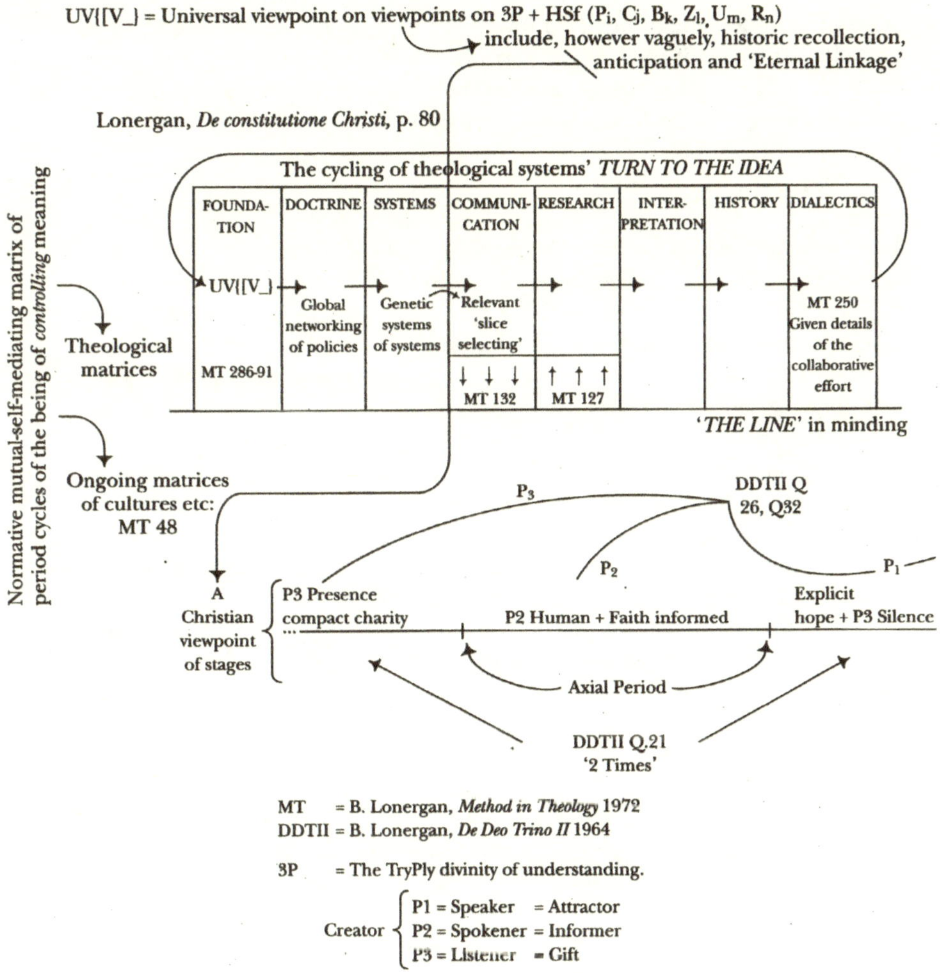

UV{[V_} = Universal viewpoint on viewpoints on 3P + HSf (P_i, C_j, B_k, Z_l, U_m, R_n)
include, however vaguely, historic recollection, anticipation and 'Eternal Linkage'

Lonergan, *De constitutione Christi*, p. 80

Normative mutual-self-mediating matrix of period cycles of the being of *controlling* meaning

The cycling of theological systems' *TURN TO THE IDEA*

FOUNDATION	DOCTRINE	SYSTEMS	COMMUNICATION	RESEARCH	INTERPRETATION	HISTORY	DIALECTICS
UV{[V_} →	Global networking of policies →	Genetic systems of systems →	Relevant 'slice selecting' →	→	→	→	MT 250 Given details of the collaborative effort
MT 286-91			↓ ↓ ↓ MT 132	↑ ↑ ↑ MT 127			

Theological matrices

'*THE LINE*' in minding

Ongoing matrices of cultures etc: MT 48

DDTII Q 26, Q32

P_3 P_2 P_1

A Christian viewpoint of stages: P3 Presence compact charity … | P2 Human + Faith informed | Explicit hope + P3 Silence

Axial Period

DDTII Q.21 '2 Times'

MT = B. Lonergan, *Method in Theology* 1972
DDTII = B. Lonergan, *De Deo Trino II* 1964

3P = The TryPly divinity of understanding.

Creator { P1 = Speaker = Attractor; P2 = Spokener = Informer; P3 = Listener = Gift }

man's polymorphic consciousness' from 'the vastly more ambitious task of directing and in some measure controlling his future history.'[43]

In conclusion, then, I give you one of my cherished images (Figure 2) in its original format, which you can find on page 124 of *A Brief History of Tongue.* My more recent effort is an image of towering cultural collaboration, rising up above common meaning, yet paradoxically no closer to Meaning, always infinitely remote in this life, but inviting all with Ultimate Suffering Praxis.[44] To reach such an image, the diagram given can be modified suggestively from its presentation in *A Brief History of Tongue*: it is a matter of suitably cutting out, connecting ends, mounting the tower on the plain of common meaning. The tower of meaning climbs with generations of cycles; its plain of meaning is – in the developed science of the hoped-for third stage of meaning – approximately uniformly remote from common meaning; it invigorates common meaning by *ex-planing*.[45]

6 Norms of Adult Growth

This topic has occupied me as a fundamental problem since 1958, when I mused over Thomas' meaning of *augmentatio*,[46] but oddly – or is it really not odd, but growth? – only in retirement have I come to grips with it both through analogies and through what might be called depth-soundings. Alessandra Gillis, thirty years my junior, has done a magnificent job in bringing together my fragmentary comments on the problem and doing so in the full context of my reflections on phylogenetic growth.[47] Both the facts that Sandy is forty-two and that she contextualizes the topic within the larger phylogenetic perspective are relevant. First, the phylogenetic context is key in many ways: the longer cycle of decline that has special significance in this second stage of meaning has combined its ills to negate the adventure of Elderhood: but that is a topic for another day. Secondly, age counts, if my position is on the ball, and it gives the problem of interpretation a curious twist. What does Sandy know about growth in her forties and fifties and sixties and beyond? What, then, of what she says of my growth? And again, that is a topic for another day, or year, or decade, of your time.

In the brief space I have allowed myself here it seems best to just take one particular statement of my position and one particular analogy that has led me on through fifty years. The particular statement: that I have become a stranger to myself of this day last week, nor could I communicate that change of meaning to myself of last week with any serious brevity. The particular analogy comes from the year 1960, when I moved from lecturing on mathematical physics to being a student of theology: a massively disturbing experience.[48] But the analogy comes from the lecturing, so let us pause over it.

Among various courses given in 1959–60 – lectures to first-year commerce students and second-year engineering students (four hundred of them!) – there stood out two courses: a first-year honours course in mathematical physics and a graduate course in the same field. In both courses we battled forwards through grim exercises towards relative mastery. But the levels were entirely different; indeed, a first-year student was well aware that wandering into even a second-year course was to wander into a strange, incomprehensible land. Furthermore, wandering, so to speak, into the next week of their own course would have left them baffled: one had to climb for a week to breath that air. Finally, a week's climbing for the graduate students involved quite a different pace: subtleties layered forward in mountain vistas.[49]

So I pose the question for your present context: why should growth in the minding of human meaning be different from growth of the meaning of the elementary conjugates of physics? Why should human self-energy be apparently so much simpler as a study than the self-energy of the electron? This is just one question of a cluster of questions concerning growth, but it is at least an interesting start. The question itself must grow in luminous darkness, in shifts through strange contexts.

> The conceptualization of understanding is, when fully developed, a system, and one must advert to the implications of systematic knowledge in the Aristotelian and Thomist *quod quid est* if one would grasp the precise nature of the concept; the concept emerges from understanding, not an isolated atom detached from all context, but precisely as part of a context, loaded with the relations that belong to it in virtue of a source which is equally the source of other concepts.[50]

What, then, of the concept and the reality of adult growth in the different stages of meaning; what of the concept of a fresh perspective on Aristotle's excellent life, on Maslow's smelling of decay, on Proust's giant-stilts tasting of tea? And what of the concept of 'the source'? Is there not a case to be made for 'a position of dynamic equilibrium without ever ceasing to drive towards fuller and more nuanced synthesis,'[51] a position that would reveal the *exigence*[52] in ever-fresher darkness? And is that freshening not an ever-accelerating post-graduate, post-retirement, business? And might this freshening not give brighter meaning to the exigent search for our concept of The Concept?[53] Might we thus rise to an interpretation of what Lonergan wrote in May 1954 at the tender age of fifty?: 'The Method in Theology is coming into perspective. For the Trinity: *Imago Dei in homine* and proceed to the limit as in evaluating $(1 + 1/n)^{nx}$ as n approaches infinity. For the rest: *ordo universi.* From the viewpoint of theology, it is a manifold of unities developing in relation to one another and in relation to God.'[54]

7 A Function of Retirement

Retirement is another name for withdrawal, and one may think of either Toynbee or Simmel.[55] But what of The Turn or The Return? If I am right about growth, then retirement is a shift in the conditions of accelerating growth.[56] I am thinking, of course, particularly of a contemplative growth that is natural to us: '*contemplatio autem veritatis competit homini secundum suam naturam, prout est animal rationale.*'[57] The multi-infolded chemical energy that is the rational animal has that natural bent,[58] and to the dynamic reach of it I return at the end of the next section. But here I wish to raise another question, relating to the rescuing operation that was the topic of section 2.

The tasks of dialectic and foundations sublate their older shadows within metaphysics, and the *per se* task of foundations emerges as *fantasy and its functional cycling.* One may think here of a sophisticated transposition of Plato's identification of guardians. But perhaps in the present context we can move with special Christian theological categories towards thinking of *imitatio theologica Christi,* and indeed '*propter necessitatem praesentis vitae,*'[59] where by the present of that life I would have you read the present of the rescue-crisis that is named in my title and talked of in section 2.

Then the 'Mission and Spirit'[60] of the retired might paradoxically be a calling forth to an imitation of those strange years of the public life of Jesus in a contemporary reach towards 'The Identification of the Solution'[61] in its lower cosmopolitan rotary blade. That component of cosmopolis, recognizable as a shift in the probabilities[62] of 'witness to the possibility of ideas,'[63] is recognizable too as a shift in hope. 'The antecedent willingness of hope has to advance from a generic reinforcement of the pure desire to an adapted and specialized auxiliary ever ready to offset every interference with intellect's unrestricted finality.'[64] So, 'intellectual collaboration would develop down the ages'[65] in a vestigial[66] global imitation of God's community.[67] That development would shift discontinuously the role of '*regina sci entiarum*'[68] towards a participation in an integral dialectic and foundational cycling that would be groundedly antifoundational in its source-openness.

That source-openness, absolutely supernatural in its 'heightened tension,'[69] calls for Elder ventures in the necessities of the present late axial period. Paradoxically, retirement may mean a move from the Nazarene shelter of the classroom to the publicity of a Socratic advocating of mystery and method. And might there not be an insignificant little hill in the vicinity of the University of Toronto where Mike could be comfortably cruxified? But let us ramble less terminally round his and our challenges.

8 Vertin's Challenge

The title here is nicely ambiguous. Mike is both challenged and challenging. How is Mike challenging? I draw attention to two of his recent papers for illustration.[70] A paper presented at a conference in California brings to the fore his logical bent. It is a challenge, regularly not met: this is not pleasant reading for those of purely literary bent. Yet are we going to get anywhere without it and its symbolic control of varieties and shades of positioning? We are back with the issue of section 3. And we are back with the rescue-operation of section 2: for this operation is to recycle Vertin's discomforting logic as it is to recycle the deeper discomforts of *Insight.* Moreover, Mike's penchant for clarity and order leads him to push towards a larger logic that would bring to the fore structures of functional specialization.[71] But I can say no more here than what I have squeezed into notes 71 and 72.

The challenge of his second interest falls within that larger logic. Mike continues to push forwards on difficult issues regarding the nature of evaluation, and the problems he faces open up towards the need for a fuller functional specialist collaboration. Again, I do no more here than give some pointers in a note: the issues here bring out the need for a massive shift towards a logic based on fuller principles of metaphysical equivalence.[72]

Then there is Mike's challenge in the other sense – clearly meshed in with the first sense – and the possibility of his sharing my existential answer to our rambles about retirement and our rambles in retirement onwards and upwards. Retirement is the liberation of a new beginning in the mood of Proust, Bachelard, von Karajan.[73] I am seven years senior to Mike and so, from a normal normative point of view, I am more a stranger to myself of last week than he is to himself of last week, if we are both lucky enough to have dawn or dusk or midday leisure in the 'obscure' 'finality' of the 'passionateness of being.'[74] Nor am I talking of something mystical, but simply of thinking, of that kataphatic contemplation that should be normative in the science of flowers or the flow of traffic. But it is a thinking that places one in the elusive *field* of the yearning cosmos. Certainly, it is not without expression, bursting forth perhaps in formulated attainments and printed achievements. But it is a following, a twining round the neurochemistry of 'an inner light that runs before the formulation.'[75] It is a growing openness to the paradoxically disappearing goal of theoretical understanding seeking 'to embrace the universe in a single view,'[76] seeking to let that groaning[77] 'universe bring forth its own unity in the concentrated form of a single intelligent view.'[78]

9 The Broader Challenge

Both senses of the challenge, of course, call you out and in, call out to you, the reader, and I would have you hold, heart-hold, the full challenge in a pragmatic envisioning of the cyclic functioning. And practicality prompts me to cut back to a tolerant minimalism: in section 11 I return to the fulsome challenge.

What do I mean by a tolerant minimalism? The meaning is perhaps decently captured in my slogan 'If a thing is worth doing then it is worth doing badly,' and such a venture is captured nicely in the poor performance of interpretation that a struggling group gave in Volume 4 of the *Journal of Macrodynamic Analysis* (2005). But, whatever one's discipline, one must come to grips realistically with what 'it' – the thing worth doing – means: it is a global effort to overcome present disciplinary fragmentation by the humility of settling for a functional role. It will be done badly in a first or second generation because the differentiations of consciousness demanded are novel and strange. So, functional history is not just an update of von Ranke: it will eventually be a new sentence-by-sentence balance between efforts of those tracking interpretations and the elder task of dialectic sifting. Here I had best say a word about intolerable minimalism, which seems to prevail in many of Lonergan's followers. That minimalism would regard the distinctions as little more than guidelines to personal work: and perhaps here one might identify quite concretely a dialogue task of elders. Lonergan did not climb grimly through the decade of his fifties to invent a filing system. What he invented was a structure of periodic functional collaboration that parallels the period table of chemistry invented a century earlier.

Above I talked of hope. 'The new man [or woman] will have to be a [woman or] man of hope, for only hope can release people from the hopelessness of warring egoisms and blundering shortsightedness.'[79] That hope is helped by a sense of what is to blossom from the shabby beginnings. The history of seventeenth-century science is a story of the puttering of individuals, and even nineteenth-century physics shows brilliant scientists struggling with basement apparatus. In chapter 4 of *Lack in the Beingstalk*, titled 'The Calculus of Variation,' I drew a useful parallel between the story told by Husserl's work under Weierstrass[80] on that subject and the future story of functional specialization. The calculus, whose nineteenth-century development is the topic of Husserl's thesis, has come a long way from the problem of the Aenead's maximizing the area within a certain boundary-length. So, we have a long way to go to maximize the effectiveness of luminous functional collaboration: in a century or three it will become a tower of able, a beauty of missionary metaphysics.

But only if we shift shabbily towards function and *praxis*, and only per haps if we are nudged doctrinally – that concrete dialogue task – by some respected few. Functional specialization as a doctrine of global collaboration in all areas of culture must become a topic, a topic of conversion, an embarrassing topic. 'Doctrines that are embarrassing will not be mentioned in polite company.'[81] The time for politeness is long past 'when philosophers for at least two centuries, through doctrines on politics, economics, education, and through ever further doctrines, have been trying to remake man, and have done not a little to make life unlivable.'[82]

10 Here I Stand

What I have written here is not within any functional speciality: it could, like most of my writing, be classed as a type of popular discourse that is to be a fallout, call out and forward, of communications. In a developed tradition of functional specialization it will be part of that formal unbearable baring, bearings-taking, that is described so brutally in the second half of page 250 of *Method in Theology*. In that tradition it may survive the baring and the refinements of communal dialectic searchings to become a component of remote metadoctrine, comprehensible only to those who climb beyond graduate meaning. It is where I stand, on an insignificant little hill in Vancouver.

And at the level of this present discourse, there should surely be a common-sense response, even if it is only the taking of a stand of interested disinterest, a stand of business as usual. Then 'here I stand' may be you going about your subtle or not so subtle avoidance of the challenge of Lonergan's greatest achievement, his structuring of historical dynamics. 'To put it bluntly, until we move onto the level of historical dynamics, we shall face our secularist and atheist opponents, as the Red Indians, armed with bows and arrows, faced European muskets.'[83] The bows and arrows, of course, can be wonderfully colourful yet quite effete. Nor does it take rocket science to detect that effete colourfulness in learned gatherings and articles that have no forward fallout. So, to my minimalism I have added here and there invitations to humour regarding what precisely we are at when we thus pursue scholarship.

But should we not lift our eyes, ayes, I-s, higher?

11 Ontic Responding

The context here is the perspective that one might reach through an integrating sublation of the two parts of *Phenomenology and Logic*. One might? 'One can go on'?[84] 'So it comes about,'[85] but perhaps not in your 'one' now. Yet a stumbling response towards taking a strange stand could enliven the luminous darkness of another generation, if only we face our personal existential gap with realistic anxiety and delicate dread.[86] 'What is this prior reality, this ontic, evident, normative something that grounds horizon, the critique of horizons, and the determination of the true horizon?'[87] It is you, the patterned chemical that is a pre-articulate yearning to embrace the universe, product of fourteen billion years, companion to fourteen billion galaxies. The cosmic reach is that a community emerge in a later millennium that is darkly luminous in regarding and guarding the yearning. But that emergence is conditioned in the lateness of its emergence by the nowTHEN[88] cultivation of a new ontic reaching in a word made fresh, the word 'I,' *Watashi wa*, whatever.

Nor is the referent of that word, or its heuristic resonant, a piece of a Noah's ark of existents and essences: it is a flowering of fourteen billion years, home nested, universe embraced. The Little Prince's flower and the Little Flower of Lisieux echo round those 14 billion gallaxies. 'The Little Prince could not restrain his admiration: "Oh! How beautiful you are!" "Am I not?" the flower responded, sweetly. "And I was born at the same moment as the sun."'[89]

Nor is each or any of the facing decisions of any I a piece of a Noah's ark, a shift in a given universe.[90] It is rather a mysteriously intimate selection of an entire integral finitude, twining with the creative Formulation and Formula that graces Bethlehem and Bethelgeuse, that gifts each I with 'a white stone and in that stone a new name written which no man knoweth save he that receiveth it.'[91]

In a later stage of meaning, such findings of Aristotle's excellent way will blossom in a larger statistics of vibrant I-sites, a common meaning of mystery lacing town and tillage, cinema and church.

I conclude by quoting from a larger shot at opening this perspective: it saves further effort and also points to a fuller context of the task of rescuing *Insight* and *Method in Theology*: I cite the conclusion of *Cantower* 38, on 'Functional History.'

> How should the story be told, of the flower born before yet with the sun, armed slowly with radiations wings and wiles and chlorophiles, painstakingly coping and copying with pigmentations plethora of possibilities? Could I perhaps talk you into an Anna Livia Florabella, a flow of worldflowers, Purefoyled, energy's hungering for wholecolour? Should I start again, like 'Oxen of the Sun,' with a primitive invocation to the sun of fertility? 'Deshil Hollis Eamus. Deshil Hollis Eamus. Send us bright one, light one.' How can one make popular a billion years of yearning?
>
> Making popular is a matter of cycling and recycling over millennia. As I wind now towards the end of the first third of the *Cantower* enterprise it seems fitting to repeat the compact invitation at the end of the second chapter of *Lack in the Beingstalk* that meshes the searchings of the elder Shakespeare with those of Joyce and Kavanagh.
>
> 'Skin-within are molecules of cos mi c all, cauled, calling. The rill of her mouth can become the thrill, the trill, of a life-time, the word

made fresh. Might we inspire and expire with the lungs of history? But the hole story is you and I, with and within global humanity, upsettling *Love's Sweet Mystery* into a new mouthing, an anastomotic spiral way of birthing better the buds of Mother.'

12 Reverierun

My title of this final section, in which I follow the editors' suggestion of reaching for some integral perspective on the volume, is a borrowed subtitle from a relevant context, recently developed.[92] But let me come to my title and my point in easy, or perhaps I should say conventional, stages.

Conventionally, then, we each pick up on the other authors to find zones of common interest and progress, even areas of conflict, the latter not being a road to popularity. In conventional terms I find, in fact, few areas of conflict, but rather eleven other people reaching out for refinements of perspective. My present interest in layers of mediations leaves me more in herenow tune with some of my colleagues than with others: Doran, Hefling, McGrath, and Morelli converge with me on the significance of zones of superstructural and infrastructural mediations, to use Morelli's distinction. Lawrence and Melchin press forwards towards sophistications of democratizing strategies. Crowe draws attention to features of willing in a manner that resonates with my own concerns.[93]

A four-month providential pause in our collaboration enabled me to round out my Quodlibet series, thus giving me a context for reading the next two papers received, those of Crysdale and O'Gara.[94] O'Gara's brief reflection impressed me as gentle and to the point.[95] Crysdale brightened my day in bringing concretely into focus the 'what to do?' question, regularly neglected in discussions of value.[96]

Yet while each of us moves forward we seem to do so in relative isolation, and certainly we reach forward in isolation from the global structuring of collaboration that was the crown of Lonergan's work.[97] So I move to my unconventional yet pragmatic response.

The response has its roots in a conversation with Dr Eileen deNeeve during the 2004 Centennial Conference in Toronto, where she raised the question of having a shot at dialectic, as described on page 250 of *Method*, simply by taking a particular author like Hayek. My brooding on the matter later in Dublin led me to a firm yes. The issue for me was conceiving the possibilities in the word 'assembly' that ends page 249, and indeed it led me then to take as the object of 'assembly' my own thousand-year-old town of Dublin.[98] But might it not lead us twelve on, to a rerun, a reverierun,[99] of this volume, within the challenge of that remarkable page of *Method in Theology*? The challenge is to position ourselves first, and then to so position ourselves in relation to each other that we are lifted towards the reverie of a new personal thematic of the hidden foundations of our cosmic selves.

This is not a pleasant challenge, and the personal experiment can bring this into raw self-exposure. That experiment, of course, can be done in total solitude and its contents hidden away in one's own files. But Lonergan's discomforting challenge is to say publicly where one stands, e.g., on extreme realism or on the significance of *theoria*, or on metaphysics as precisely explanatory, on the prospective narrative of one's own life: all zones of conversion-challenge.[100]

From what I have written in this essay, it is evident that my key interest is in people's stands on the significance and the implementation of functional specialization. The issue of implementation[101] or effectiveness can be raised quite bluntly by us, each and all, asking, To what does this volume lead? What might be its fallout, its street value? The question stirs up immediately the topic of the missing forward specialties, of the complexity of the necessary genetic systematics and the larger difficulty of a globalization of the eighth specialty.[102] At all event, this is what my title points to: a re-cycling of our efforts that might lead slowly to a quite different *ethos* of future efforts.

But it seems to me worthwhile to raise here the curious issue of our differing positions regarding Lonergan: if you like, taking as the *assembly* of page 250 his 'Complete Works.' I have been stating my own position since 1961,[103] but perhaps there is no harm in adding recent particular embellishments. As I continue to grapple with the remote meaning of *Insight*, I am increasingly astonished at the lonely achievement of the forty-nine-year-old Lonergan. My present focus is contemporary physics, with an eye towards an explanatory eschatology. I returned to *Insight*, chapter 5, including the original text with its corrections, exclusions, cancellations, back-up scribbles.[104] I find him reaching out to refinements about algebraic geometry and electrodynamics and distant galaxies and spans of time of the order of 10^9 years and statistical control of cosmic meaning.[105] He leads me to fresh light on the overestimation of the energy-momentum tensor, a massively coincidental affair,[106] and on the damage to both theoretic and popular consciousness that stems from the missed perspective on the concrete intelligibility of Space and Time.[107] Grand Unification Theory is to be, not some brief history of time, but 'an abstract relational field'[108] meshing the four fundamental forces into the laws of a complex of fibre-bundle geometries.[109] But I am, perhaps, losing my general reader here.[110]

Yet I would note that Lonergan considered chapter 5 to be a bridge[111] to the rest of the book, a bridge that would make possible and probable the 'comeabout'[112] to the explanatory heuristics that he achieved before his fiftieth year, that I am still struggling towards after fifty years of reading *Insight*. This seems to me to make quite probable a detail of my position on Lonergan: that the Lonergan school generally under reads him, or indeed misreads him. One instance can be identified and corrected by attending to a brief exchange at the 1970 Florida Conference. I still recall the silly fellow who asked Lonergan whether he discovered feelings through Scheler. Lonergan eyed him for a moment before claiming in his up-toned rhythm. 'I've got feelings too.' Then he made clear, one might say in anticipation of an established misreading of *Insight*, his stand and effort in *Insight*: 'There is in *Insight* a footnote to the effect that we're not attempting to solve anything about such a thing as personal relations. I was dealing in *Insight* fundamentally with the intellectual side – a study of human understanding – in which I did my study of human understanding and got human intelligence in there, not just a sausage machine turning out abstract concepts. That was my fundamental thrust.'[113]

The rest of his career, under the pressure of a subtle demand for *haute vulgarization*, gave him no opportunity to express publically a thematization of that heart of matter. But he did live within that *field*, as self-luminous subject, luminous indeed regarding what he meant by random phrases like 'a room filled with music.'[114]

S.J. McGrath rightly talks about infinities, a zone of layers of intimacy with the Subjects that are not objects.[115] One can suspect that Bernard Lonergan edged towards those infinities, especially in music, from his childhood days of pausing in his family garden as his mother played a piano version[116] of the Kreutzer Sonata, to his last years of 'feeling' Beethoven's Late Quartets.[117] So he could write of a need in him and in each of us that is at once personal, interpersonal, and historical. 'What then is needed is a qualitative change in me, a shift in the centre of my existing from the concerns manifested in the *bavardage quotidien* towards the participated yet never in this life completely established eternity that is tasted in aesthetic apprehension.'[118]

Notes

1 A relevant context for this article is P. McShane, 'Asia Una Obscuridad Luminosa de la Circumstantia: *Insight* despues Cuarante Annos,' *Universidad Philosophia* 32 (1999). The English version, 'Towards a Luminous Darkness of Circumstances: *Insight* after Forty Years,' is available on various Lonergan websites, including www.philipmcshane.ca. The *Cantowers* and *Quodlibets* mentioned below are also available there. I should also mention a work, available on the website, that meshes with the drive of the present volume: *Joistings* 1–8 is a hundred-page essay towards the genesis of a

kataphatic spirituality. Its drive is towards the rescue of Lonergan's Latin works – now appearing in translation – from the inadequacies of traditional expression.

2 Bernard Lonergan, *Method in Theology* (Toronto: University of Toronto Press, 2003), 163.

3 Ibid., 88, n. 34.

4 Bernard Lonergan, *Philosophical and Theological Papers 1965–1980*, vol. 17 in *Collected Works of Bernard Lonergan*, ed. Robert C. Croken and Robert M. Doran (Toronto: University of Toronto Press, 2004).

5 Ibid., xiv.

6 Ibid., 366. The essay, titled 'Questionnaire on Philosophy: Response,' was written in 1976, expressing Lonergan's position on philosophy in Jesuit education.

7 Ibid., 370.

8 Ibid., 403. I now quote from the second essay, written sometime in the winter of 1977, 'Philosophy and the Religious Phenomenon.'

9 I draw attention in this note to the parallel between 'context' and 'notion': the parallel draws attention to problems in the meaning of 'ontic.'

10 Lonergan, *Philosophical and Theological Papers 1965–1980*, 403.

11 'Metamusic and Self-Meaning.' It was one of two papers presented at the International Florida conference of 1970, both later published as chaps. 1 and 2 of *The Shaping of the Foundations* (Washington: University Press of America, 1976).

12 The shift is discussed in *Sofdaware* 1, the first of eight essays focused on p. 250 of *Method*, as background for dialogue with an Australian group of Lonergan students. The work gradually led me to a fuller appreciation of the function of foundational work as cycling and recycling fantasy.

13 I give leads to this in *Cantower* 30.

14 For my most recent effort here, see *Quodlibet* 6.

15 The asymmetric sloping process would require at least a separate essay. A useful image is a set of converging lines up from varieties of research to an integral fourth specialty. The creative base here is geographically random (think of the Councils of the Church, or the emergence of modern sciences). The descending slopes, on the other hand, aim at reaching global landmasses – and even waters – with some uniformity.

16 See Bernard Lonergan, *Insight*, vol. 3 in *Collected Works of Bernard Lonergan*, ed. Frederick E. Crowe and Robert M. Doran (Toronto: University of Toronto Press, 1992), 599. A context for reflection on technique's relation to the need, even in the initial stages of a science, for the push for explanatory control-patterns of investigation is *De Deo Trino II: Pars Systematica* (Rome: Gregorian Press, 1964), 308–9: '*Quod relationes non dividuntur in predicamentales et transcendentales nisi in stadio scientific intermedio, neque valde convenienter ita dividuntur, etiam in illo stadio.*'

17 Lonergan, *Insight*, 301.

18 I quote from unpublished scribbled sketchings of a chap. 1 of *Method in Theology*, dating from early 1965. These sketchings are available in chap. 2 of

Darlene O'Leary, *Lonergan's Practical View of History* (Halifax: Axial Press, 2005).

19 The symbolism first appeared in the early 1970s on p. 106 of *Wealth of Self and Wealth of Nations* (New York: Phoenix Press, 1975), where it is explained in some detail. It is presented again in chapter 4 of *A Brief History of Tongue* (Halifax: Axial Press, 2000) with more complex *words* such as that given on 124, a controlling *word* of functional collaboration.

20 Bernard Lonergan, *The Ontological and Psychological Constitution of Christ*, vol. 7 of *Collected Works of Bernard Lonergan*, trans. and ed. Michael G. Shields (Toronto: University of Toronto Press, 2002), 151.

21 Lonergan, *Method in Theology*, 287. This is a key paragraph in the book.

22 Lonergan, *Insight*, 755.

23 I pointed this out originally in the concluding section of *Cantower* 33. It was to have been the topic of the *Cantowers* of 2008.

24 The role of fantasy in foundational work was first introduced in 'Instrumental Acts of Meaning and Fourth Level Functional Specialization,' a Boston paper that became chapter 4 of *The Shaping of the Foundations*.

25 'It is quite legitimate to seek in the efficient cause of the science, that is, in the scientist, the reason why a science forms a unified whole.' Bernard Lonergan, *Topics in Education*, vol. 10 of *Collected Works of Bernard Lonergan*, ed. Frederick E. Crowe and Robert M. Doran (Toronto: University of Toronto Press, 1993), 160. From this one can move to a glimpse of a new unity and beauty given to metaphysics by Lonergan's functional suggestion.

26 The title of sec. 3.6 of chap. 17 of *Insight*.

27 Lonergan, *Insight*, 602.

28 John Benton does this very successfully in his article in *Journal of Macrodynamic Analysis* 4 (2004), http://www.mun/jmda.

29 'Indigo' could pass for a certain way of speaking, in some sections of the Irish population, about the shift to interiority: 'In they go.'

30 Recall Lonergan: 'The use of the general theological categories occurs in any of the eight functional specialties.' *Method in Theology*, 292. They may not be great in the initial stages of collaboration, and in that case there comes into play my slogan, 'If a thing is worth doing, then it is worth doing badly.'

31 I realize that this is all too hurried and doctrinal. One has to unpack both the brief statement of the function of communications on p. 132 of *Method in Theology* and the brief statement regarding the functioning of dialectic on p. 250. The latter page has preoccupied me for some time and is the topic of the website series (www.philipmcshane.ca) *Sofdaware*. Other views are handled in both specialties, but quite differently. See especially the website *Quodlibet* 6 on the precise meaning of p. 250's *Comparison*.

32 A parallel may help here. Imagine Butterfield's *Origins of Modern Science* compressed into a page and presented to the medievals; fantasize now about reading 250 of *Method in Theology* in AD 2500.

33 *Searching for Cultural Foundations*, ed. Philip J. McShane (Washington: University Press of America, 1984). The authors of the five chapters were Frederick

E. Crowe, Robert M. Doran, Frederick Lawrence, Philip J. McShane, and Michael Vertin.

34 *Gregorianum* 50 (1969), 485–505. I must draw attention to Karl Rahner's brief comments on that article. Rahner was right on about the multidisciplinary power of Lonergan's achievement: 'Die theologische Methodologie Lonergan's scheint mir so generish zu sein, dass sie eigentlich auf jede Wissenschaft passt.' 'Kritsche Bemerkungen zu B.J.F. Lonergan's Aufsatz: "Functional Specialization in Theology,"' *Gregorianum* 51 (1970), 537.

35 It is worth recalling Lonergan's comment – in a powerful paragraph of *For A New Political Economy* – on the need for speculation: 'It must lift its eyes more and ever more to the more general and more difficult fields of speculation, for it is from them that it has to derive the delicate compound of unity and freedom in which alone progress can be born, struggle, and win through.' Bernard Lonergan, *For A New Political Economy*, vol. 21 of *Collected Works of Bernard Lonergan*, ed. Philip J. McShane (Toronto: University of Toronto Press, 1999), 20.

36 Bernard Lonergan, 'Theology and Praxis,' in *A Third Collection*, ed. Frederick E. Crowe (New York: Paulist Press, 1985), 184.

37 Lonergan, *Method in Theology*, 355.

38 Lonergan, *Topics in Education*, 230.

39 The title of the second section of chap. 14 of *Method in Theology*.

40 See the index under 'Field' in Bernard Lonergan, *Phenomenology and Logic*, vol. 18 of *Collected Works of Bernard Lonergan*, ed. Philip J. McShane (Toronto: University of Toronto Press, 2002).

41 McShane, *Cantower* 7, 'Systematic and General Systems Theory' (www.philipmcshane.ca), gives indications of the nature of this genetic logic within the seventh specialty. The full logic, of course, is the dialectic hodic logic that assures the circulation of the systematic genetic logic through all eight specialties.

42 Lonergan, *Insight*, 649. I think here also of the 2001 film *Wit*, and the lead character's appeal that fits the title and the circumstances of this volume: 'We are discussing life and death, and not in the abstract either. We are discussing my life and my death. And I cannot conceive of any other tone. Now is not the time for verbal thought-play. Nothing could be worse than a detailed scholarly analysis of erudition, interpretation, complication. Now is the time for simplicity. Now is the time for, dare I say it, kindness.'

43 Ibid., 258.

44 See Lonergan's brief, powerful expression of this in *Understanding and Being*, vol. 5 of *Collected Works of Bernard Lonergan*, ed. Elizabeth A. Morelli and Mark D. Morelli (Toronto: University of Toronto Press, 1991), 374–7.

45 The meaning of 'ex-planing' and its relation to the problem of popularization is a topic of the conclusion of chap. 3 of *Lack in the Beingstalk: A Giants Causeway* (Halifax: Axial Press, 2004). Perhaps it is worth remarking that all the planes of meaning in this life are infinitely remote from Meaning, with a strange power of infinity.

46 The text was a. 11 of *Quaestio Disputata, De Virtutibus in Communi: Quaeritur quomodo virtus infusa augeatur.* I discuss this context at some length in sec. 2.0 of *Process: Introducing Themelves to Young Christian Minders.* The book, written in 1989, is available on the website www.philipmcshane.ca.

47 See Alessandra Drage, 'Philip McShane's Axial Period,' *Journal of Macro dynamic Analysis* 4 (2004), http://www.mun/jmda.

48 I must pass over that experience and its meaning here. But you might call on the analogy with physics in trying to understand why, in physics, the second, third, and fourth years are necessarily separated since a climb is involved, while in the theology of my day, they shared a common course. Was there not a climb? And why is it that theological and philosophical topics are generally considered fair game for multileveled audiences?

49 I am thinking here of the work of Richard Feynman, both advanced and popular. In what is his best effort at popularization he talks of certain techniques 'that take graduate students three or four years to master.' See his *QED: The Strange Theory of Light and Matter* (Princeton: Princeton University Press, 1988), 125. The level of difficulty of his advanced work on path integration in quantum theory and relativity goes quite beyond his little book, beyond nor mal graduate students in physics. Further, I would note that there are problems in his presentations – in this book or in his famous three volumes of *Lectures in Physics* – that reach into larger questions of popularization. Does he imply, for instance, in that remark just quoted, that there is a serious competence that can be attained without the control of technique?

50 Bernard Lonergan, *Verbum: Word and Idea in Aquinas*, vol. 2 of *Collected Works of Bernard Lonergan*, ed. Frederick E. Crowe and Robert M. Doran (Toronto: University of Toronto Press, 1997), 238.

51 I quote from the final page of *Insight.*

52 The index entry on 'Exigence' in *Phenomenology and Logic* opens up this topic.

53 See the end of the last paragraph of *Quaestio XXXII* in Bernard Lonergan, *De Deo Trino II: Pars Systematica,* to appear shortly in English as vol. 12 of *Collected Works of Bernard Lonergan.*

54 I quote from a letter of Lonergan to Fr Fred Crowe that he kindly made available to me. I quoted it previously in a relevant context: the context of the fullest meaning of *Completeness* of p. 250 of *Method in Theology* (see *Sofdaware* 5, 'Care Reaching for *Completeness*,' especially nn. 2, 3, 10, 12, 22, 35). Where I quoted it thus previously continues in a manner that helps come to grips with our present reach: 'What is the growth curve of completeness. The limit of which Lonergan writes springs forth as e^x, and it is a measure of its own growth: $d/dx(e^x) = e^x$. "Doctrines that are embarrassing will not be mentioned in polite company" (*Method in Theology,* 299), and this is an embarrassing doctrine for any version of satisfied *completeness.* The exigence buried in the battered heart of every serious axial theologian is to be increasingly a stranger to the present self-completenesss through the rhythms of evaluation of each sacramental day.'

55 Interestingly, Lonergan, in *De Deo Trino I: Pars Dogmatica* (Rome: Gregorian

Press, 1964), n. 10, parallels Simmel's *die Wendung zur Idee* with displacment towards system, which captures something of the *ethos* of functional specialization.

56 My simplest imaging of this is of a balloon growing outwardly at uniform rate of change of its radius: the volume is an increasing function of age.

57 Thomas Aquinas, *Summa Theologiae* (hereafter *ST*), 2-2 q. 180, a. 7c. Question 182, comparing the active and the contemplative lives, is a useful context for the rest of this section. See also *ST*, 3, q. 40, a. 1, ad 2m (on the style of Christ's conversation).

58 Obviously a tricky topic: I had best refer you to Lonergan's treatment of it in *De Ente Supernaturale.*

59 *ST*, 2-2 q. 182, a.1c.

60 I am recalling the context of the article of that title in *A Third Collection*, 23–34.

61 The title of the final section of chap. 20 of *Insight.*

62 Lonergan, *Insight*, 144, speaks of a shift of probabilities from products to sums that is related to the cyclic structuring of inquiry.

63 Ibid., 264.

64 Ibid., 747.

65 Ibid., 748.

66 On varieties of vestiges of the Trinity, see *ST*, 1, q. 45, a. 7.

67 A context here is *Quaestio* XXX of Lonergan, *De Deo Trino II: Pars Systematica.*

68 Lonergan, *Insight*, 764. See further *Phenomenology and Logic*, 126–7, 130, on this problem.

69 Lonergan, *Insight*, 749.

70 I refer to two of his recent efforts: 'Seven Families of Basic World Views,' presented at the 19th Annual Fallon Memorial Lonergan Symposium, Loyola Marymount University, Los Angeles, March 2004; 'Images, Symbols, and Signs: Concrete Mediators of Human Living,' in *Image Makers and Image Breakers*, ed. Jennifer Harris (Ottawa: Legas, 2004), 155–70.

71 See Vertin, 'Acceptance and Actualization: The Two Phases of my Human Living,' *Method: Journal of Lonergan Studies* 21 (2003), 67–86. The article opens up complexities of functional collaboration, with diagrams pointing to subtle and necessary correlations. This is a key contribution of his efforts over the years: his listings and diagrams, far from being unnecessary complications, as some may think, point to the larger need, a fuller symbolic expression of the intricacies of the metaphysical control of meaning. Add the comments in the following note.

72 This is the massive task sketched briefly by Lonergan in *Insight*, chap. 17, sec. 3.3. Relevant to Vertin's push on evaluation, for example, are the metaphysical equivalents of the various steps of evaluation described by Thomas (*ST* 1-2 qq. 7–17). One key zone that needs attention here is perhaps worth a mention. The whole issue of the emergence of judgments of value within the dynamic of feelings obviously comes under the general account of capacity-for-performance that Lonergan gives in chap. 15 of *Insight.* But capacity-for-performance needs the enriched context of a metaphysics that would trans-

pose Aquinas's struggle with *potentia activa*, detailed by Lonergan in *Verbum*, 121–51. That context would lead to a transposition of Aquinas's view (see ibid., 145) of the 'natural resultance' of, e.g., the forms of neuro-dynamics from the human soul, and that transposition would enrich the introspective and metaphysical analysis to which Thomas's treatment of the *Prima Secundae* (qq. 7 -17) invites. This would also give a metaphysical precision both to the *exigence* that Lonergan describes in *Phenomenology and Logic* and to the psychic dimensions of that exigence that concern Doran and McGrath.

73 Proust is familiar. Bachelard talks of labouring to build a house late in life; von Karajan in his elderhood approached old works as if they were 'entirely new.'

74 See n. 60. The references here are to *A Third Collection*, 26, 29.

75 Lonergan, 'Theology and Praxis,' in *A Third Collection*, 190; 'A Post-Hegelian Philosophy of Religion,' ibid., 219.

76 Lonergan, *Insight*, 442.

77 The context is Romans 8:19–23.

78 Lonergan, *Insight*, 544.

79 Lonergan, *Philosophical and Theological Papers 1965–1980*, 367, in 'Questionnaire on Philosophy: Response.'

80 'The Calculus of Variation,' chap. 4 of McShane, *Lack in the Beingstalk: A Giants Causeway*, deals with that topic, drawing parallels with the calculus of variation that is functional specialization.

81 Lonergan, *Method in Theology*, 299.

82 Lonergan, *Topics in Education*, 232. I note that, since writing the present essay, I have provided a fuller perspective on the matter, 'The Origin and Goal of Functional Specialization,' presented at the 20th Annual Fallon Memorial Lonergan Symposium, Loyola Marymount University, Los Angeles, April 2005. It is available on www.philipmcshane.ca as *Quodlibet* 17. *Joistings* 8, also available there (see n. 1 above), puts the collaborative effort in the supernatural context of our sharing in the Satisfaction of Jesus.

83 Lonergan, *Philosophical and Theological Papers 1965–1980*, 366.

84 Lonergan, *Method in Theology*, 287.

85 Lonergan, *Insight*, 537.

86 'Existential gap,' 'anxiety,' 'dread': words from those last two chapters in *Phenomenology and Logic*.

87 Ibid., 313–14.

88 The title of *Cantower* 5 is 'Metaphysics THEN.' It contrasted with both Zen and Ken traditions. Later I preferred to use the word 'VEN,' which echos the *praxis* orientation of which I write.

89 Antoine de Saint Exupery, *The Little Prince* (New York: Harbrace, 1973), 32–3.

90 An initial lead on this complex topic could be Lonergan, *Phenomenology and Logic*, 349–51.

91 Revelations 2:17.

92 'Reverierun' is the title of section 2 of *Quodlibet* 8, 'The Dialectic of My Town, Ma Vlast.' See further n. 98 and 99.

93 In the centre of his paper in this volume, Fr Crowe makes the point: 'I have

been prolix on the will of the end in human decisions because it is not given due attention in studies of Thomas and Lonergan' (p. 90). Here and there in my own essay I point to a like gap concerning the willing of means. Fr Crowe is one of the few who has paid serious attention to that topic and to those neglected questions 6–17 of the *Prima Secundae.* See n. 72 above and n. 96 below.

94 The three final *Quodlibets* are: 19, 'The Solution to the Problem of Feelings and Values in Lonergan Studies'; 20, 'The Application of Lonergan'; 21, 'Recycling Ancient Meaning.'

95 Underneath the brief comments lurk, as O'Gara could say at length, deep problems of the hermeneutics of the Church's Rock, problems raised by Sean McEvenue and myself in *Quodlibet* 21.

96 See n. 93 above. I raise the issue in a broad but elementary manner in *Joistings* 3: 'What-to-do questions' (see n. 1 above). It is treated in a more complex form in *Quodlibet* 19, 'The Solution to the Problem of Feelings and Values in Lonergan Studies.'

97 I like to think of the twenty-nine occurrences of the word 'collaboration' in 'Resumption of the Heuristic Structure of the Solution' (Lonergan, *Insight,* chap. 20, sec. 5) as a dynamic indeterminate reach, within grace, for his later discovery of this beautiful global vortex of meaning.

98 DeNeeve's question was the driving force in *Quodlibet* 7, '*Method in Theology* page 250, for Beginners.' *Quodlibet* 8 applies it to a town in a manner that extends an earlier reflection on the metaphysics of Manhattan: see *Cantower* 14, 'Communications and Ever-Ready Founders,' sec. 3, 'Founders of New York.' For its relevance to the present essay, see n. 102 below.

99 The first word of *Finnegans Wake* is 'riverrun,' a huge topic by itself. But it is worth noting at least that the meaning of 'run' in Gaelic (pronounced *roon*), is related to northern European meanings. 'Roon' has the meaning both of beloved and of mystery. *Reverierun* relates to the re-run of *Finnegans Wake* that the structure of the book invites and to categorial fantasy, the core of foundations.

100 This is not the place to try to hint at the developed metaphysics of such topics that lurk in Lonergan's sketchy principles of metaphysical equivalence. Still, it is worth noting that a new distant control of meaning will make it possible to thematize the orientations listed above within that context. What, for instance, are the metaphysical equivalents of claims regarding conversions, distinctions, progressions, etc.? It takes a great deal of innovative focus to thematize any such suggested reality in terms of metaphysical equivalents, yet without that focus one is trapped in vulnerable metadescription. Pointers regarding this problem are in my essay 'Obstacles to Metaphysical Control,' part of *Quodlibet* 20. The essay is available also in *Method: Journal of Lonergan Studies* 23 (2005).

101 The topic is in fact central in *Insight* – the need for 'a practical theory of history' (*Insight,* 258) – and deserves fuller indexing in a later edition. My random reading gives relevant occurrences of the word 'implementation' itself on 254, 259, 261, 263, 416, 517, 530, 544, 547, 708, 748.

102 See Philip McShane, 'Systematics, Communications, Actual Contexts,' *Lonergan Workshop* 6 (Chico, CA: Scholars Press, 1986). One needs to keep psychically present the concretely efficient reference of a unified metaphysics. So, each of us must think in terms of his or her own street, own nation. In my own case, I may point to Lloyd Axworthy, *Navigating a New World: Canada's Global Future* (New York: Alfred A. Knopf, 2003). One must think like him that 'there can be a resurrection of a failed state and a crucified population' (284); indeed, 'From the Isle of Light. How to bring about this change? How to move from ideas, principles, blueprints and prescriptions to serious reform of the system? And what can we do as Canadians to help bring this about?' (403). We need to add to his subtitle the hope within 'Lonergan's Global Future,' and fantasize about a resurrection of a failed Lonerganism.

103 My first enthusiastic survey of significance in such areas as physics, philosophy, theology, was 'The Contemporary Thomism of Bernard Lonergan,' *Philosophical Studies* 11 (1962), 63–80.

104 There is doctorate work to be done here, to get beyond my random foraging. Fragments are to be found in stray places: for instance, the key correction to Aristotle's view of motion is found on the last page of item A296 in the Archives. I quoted it in Lonergan, *Phenomenology and Logic*, n. 13 of p. 13. There are the fragments to which I draw attention in the following note.

105 I am referring here to stray pieces of the original typescript of *Insight*, chap. five, but also to the fragments in the archival items, A283–A289.

106 The context is Lonergan's considerations of coincidences' rapid divergences, but it is helpful to muse over, contemplate seriously, Feynman's description of a single room's randomly meshed radiations, in *Feynman's Lectures on Physics*, vol. 2 (Toronto: Harper Collins, 2003), 20.8: 'Flying across the room are electromagnetic waves which carry music of a jazz band,' etc. There is radiation from cold blackboards and sweaty foreheads. Boulder Dam is present, and 'electric and magnetic fields that are waves originating billions of light years away. That this is true has been found by 'filling the room with wires – by building antennas as large as this room.' And what of the controlling 'music without sound'? (John of the Cross, *Songs between the Soul and the Bridegroom*). See n. 110 below. On the eternal control of the coincidental, see Lonergan, *Insight*, chap. 19, sec. 7.

107 Lonergan, *Insight*, chap. 5, sec. 5. The book by Greene mentioned in n. 109 below is typical of the general confusion.

108 *Ibid.*, 517.

109 A context here is Lochlainn O'Raifeartaigh, *The Dawning of Gauge Theory* (Princeton: Princeton University Press, 1997). In contrast there are the muddles of Brian Greene, *The Fabric of the Cosmos: Space, Time and the Texture of Reality* (New York: Alfred A. Knopf, 2004). A useful exercise here is to bring to bear the precision of Lonergan's brief consideration, in *Insight*, of Newton's bucket on Greene's prolonged messing about the same topic. See the indices. I suspect that later centuries will note Lonergan's shift of perspective in physics as a parallel to his shift of economic perspective away from 'the

conventional nostrums of today's international economic theology' (Axworthy, *Navigating a New World*, 299).

110 Still, it is worth noting that we are not dealing here just with a problem in physics. Such notes here as nn. 100 and 106 bear that out and give a context. Present physicists struggle with anthropic principles (see *Lack in the Beingstalk*, chap. 3, sec. 5). Have we something to say to them about the vestiges of God? (See n. 66 above.) The issues of n. 100 implicitly raise questions of a deeper appreciation of the finality of energy and n. 106 ends with the problem of divine control. Is there not an elegant control staring the physicist in the face through the Principle of Least Action that gives a concrete dynamic balance between radiant coincidentality and nomic reaching? Are we to leave popular culture in the hands of pop-physics myth-makers, or should we not mediate the mysterious freshness of a dream?

111 The first paragraph of chap. 5 of *Insight.*

112 The text is worth quoting here. It points to the fundamental existential come-about, conversion, of Lonergan's climb, a fundamental biographic challenge to each of us. 'So it comes about that the extroverted subject visualizing extensions and experiencing duration gives place to the subject oriented to the objective of the unrestricted desire to know and affirming beings differentiated by certain conjugate potencies, forms, and acts grounding certain laws and frequencies' (*Insight*, 537).

113 Bernard Lonergan, 'An Interview with Fr. Bernard Lonergan S.J.,' in *A Second Collection*, ed. William F.J. Ryan and Bernard J. Tyrrell (London: Darton, Longman & Todd, 1974), 221–2. I note that I omitted names of questioners in my editing. The reference to 'personal relations' is to the note on the first page of the epilogue.

114 Recall n. 106. The second-last paragraph of sec. 11 above points to the elder Shakespeare's reaching, in *Pericles*, for 'the music of the spheres!'(V.ii.231). And does it not enrich our *contemplatio ad amorem obtinendam* to reach for an understanding of how God manages this *pati* through their thalamic lift of typhanic membrane and cochleal loop? A contemporary beginning here could be 'Music and the Brain,' *Scientific American*, November 2004, 89–95. All this leads to a contextualization of the final paragraph below. It is the network of mediation that I mentioned at the beginning of this section. Hefling's article adds a further rich context.

115 Lonergan, *Method in Theology*, 342. Recall n. 100 above. To attain clarity here one must push for metaphysical equivalents of claims to 'infinity' or 'intimacy.' Such clarity, paradoxically, can give larger licence to poetic reachings. Is the world charged with the grandeur of God, as Hopkins claims? And was it so from its clouded origin? One needs a heartheld thematic of energy's destiny to tune one to the longings of thirteen billion years ago, of this morning's minions. Lonergan left evident unfinished business here, not only with regard to the Eschaton, but with regard to the present reachings of those entwined dynamics, entropy and negentropy, in the flowering of the fleshWord.

116 A favourite recollection of mine is of an evening when we listened to the Kreutzer and he told me of the first time he had heard it, a small boy poised

in a garden. It was some years before I tracked down the music: musicians simply did not believe me about its existence. The piano version was the achievement of Czerny, the famous 'piano exercise' man, a young friend of Beethoven.

117 I recall phoning him after I had given him a recording of these quartets to talk of his reaction. I asked the conventional question, 'What do you think of them?' His immediate response: 'I don't think. I feel!'

118 I quote from a review by Lonergan in *Gregorianum* 36 (1956), 138, of Jules Chaise-Ruy, *Les dimensions de l'etre et du temps.*

Michael Vertin Bibliography

I Books edited

Frederick E. Crowe. *Appropriating the Lonergan Idea*. Washington, DC: Catholic University of America Press, 1989. Reprinted with new Editor's Introduction. Toronto: University of Toronto Press, 2006.

– *Three Thomist Studies*. Boston: Lonergan Center of Boston College, 2000.

– *Developing the Lonergan Legacy*. Toronto: University of Toronto Press, 2004.

II Articles

'"Immateriality," "Self-Possession," Phenomenology, and Metaphysics.' *American Catholic Philosophical Association Proceedings* 52 (1978), 52–60.

'The Doctrine of Infallibility and the Demands of Epistemology.' *The Thomist* 43 (1979), 637–52.

'Philosophy-of-God, Theology, and the Problems of Evil.' *Laval theologique et philosophique* 37 (1981), 15–31; and *Lonergan Workshop* 3 (1982), 149–78.

'Dialectically-Opposed Phenomenologies of Knowing: A Pedagogical Elaboration of Basic Ideal-Types.' *Lonergan Workshop* 4 (1983), 1–26. (Also in P. McShane, ed., *Searching for Cultural Foundations*: see section III below.)

'Transcendental Analysis, and the Objective Study of Religion.' *Method and Theory in the Study of Religion* 1 (1989), 106–14.

'Lonergan's "Three Basic Questions" and a Philosophy of Philosophies.' *Lonergan Workshop* 8 (1990), 213–48.

'"Knowing," "Objectivity," and "Reality": INSIGHT and Beyond.' *Lonergan Workshop* 8 (1990), 249–63.

'Lonergan on Consciousness: Is There a Fifth Level?' *Method: Journal of Lonergan Studies* 12 (1994), 1–36.

'Diverse Readings of Evil.' *Catholic Theological Society of America Proceedings* 50 (1995), 93–104.

'Judgments of Value, for the Later Lonergan.' *Method: Journal of Lonergan Studies* 13 (1995), 221–48.

'The Holy Spirit's Assistance to the Magisterium in Teaching: Theological and Philosophical Issues.' With M. O'Gara. *Catholic Theological Society of America Proceedings* 51 (1996), 125–42.

'Lonergan's Metaphysics of Value and Love: Some Proposed Clarifications and Implications.' *Lonergan Workshop* 13 (1997), 189–219.

'Is There a Constitutional Right of Privacy?' *Lonergan Workshop* 16 (2000), 1–47.

'Interpreting the Constitution.' *Method: Journal of Lonergan Studies*, 18 (2000), 161–77.

'Transcendental Philosophy and Linguistic Philosophy.' *Method: Journal of Lonergan Studies* 19 (2001), 253–80.

'Acceptance and Actualization: The Two Phases of My Human Living.' *Method: Journal of Lonergan Studies* 21 (2003), 67–86.

'The Two Modes of Human Love: Thomas Aquinas as Interpreted by Frederick Crowe.' *Irish Theological Quarterly* 69 (2004), 31–45.

III Parts of Books

'Maréchal, Lonergan, and the Phenomenology of Knowing.' In M. Lamb, ed., *Creativity and Method: Essays in Honor of Bernard Lonergan*, 411–22. Milwaukee: Marquette University Press, 1981.

'Dialectically-Opposed Phenomenologies of Knowing: A Pedagogical Elaboration of Basic Ideal-Types.' In P. McShane, ed., *Searching for Cultural Foundations*, 65–85. Lanham, MD: University Press of America, 1984. (Also in *Lonergan Workshop* 4: see section II above.)

'Freedom.' In J. Komonchak et al., eds., *The New Dictionary of Theology*, 404–6. Wilmington, DE: Michael Glazier Books, 1987.

'Transcendentals.' In J. Komonchak et al., eds., *The New Dictionary of Theology*, 1043–4. Wilmington, DE: Michael Glazier Books, 1987.

'Truth.' In J. Komonchak et al., eds., *The New Dictionary of Theology*, 1062–3. Wilmington, DE: Michael Glazier Books, 1987.

'Is God in Process?' In T.P. Fallon & P.B. Riley, eds., *Religion and Culture: Essays in Honor of Bernard Lonergan*, 45–62. Albany: State University of New York Press, 1987.

'Dialectic, Hermeneutics, and "The Bible as the Word of God."' In S. McEvenue and B. Meyer, eds., *Lonergan's Hermeneutics: Its Development and Application*, 38–46. Washington, DC: The Catholic University of America Press, 1989.

'Freedom.' In M. Downey, ed., *The New Dictionary of Catholic Spirituality*, 418–19. Collegeville, MN: Liturgical Press/Michael Glazier Books, 1993.

'Intention, Intentionality.' In M. Downey, ed., *The New Dictionary of Catholic Spirituality*, 542–3. Collegeville, MN: Liturgical Press/Michael Glazier Books, 1993.

'Mind.' In M. Downey, ed., *The New Dictionary of Catholic Spirituality*, 655–8. Collegeville, MN: Liturgical Press/Michael Glazier Books, 1993.

'Gender, Science, and Cognitional Conversion.' In Cynthia Crysdale, ed., *Lonergan and Feminism*, 49–71. Toronto: University of Toronto Press, 1994.

'La finalité intellectuelle: Maréchal et Lonergan.' In Paul Gilbert, ed., *Joseph Maréchal: Entre la critique kantienne et l'ontologie thomiste*, 447–65. Bruxelles: Éditions Lessius, 2000.

'Images, Symbols, and Signs: Concrete Mediators of Human Living.' In Jennifer A. Harris, ed., *Image Makers and Image Breakers*, 155–70. Ottawa: Legas, 2004.

'Foreword: Euthanasia, Ethics, and General Valuative Studies.' In William Sullivan, *Eye of the Heart: Knowing the Human Good in the Euthanasia Debate*, xvii–xxiv. Toronto: University of Toronto Press, 2004.

'Affirming a Limit and Transcending It.' In Joseph Goering, ed., *LIMINA: Thresholds and Borders*, 117–26. Ottawa: Legas, 2005.

'Preface' and 'Introduction. Employing Functional Specialization: Overview of a Group Experiment.' In H. Daniel Monsour, ed., *Ethics and the New Genetics: An Integrated Approach*, vii–xi, 3–12. Toronto: University of Toronto Press, 2007.

Contributors

Frederick E. Crowe, SJ, Professor Emeritus of Systematic Theology, Regis College, Toronto School of Theology

Cynthia S.W. Crysdale, Associate Professor, School of Theology and Religious Studies, Catholic University of America, Washington, DC

Robert M. Doran, SJ, Professor, Emmett Doerr Chair in Catholic Systematic Theology, Marquette University, Milwaukee, Wisconsin

Charles Hefling, Associate Professor of Theology, Boston College

John Heng, Assistant Professor of Philosophy, King's College, University of Western Ontario, London, Ontario

Matthew Lamb, Professor of Theology and Chairman of the Theology Department, Ave Maria University, Naples, Florida

Fred Lawrence, Professor of Theology, Boston College

S.J. McGrath, Assistant Professor of Philosophy, Mount Allison University, Sackville, New Brunswick

Philip McShane, Professor Emeritus of Philosophy, Mount St Vincent University, Halifax, Nova Scotia

Kenneth R. Melchin, Professor, Faculty of Theology, Saint Paul University, Ottawa

Mark D. Morelli, Professor of Philosophy, Loyola Marymount University, Los Angeles

Margaret O'Gara, Professor, Faculty of Theology, University of St. Michael's College, Toronto

William F. Sullivan, Assistant Professor, Department of Family and Community Medicine, University of Toronto

www.ingramcontent.com/pod-product-compliance
Lightning Source LLC
LaVergne TN
LVHW042156080826
844660LV00042B/1141

* 9 7 8 1 4 8 7 5 8 7 2 5 3 *